ROMMEL'S
PANZERS

Rommel and the Panzer Forces of the Blitzkrieg 1940–1942

Christer Jörgensen

MBI

This edition first published in 2003 by MBI, an imprint of
MBI Publishing Company, Galtier Plaza, Suite 200, 380 Jackson Street,
St. Paul, MN 55101-3885, USA

The information in this book is true and complete to the best of our
knowledge. All recommendations are made without any guarantee on the
part of the author or Publisher, who also disclaim any liability incurred in
connection with the use of this data or specific details.

We recognize that some words, model names and designations, for
example, mentioned herein are the property of the trademark holder. We
use them for identification purposes only. This is not an official
publication.

MBI titles are also available at discounts in bulk quantity for industrial or
sales-promotional use. For details write to Special Sales Manager at
Motorbooks International Wholesalers & Distributors, Galtier Plaza,
Suite 200, 380 Jackson Street, St. Paul, MN 55101-3885 USA.

ISBN: 0-7603-1481-0

Printed in China

Editorial and design:
The Brown Reference Group plc
8 Chapel Place
Rivington Street
London
EC2A 3DQ
UK

Senior Editor: Peter Darman
Editor: Alan Marshall
Picture research: Andrew Webb
Design: Jerry Udall
Maps: Bob Garwood
Production Director: Alastair Gourlay

This book is dedicated to the memory of British Eighth Army veteran John Byott

Contents

Key to Maps

Military units – types

⊠	Infantry
▱	Armoured
▱	Mechanized/panzergrenadier
⊞	Fortress
◨	Mountain
⧄	Cavalry

Military units – size

XXXXX ☐	Army group
XXXX ☐	Army
XXX ☐	Corps
XX ☐	Division
X ☐	Brigade
III ☐	Regiment

Military movement

▬▬➤	atttack/advance
▪▪▪➤	retreat

Military unit colours

▦	German
▦	British and Commonwealth
▦	US
▦	French
☐	Italian

Geographical symbols

————————	road
– – – – – –	track
⬤	urban area
•	urban area
⬤	trees
⌇	ridge
⛰	mountain
– · – · – · –	national boundary
————————	river
⊢⊢⊢⊢⊢⊢	railway

6

List of Maps

Introduction

During the darkest days of World War II (early 1942) the British Prime minister and war leader, Winston Churchill, usually an optimistic, self-confident and ebullient character, was brought to despair by British setbacks in the Desert War in North Africa at the hands of his country's worst enemy: the "Desert Fox". The Fox was none other than General Erwin Rommel, the commander of the German Africa Corps whose prowess in war inflicted defeat upon defeat on the British. In early 1942 Churchill shouted to his aides: "Rommel, Rommel, Rommel – what matters but beating him."[1]

For Churchill, defeating Rommel became an obsession that would dominate his conduct of the war during 1941 and 1942. So desperate was he to rid himself of this German thorn in his side that he allowed himself to be persuaded to launch a most secret and clandestine operation to take place: to abduct or kill Rommel in his African headquarters. The operation, launched in November 1941, failed.[2] Yet in public Churchill would not admit to such methods in war and admitted, in early 1942 to the British Parliament, in a rare display of generosity towards Rommel: "We have a daring and skilful opponent against us, and may I say across the havoc of war, a great general."[3]

No German general, before or since, had been the subject of such praise by the British, or such calculated acts of vengeance, as the Fox. What made Rommel so special? He had been an outstanding infantry commander during World War I with a string of spectacular Alpine victories to his name. The hallmark of his style of command was to lead from the front and pursue the enemy mercilessly, through daring thrusts and attacks, until the foe was forced to capitulate. Rommel, appointed to command the legendary 7th Panzer Division in early 1940, proved a born leader of men and proved during the French campaign (May–July 1940) that he was an outstanding panzer commander. Even though Rommel came out of that campaign with an enhanced reputation for bold and imaginary leadership, it was in North Africa that he became the legendary "Desert Fox". It was in Africa that he and his men of the equally legendary Deutsche Afrika Korps (DAK) outfought, outsmarted and outmanoeuvred the British again and again during a series of brilliantly fought battles. The British recognized that they were dealing with an exceptionally talented and tough army led by a military genius. Indeed, once the Fox had been defeated the British, good sportsmen that they were, lavished praise on him and the DAK.

To friend and foe alike Rommel was a gentleman warrior, a tough but humane professional soldier, who fought for his country and his soldiers whatever the odds stacked against him. He inspired enormous loyalty in those who served under him and even won the admiration of his enemy – the highest form of praise there is – and in the end let his patriotism and loyalty to his country override his sense of gratitude to the man who in part had created him. But at all times Rommel was a warrior at heart and a soldiers' general. We are very unlikely to see his like again.

This is the story of Rommel, his panzers and the men who fought under his command on two continents and in two world wars.

Notes

1 Wolf Heckmann, *Rommel's War in Africa*, London, 1981. p.16. According to the diary of General Sir Ian Jacob.

2 *Purnell's History of the Second World War*, Vol. 6. Michael Mason, *Target Rommel: The Keyes Raid* (Nov. 1941). pp.653-655

3 Heckmann, p.16

The Useful Soldier

Rommel's background and the battlefields of World War I *(1914–18)*

F amily and background have a great influence on later life since they create the mould that shapes an individual. Erwin Rommel was born in 1891 in the small south German region of Swabia, whose inhabitants were known for their dour, hard-working and tenacious characters. During his long military career, Rommel showed exactly these qualities of endurance, toughness and ingenuity. He also retained throughout his life a strong regional patriotism and his distinct Swabian accent, despite living in other parts of Germany.

Rommel's father, a strict and demanding schoolmaster, instilled in the boy good Protestant values such as hard work, discipline, loyalty and patriotism. He was also responsible for his son becoming a soldier, and in July 1910 Rommel joined the 124th Würtemburg Infantry Regiment (Swabia then being part of the Kingdom of Würtemburg). A year later he passed out of the Danzig Cadet School, and the commandant noted that officer cadet Rommel was a "useful soldier". He had "immense willpower, was keen and enthusiastic [and had] a strict sense of duty and a very comradely attitude".

At this time, Rommel met, fell in love with and married the love of his life, Lucie Mollin, a dark-haired German beauty of Italian and Polish descent. She was to be his companion for the rest of his life, and he returned her support with undying affection and devoted loyalty.[1]

Rommel's regiment was stationed near Stuttgart where he trained recruits until, in March 1914, he was attached to the 49th Field Artillery Regiment.[2] World War I broke out in August 1914. Rommel's regiment was part of the German Fifth Army that invaded eastern France in the region of the southern Ardennes, an area with which Rommel would become very familiar during his later French campaign in World War II.

He relished the mobile phase of the war and conducted operations as if he were a cavalry, not an infantry, commander. On 22 August, he captured the

Left: Erwin Rommel, seen here after the 1918 armistice with his "Blue Max" and Iron Cross, had a "good war" with spectacular victories against Italy and Romania. This "useful soldier" displayed much of the aggression, courage and cunning that later gave him a fearsome reputation in World War II.

village of Blied with a small detachment, killing 30 and taking 12 French prisoners. For his personal bravery and the dash of his troops, Rommel was awarded the Iron Cross II Class. Like a bloodhound, he had a nose for the enemy's weakness. He was always keen to attack, and took charge of operations himself – often to the fury of his superiors. He believed in initiative and independence, even at the expense of strict hierarchical "discipline".[3]

Romania: how Rommel learnt to fight and command (1917)

In September 1915, Rommel joined the Würtemburg Mountain Battalion. It was while in service with this unit that he became an independent and bold commander of men in the most arduous of circumstances. The Kingdom of Romania, after some indecision, had joined the Allies in late August 1916 and had invaded the Romanian-populated province of Transylvania. Victorious at first, the Romanians, badly led and poorly supplied, were defeated when Germany sent its beleaguered ally, Austria-Hungary, military support. Shaped like a triangular wedge, Rumania was surrounded by enemy territory to the south (Bulgaria) and the Austro-Hungarian Empire to the north. While the Bulgarians crossed the Danube in force, thus threatening the whole southern part of Romania, an Austro-German army under General Falkenhayn invaded Romania from the northwest through the passes of the Transylvanian Alps. It was able to outflank and defeat the enemy, despite Russian support for the Romanians. On 6 December 1916, the capital, Bucharest, fell to Falkenhayn.[4]

Rommel's battalion had been sent to the Romanian front in October 1916 and took part in Falkenhayn's advance on Bucharest. But, without proper tents

Below: German infantry wait patiently on a wooded hilltop in the Ardennes for the signal to advance farther into France in August 1914. Rommel's regiment was part of the German Fifth Army that invaded eastern France in the region of the southern Ardennes.

Left: Romanian troops on the march in the Carpathian mountains, 1916. Rommel's battalion had been sent to the Romanian Front in October 1916 and took part in General Falkenhayn's successful advance on Bucharest.

and equipment, his men suffered from frostbite and hunger. Rommel learnt a valuable lesson about troop management. In order to perform to the maximum level, the troops had to be cared for by their commander. He also discovered that a commander would earn his troops' respect and loyalty only if he shared their burdens and problems. "Never ask of others what you would not or could not do yourself." From now on this would be Rommel's motto.[5]

On 7 January, Rommel advanced some 6.4km (4 miles) east of the German frontline and penetrated deep inside Romanian territory with a company of mountain troops, supported by a machine-gun unit. Rommel took the village of Gagesti and the surrounding heights. He did so by attacking on a narrow front and concentrating fire against a single point. Once through enemy lines, he established fire points to break the Romanians' resistance. Rommel taught his subordinate officers to ignore possible attacks from the rear and flanks in order to maintain the all-important momentum of the attack. This was to be Rommel's style in France and North Africa during the next war. It was here, around a small and insignificant Romanian village in the Transylvanian Alps, that Rommel had for the first time applied the techniques and leadership style that would later make him such a remarkable commander.[6]

After a short spell on the Western Front, Rommel returned to Romania in August 1917. On 9 August the entire battalion was ordered to attack Mount Cosna, at the easternmost tip of the German-held front in Romania. That day Rommel and his unit drove the Romanians out of five forward positions in front of the mountain. The following day, Rommel was given command of six rifle and two machine-gun companies. Advancing boldly along an exposed

Below: General Falkenhayn led an Austro-German army into Romania from the northwest through the passes of the Transylvanian Alps. He was able to outflank and defeat the Romanian forces.

ridge, his objective was the summit of Mount Cosna. He deployed his machine-gun companies and two of his rifle units to pin down the Romanians and prevent them from attacking his flanks. With his remaining four companies, Rommel outflanked the Romanians by climbing a wooded ridge to the north of the enemy's positions. In the space of a few hours, Rommel had captured Mount Cosna while the Romanians fled in disorder to their own lines.[7]

Italy: Rommel's spectacular mountain victories (1917)

Mount Cosna was Rommel's first mountain victory, but it would not be his last or his most spectacular. The Italians had opted at the outbreak of war for a dubious kind of neutrality. Having forfeited the trust of the Central Powers (Germany and Austria-Hungary), especially their old enemy Austria-Hungary, the Italians had finally declared war in 1915. The fighting didn't go well and the Italians, who had hoped for spectacular results, were bogged down in a bloody stalemate along the Isonzo River and in the mountains and foothills of the Alps. Rommel, after a short stay with Lucie in Germany, returned to frontline duty in October 1917.

The Austrians, who were proving a costly liability to Germany, were in almost as much trouble as the Italians and appealed for German assistance. Germany, itself increasingly short of troops, could not abandon its ally. The German high command created the Fourteenth Army of seven divisions for service on the southern front. Soon promoted to captain, Rommel was given his own "Rommel Detachment" of three mountain companies and one machine-gun company. Unlike other armies, Germany had a highly trained and motivated corps of junior officers. Such officers were given tasks entrusted only to more senior soldiers in the armies of other countries.[8] This unusual, but effective, tradition was to assist Rommel's rapid rise through the ranks.

On 24 October the Germans opened the Battle of Caporetto with a massive artillery barrage from 1000 guns. Rommel, leading from the front, advanced undetected along the Kolovrat Ridge towards Mount Matajur, his ultimate objective. He captured 500 surprised Italian troops. Again and again, he would

Below: Germany opened the Battle of Caporetto with a heavy artillery barrage, before Rommel and his detachment advanced undetected along the Kolovrat Ridge to the surprise of the defending Italian troops.

face the same problem where an overwhelming and surprising victory would leave him and his formation in a dangerous and exposed position. He had only three choices: retreat; make a stand; or attack. Rommel's decision was simple: to attack at all times if possible. He seized the village of Luico, with 100 prisoners taken, advanced down the ridge and captured the Italian supply road. He had only 150 men, but when the rest of the battalion arrived at Luico to take over the guarding of 2000 Italian prisoners he decided to press on.

Rommel made a spectacular night attack against Mount Cragonza and the village of Jevszek. Not only were these two objectives captured, but Rommel's victory was still more remarkable in that his detachment attacked uphill, without cover and in the face of withering fire. His courage and cunning paid off with spectacular results. Putting his life at risk, Rommel, carrying a white flag of truce, approached the Italian lines, spoke to the troops and persuaded them to surrender. From now on Rommel's other motto would be: why fight it out with the enemy if a parley or a sheer bluff would secure a bloodless victory?[9]

Due to the enormous number of prisoners pouring into his hands, the battalion's commander, Colonel Sprosser, assumed erroneously that Mount Matajur had fallen and ordered Rommel to return. When he received the order, Rommel, assessing that Sprosser had misjudged the situation through a lack of information, decided to disobey and continue the attack until Matajur was captured. Here was Rommel at his most rebellious, when his inherent aggressiveness overrode his strong sense of obedience and

Above: German troops on the move during the Battle of Caporetto (top). During 52 hours of non-stop fighting, Rommel's detachment suffered just six dead and 30 wounded, but captured 9000 Italians (above).

Above: The Battle of Soissons, June 1918. German troops are seen crossing the road, while others rest on the Chemin des Dames. Rommel served on the Western Front during the final year of World War I. He was indeed fortunate to have fought in theatres where the warfare was of a more fluid nature.

respect for discipline. If an order stopped him from achieving his goals, Rommel would ignore it – as he was to do time and time again in France and in the North African desert.

The area around the summit was held by the crack 2nd Battalion of the Salerno Brigade. Again, Rommel believed that the enemy should be bluffed and tricked if possible to abandon territory or surrender without resistance. Once more he approached the Italians under a white flag and urged them to capitulate. To his utter amazement, 1200 troops, defying their infuriated and humiliated officers, lined up and laid down their arms before Rommel. He went on with his detachment and captured the summit, which yielded another 120 prisoners. At 11:40 hours on 26 October, two days after the offensive had begun, Rommel's men fired a flare that signalled that Mount Matajur was in German hands. During 52 hours of non-stop fighting, Rommel's losses were just six dead and 30 wounded, but his detachment had captured 9000 Italians. In December, Rommel and Sprosser were belatedly awarded the "Blue Max" (*Pour le Mérite*), Imperial Germany's highest decoration.[10]

Rommel: a victorious and undefeated officer

Rommel remained at the Italian Front for the rest of 1917. He served on the Western Front during the following year, but was spared the worst of the nightmare of trench warfare that dulled the minds of so many contemporaries, making them timid and slow. Rommel had spent most of his time on fluid fronts, where mobile warfare could still be conducted with great effect. Unlike his French and British opponents, he believed in the potential and validity of mobile warfare during the next major conflict. It was ironic that Rommel won his reputation for boldness and panache fighting two of Germany's most important allies in World War II, Italy and Romania. In the case of the Italians, this was a mixed blessing as it made Rommel wary of trusting them in modern warfare, given their poor showing against him in the Alps. In spite of his enemies' claims, though, he was no hater of Italians, admiring their stoicism during the desert war. He even allowed his daughter, Gertrude, to marry an Italian.

When the war ended in November 1918, Rommel did not feel part of a defeated army because of his spectacular victories. His was a "good" war. Unlike Hitler, he wasn't burdened with a sense of personal shame and humiliation. Rommel was ready for another round.

Chapter notes

1 It has emerged only recently that Rommel had a serious romance before World War I that led to the birth of a daughter, Gertrude, whom Rommel acknowledged as his own and to whom he gave financial and emotional support. Her mother died tragically in 1928 of a broken heart. That Rommel was a vital part of his daughter's life was shown by the fact that she asked him for permission to marry an Italian. Rommel had no problem with this as long as he was a "real and honest man". TV documentary, "The Real Rommel", interview with Rommel's grandson.

2 Irving, *The Trail of the Fox*, pp.8-11. Like Hitler, Rommel was known among the troops as a non-drinker, non-smoker and as a man who abhorred womanizing. However, unlike his future Führer, he was married and therefore quite normal.

3 Fraser, *Knight's Cross*, pp.23-44.

4 Basil Liddell Hart, *History of the First World War* (London, 1997), pp.264-268.

5 Fraser, pp.48-51.

6 Ibid, p.52.

7 Ibid, pp.54-56. Due to the threat of a Russian advance, the Germans – to Rommel's chagrin – had to leave Mount Cosna which was occupied by the Romanians on 19 August.

8 Ibid, pp.61-65.

9 Ibid, pp.65-71.

10 Ibid, p.72, p.77. Ferdinand Schörner was awarded the "Blue Max" before Rommel for supposedly reaching Matajur first. Rommel protested, thus beginning a lifelong rivalry between him and Schörner – known as Hitler's last general because he commanded Army Group Centre in Bohemia in May 1945.

CHAPTER 2

The Political Soldier

Rommel, the rise of Hitler and the panzer army (1918–39)

In 1918 Rommel was still only 27 years old, but a highly decorated officer in the new post-war German Army, known as the "Reichswehr" (literally National Defence Force). The young officer, whose life was devoted to his wife and his career, was lucky to remain in the army. As a highly patriotic soldier, Rommel was put to good use. In March 1919 he took over a disaffected "Red" naval detachment, which he soon converted into a loyal fighting unit. In the spring of 1920, Rommel was fighting against Communist rebels in Westphalia. Between 1920 and 1929, he was commander of a rifle company in Stuttgart and in charge of training. He also devoted a lot of time to understanding the internal combustion engine and the tactical use of the machine gun. Both these areas of interest and his technical flair were put to good use later in his career. Rommel was an outstanding lecturer and viewed as an exacting, but inspiring, troop trainer. It was at Stuttgart that his son, Manfred, was born in 1928. During 1933–34 Rommel was commander of a jäger (light infantry) battalion at Goslar – a time he described as the best years of his life. In September 1934 he became commander of the Rommel Battalion.[1]

During these years another war veteran, Adolf Hitler, had put his mark on the political map of Germany. In 1928, Hitler was an obscure south German political extremist whose only claim to fame was to have orchestrated and led a failed coup, "the Beerhall Putsch", in Munich five years earlier. In 1931 Hitler's party, the National Sozialistische Deutsche Arbeiter Partei (NSDAP) (National Socialist German Workers' Party), was the country's largest; it gained inexorably in the polls due to a combination of unemployment, despair and the worldwide economic depression that had left Germany prostrate. In January 1933, Hitler finally took power and became Chancellor of Germany. Rommel admired Hitler as a leader of men and liked Nazi radicalism since he had an abiding hatred of Germany's arrogant and selfish upper classes. But he viewed the Nazis' anti-Semitism as repulsive and the

Left: The Panzer I was a thinly armoured, poorly armed light tankette that could hold its own only against armoured cars. Despite these flaws, 1500 were produced by 1939 as Hitler tried to convince the world that he had a formidable tank force. The failings of the Panzer I were highlighted in the Spanish Civil War.

"Night of the Long Knives", the June 1934 purge of the SA Brownshirt leadership, as altogether unnecessary. Rommel was to remain largely supportive of Hitler until El Alamein, but thereafter grew ever more critical. However, in September 1934 at Goslar, Rommel met Hitler for the first time and was from that point on viewed as a pro-Nazi officer and Hitler's protégé.[2]

Rommel was transferred to the Infantry School at Potsdam outside Berlin where he became a popular and respected lecturer. What the students apparently admired most was his independence of mind and his clear streak of individualism, seen as hallmarks of a successful leader and of a man of principle. Rommel and his family did not mix with Berlin society, and his relationship with the general staff and their clique was never an easy one. As a middle-class Swabian, Rommel had nothing, except his military career, in common with the Prussian noblemen who still, even in Hitler's Third Reich, dominated the general staff. He did share their conservatism, their ethos and their political views, but he remained a rank outsider all his life. In 1937 Rommel wrote and published a very successful book *Infanterie Greift an* (*The Infantry Attacks*) that brought him some fame and rather more money. To many of his jealous and narrow-minded colleagues, this was "commercialism" and quite unacceptable. Rommel relished the fame and laughed all the way to the bank.[3]

In 1937 Rommel was given the duties of liaison officer with the Hitler Jugend (Hitler Youth), under the charming but arrogant Baldur von Schirach. The two men did not like each other. Schirach, who was American-educated, disliked the ramrod-stiff Rommel whom he saw as a caricature of the Prussian officer. He was surprised when Rommel opened his mouth and spoke with a broad Swabian accent, and proved far less stiff than he had expected. Rommel, whose relationship with Hitler was far more congenial, was promoted to head Hitler's security staff. During the occupation of Bohemia in March 1939, Rommel urged a reluctant Hitler to brave a possible assassination attempt by driving into Prague with only his small bodyguard for protection. Hitler's entry into the Czech capital was a propaganda coup, and the chancellor remarked that Rommel was an officer with guts and made of the "right stuff".[4]

Tank development in Great Britain, France and Germany (1918–39)

Although he was to become more famous than other officers as a daring tank commander and the archetypal panzer general, Rommel was not actually involved during the interwar years in the creation of the German panzer forces. That was the work of another brilliant maverick, General Heinz Guderian, and his associates. Before looking at tank developments in Germany, we first have to consider events in Great Britain and France.

Below: Reichsjugendführer Baldur von Schirach, the charming but arrogant American-educated officer to whom Rommel reported in 1937 when appointed liaison officer with the Hitler Youth.

Great Britain was the pioneer in the construction, design, development and practical use of the tank. It had been the first nation to use the tank in real combat, in Flanders in 1916, and the first to stage a mass attack with tanks at Cambrai in November 1917. By contrast, the Germans had scant interest in tank design before the war, and were not particularly adept at their use during World War I. The British therefore had a lead over the other combatant nations in 1918 that they could have put to good use. But after 1918, British military thinking regressed. Traditional bias towards the horse and infantryman prevailed over the concept of mechanization and the use of tanks. This was typified by Field Marshal Haig's claim in 1925 that the tank and aircraft, while useful, would always be mere accessories to the soldier and the horse on the battlefield.[5]

Above: Adolf Hitler (right) rides with President von Hindenburg in the early 1930s. Rommel admired Hitler as a leader of men and liked Nazi radicalism since he had an abiding hatred of Germany's arrogant and selfish upper classes. However, he viewed the Nazis' anti-Semitism as repulsive.

Those not sharing Haig's prejudices and advocating the mechanization of the armed forces with the emphasis on tanks and aircraft, such as Colonel John F.C. Fuller and Captain Basil Liddell Hart, were marginalized, ostracized and forced eventually to leave the military altogether. Fuller was a brilliant and profound thinker who tried to convince the traditionalists and reactionaries on the British general staff not only to retain the tank forces set up during World War I but to increase them in size, role and responsibility. Fuller's abrasive and messianic style, as much as his unwelcome message of modernization, led to the rejection of his ideas for mechanized armies led by tank divisions formed into tank corps. Strapped for money, the suspicious and financially prudent British military establishment rejected Fuller's ideas, only to see them used by Great Britain's enemies instead.

In Germany, Guderian embraced Fuller's ideas and put them partly into practice, while Soviet tank warfare specialists, such as Marshal Tukhachevsky, did the same. In both countries Fuller was a name that was respected, and he was later viewed as something of a military guru and as a genius on a par with Clausewitz.[6]

The victory of the traditionalists and a shortage of money ensured a steady erosion of the lead Great Britain had in 1918. In the 1920s, with an apparent absence of any threat to world peace, this deterioration hardly mattered, only becoming an issue in the next decade when both the USSR and Germany recovered their military strength. In 1926 two

Below: The British Mk VI tank, many of which fought in France in 1940. In 1927, Britain was the leading country in tank design and production, but during the 1930s it slipped behind friend and foe alike. Britain's weakness did not lie with the machines, but with a lack of ideas.

Royal Tank Corps (RTC) battalions, supported by a motorized battalion of infantry, took part in the exercises on Salisbury Plain and showed the worth of such units on a modern battlefield in terms of firepower, mobility and speed.

In 1931 the 1st Tank Brigade, with 95 light and 85 medium tanks, was formed but had, within a year, been disbanded.[7] The brigade's apparent failure to perform could be explained by the choice of commander. He had no experience with tanks and therefore showed little confidence or ability in handling them on exercise.[8] It was not until November 1933 (after Hitler had come to power) that the British set up a permanent Tank Brigade with 230 light Mark II tanks under the command of a brilliant leader, Colonel Percy Hobart. Like Fuller, Hobart did not suffer fools gladly, was outspoken and radical in his views on mechanization. This earned him enemies, and in 1936 Hobart was "deported" to Egypt to command the tank forces there.[9]

In 1927 Great Britain was still the leading country in the production and design of tanks, but during the 1930s it would slip behind friend and foe alike. Models such as the Mark I (A9) and Mark II (A10) were fast at 27km/h (17mph), but poorly protected and armed. The Mark III (A13) was also fast yet quite poorly armed, with a single 2lb (40mm) gun and a light Vickers machine gun.[10] The British weakness did not lie with the machines or even with the men who manned them, however, but with a lack of ideas. The British seemed to have forgotten how to use their tanks; and, since it was cavalry officers who dominated the tank forces in the 1930s, the tank was seen as something of a mechanized "horse".

The vehicles were used for reconnaissance, screening and raiding enemy lines of communication – the roles the cavalry had been assigned since the introduction of the machine gun, repeater rifle and breech-loading artillery. This was a fatally flawed view of the tank, which was actually a revolutionary new weapon of war. The correct role for the tank was to attack the enemy en masse, outflank him, surround him, and then force him to surrender through lack of water, food and ammunition. This could be achieved only if the tanks had the support of mechanized infantry, artillery and the close cooperation of air power. The British, like their French allies, failed completely to integrate the Royal Air Force (RAF) with the land army and the tank arm. The RAF had struggled to achieve its independence as a strategic arm on its own, and its leadership was terrified at the thought that it could lose that independence through too close a relationship with the British Army. Strafing enemy ground forces and dive-bombing was seen as a threat to the RAF's strategic independence. Air force command chose instead to stick to high-altitude bombing, aerial dogfights and reconnaissance.

Above: Captain Basil Liddell Hart. Along with other supporters of British military mechanization such as Colonel John F.C. Fuller, he was marginalized, ostracized and eventually forced to leave the military altogether.

Left: French *Chasseurs d'Afrique* on parade. In France, tanks were treated as mechanized horses and were only to be used in small groups or as part of a cavalry formation.

Below: The French H-38 light tank. Its armament consisted of one 37mm gun and one 7.5mm machine gun. It only had a crew of two, which hampered battlefield effectiveness.

In late 1937, the chief test pilot of British aircraft manufacturer Vickers returned from Germany, where he had tested the Junkers Ju 87 Stuka dive-bomber. He submitted a glowing report on the need for Great Britain to build its own equivalent, but the Air Ministry wrote back and told him "to mind [his] own bloody business".[11] The lack of air support and lack of coordination between the army and the air force would ensure that the British snatched many a bloody defeat from the jaws of victory during the campaigns in France and North Africa. In fact, the British never learnt to handle their tanks properly since they persisted in using their machines as cavalry, while the lack of dive-bombers ensured that the Germans could get away from many a trap laid for them.

In France, the situation, except for the quantity and quality of material, was no better. Having won World War I, the French believed they had been particularly clever and weren't about to be told what to do by the Germans. In France there was no need or compulsion, as in Germany and Russia, to question either the existing political order or military dogma. The French were not only lumbered with surplus equipment but with outdated ideas from the Great War.[12] In France, as in Great Britain, a few voices dared to raise the question of tanks and modernization. As early as 1922, World War I veteran Colonel Estienne called for the establishment of a tank corps with 100,000 men and 4000 machines. In 1928, with the support of Paul Reynaud (later to become French premier), came a similar call from General Doumenc. The response was complete silence.[13]

Above: French Morane-Saulnier M.S. 406 fighters. In May 1940 France had 1200 aeroplanes facing 3000 German aircraft. Many French aircraft were much slower and less reliable than their German adversaries.

Main picture: By May 1940, France had built up a formidable arsenal of tanks. Its army could claim to have the two best medium tanks in the world: the Somua (S-35) and the Char-B (pictured).

Above: During the 1930s, many in the German military high command shared an aversion to, and contempt for, the cardboard and wooden dummy tanks the Reichswehr used in its exercises.

Instead, the French adopted strategic defence as the response to a then unlikely German threat by building the Maginot Line from the Swiss border to Malmédy. It was "completed" in 1934 at a cost of £30 million.[14] Immediately, an argument broke out over whether or not to extend the line to the English Channel. Marshal Foch wanted a line of fortified zones to be extended all the way to the coast. Marshal Philippe Pétain wanted only a continuous line along the northeastern sector. He argued that the frontier north of Malmédy should be left unfortified since the French Army needed to confront German invaders on Belgian soil.[15]

This then created the problem of what sort of a French army would confront any German invaders in Belgium. The overwhelming majority of the French military establishment came to the wholly erroneous conclusion that the Maginot Line was impregnable and thus ensured the security of France's eastern frontier. They believed that their army, as it stood, was the best in the world and that only very minor changes were needed.

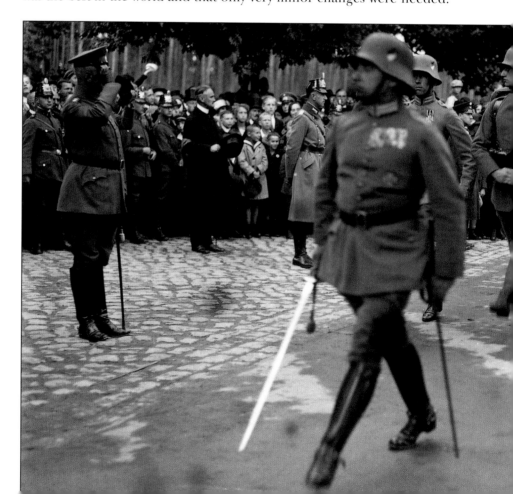

Compounding this complacency was the acceptance, without question, of two Pétain ideas. The first was that the use of anti-tank guns and mines in combination would render any massed tank attack by the enemy "impossible".[16] This was utter nonsense, and it was only in 1943 at Kursk that such a tank attack would be stopped by anti-tank guns and mines in combination with huge numbers of tanks and aircraft. The other unrealistic Pétain notion was that the Ardennes region was impenetrable to tanks. In May 1940, though, seven entire panzer divisions poured through the Ardennes without much effort.

Despite inadequate leadership, as exemplified by the outdated ideas of Pétain, the French had built up a formidable arsenal of tanks by May 1940. In 1932 they developed the mechanized cavalry division – *division légère mécanique* (DLM). The DLM consisted of one armoured brigade, one

Above: The French Air Force may have been no match for Germany's Luftwaffe, but the British Spitfire was more than a match for the German Bf 109. Shown here, a group of Spitfire I test aircraft fly over England in the summer of 1938.

Left: German soldiers march through Berlin in the 1920s. In Germany following the imposition of the Treaty of Versailles the new army, called the Reichswehr, was reduced to 100,000 men and not allowed to train any reserves. It was deprived of all heavy arms, chemical weapons, aircraft, submarines and tanks. However, it retained a cadre of excellent officers, including Rommel.

motorized infantry brigade, one artillery regiment and one regiment of armoured cars – representing a full complement of 13,000 troops, 4000 horses and 1550 motorized vehicles.[17] Of its 250 tanks, though, only 90 were earmarked for combat while the rest were reconnaissance "vehicles".[18] This misuse of resources reflected the French school of thought concerning tanks, which was similar to that of the British. Tanks were supportive weapons for infantry and cavalry and had a subordinate role in battle. They were there to provide a screen for the infantry, artillery (drawn by horses) and the cavalry proper. The tanks were treated, as in Great Britain, as mechanized horses and were only to be used in small groups or as part of a cavalry formation. The combination of horse and tank did not work in practice since the horse slowed down the tank and was vulnerable to enemy fire. French tanks often lacked radios, and during May 1940 would operate in small, vulnerable groups at the mercy of massed German panzers and devoid of infantry, artillery or aerial support.

The French debacle of May 1940 was therefore due very much to outdated thinking and military conservatism and not, as was thought at the time, to the inferiority of French tanks. It is true that prior to 1935 most of France's tanks consisted of the small, poorly equipped and slow Renault FT machines. After 1935, in the face of an ever-growing German threat, the French began to build

Main picture: The Panzer II was first issued to German armoured units in the spring of 1936. These are Ausf C models, which had five independently sprung, large-diameter road wheels. Armament consisted of one 20mm gun and one 7.92mm machine gun.

Left: Hitler sent 25 Panzer I tanks to support Franco in the Spanish Civil War. Lieutenant-Colonel von Thoma reported that these light tanks were completely useless in modern warfare and should be replaced by more heavily armed panzers as quickly as possible.

Below: Heinz Guderian was a dynamic officer who believed strongly in the future of tanks, even though he lacked any technical understanding of them. He was an inspired choice as chief of staff to General Lutz, the inspector-general of transport troops.

Above: Germany's Junkers Ju 87 Stuka, the ultimate dive-bomber. Neither Britain nor France felt that the development of a purpose-built dive-bomber was necessary, but Hitler's forces quickly showed how the Stuka could work with tank divisions in delivering a knock-out blow.

en masse some modern and very good tanks. Within five years the French could match the Germans in numbers and even surpass them in the quality of their vehicles.[19] In May 1940 the French had the two best medium tanks in the world – the Somua (S-35) and the Char-B. The Somua weighed 19.7 tonnes (20 tons) but could reach an impressive top speed of 40km/h (25mph). The Char-B had formidable armour, weighed 31.5 tonnes (32 tons), had a 75mm gun in the hull and an excellent 47mm gun in the turret. But it was slow compared with the Somua, and its overall performance was hampered by its small, one-man turret. That said, both machines were superior in most respects to the German panzers.[20]

So much for the quality of the tanks, but what about the quantity? The argument raised in defence of the Allies in May 1940 was that they were inferior in numbers to the Germans. This is an erroneous claim since the French had a large number of good tanks. They had 260 Somua tanks, 311 Char-Bs, 545 Hotchkiss H-35s and 276 H-39s, as well as 850 Renault (R-35) tanks. This was a grand total of 2242 French tanks, to which had to be added some 231 British tanks.[21] The French lost because their tanks were misused. Their crews had to fight a battle that was no longer relevant and against an enemy that applied the tank in a more effective manner, thus completely outclassing the French despite their superior machines.

French forces were far from inferior on the ground. That was not the case in the air, where the French inferiority, both in terms of quality and quantity, was fatal. In total, the Allies had 800 fighters facing 1000 German ones, but the French had only 150 medium and heavy bombers facing 10 times that number of German ones. Overall, the French had 1200 aeroplanes facing 3000 German aircraft. These were poor odds considering that the French machines were often slower and less reliable than the German models.[22]

The French, unlike the British and Germans, persisted in producing their aircraft by hand. In September 1939 the French produced only 60 aircraft, and there was no quickening of pace during the following months. When France fell, the Germans were astonished to find warehouses filled with aircraft that had either been stockpiled or hadn't been assembled. This was most unfortunate, as France had one fighter design, the Dewoitine D520, that was equal to the British Spitfire and therefore a match for the German Bf 109 model. Due to the slow rate of production and other organizational problems, there were only 79 of these machines in service with the French Air Force in May 1940.[23]

Again, it wasn't just the numbers or quality of French aircraft that contributed to France's defeat, but a failure of strategic and tactical application of airpower. This was exemplified by the views of the French

Below: The first phase in a Blitzkrieg assault involved infantry forces engaging the defenders whilst dive-bombers attacked the reserves and mobile artillery and armoured spearheads crossed the river/obstacle with the aid of sapper units.

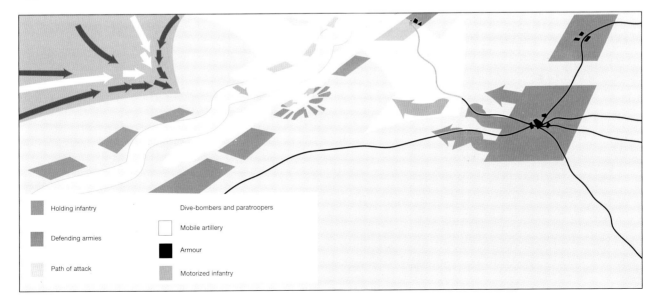

Holding infantry

Defending armies

Path of attack

Dive-bombers and paratroopers

Mobile artillery

Armour

Motorized infantry

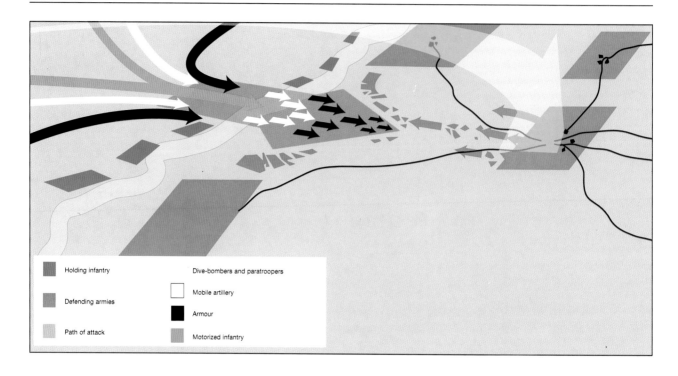

Key:
Holding infantry

Defending armies

Path of attack

Dive-bombers and paratroopers

Mobile artillery

Armour

Motorized infantry

Above: As more units crossed the river, assault troops and demolition squads knocked out enemy strongholds and attempted to widen the bridgehead. Armoured units then punched into the enemy rear, closely followed by mechanized infantry and artillery support. Meanwhile, dive-bombers continued to soften-up the path ahead.

commander-in-chief, General Maurice Gamelin. He, along with many other French commanders, believed that the aircraft, like the tank, was a mere auxiliary to traditional arms. Gamelin predicted that the rival air forces would knock each other out of the contest, leaving the land battle to French and German armies alone.[24] With views like these, it is no wonder that the French, even more so than the British, failed to develop any notion of land-to-air cooperation or a modern dive-bomber. The contribution of the French Air Force during the May campaign was to be quite marginal, and almost from the outset the skies over France and Belgium were German.

Germany, besides Russia, was the main loser in the Great War and had been deprived of territory, colonies and inhabitants by the Treaty of Versailles (1919). Without doubt, the most hated of all the impositions of the treaty was Germany's state of disarmament. What was supposed to be an assurance against future German aggression was, to the Germans, akin to being defenceless. The new army, called the Reichswehr, was reduced to a mere 100,000 men and not allowed to train any reserves. It was deprived of all heavy arms, chemical weapons, aircraft, submarines and tanks.[25] By prohibiting them from having tanks, the Allies mistakenly convinced the Germans that the secret of their victory was the tank. The Germans thus did more to get round this ban than for any other forbidden weapon. This prohibition was to prove as ineffective as the rest, although the dismantling of the German armaments industry, which included a French occupation of the Ruhr (1923–25), crippled tank production in the 1930s.[26]

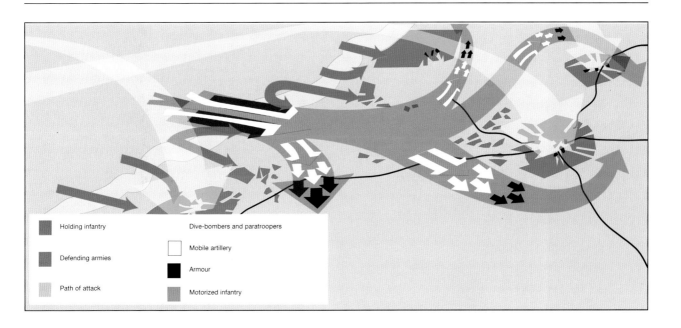

Holding infantry

Defending armies

Path of attack

Dive-bombers and paratroopers

Mobile artillery

Armour

Motorized infantry

Stripped of vital border areas and fortifications, the Germans felt exposed and unprotected. This forced them, unlike the British and French, to rely on a system and strategy of mobile defence to protect their open and extensive borders to the east and west. In addition, this emphasis upon mobile war was reinforced by the earlier defeat in World War I, which had raised doubts over strategy, methods and technology. Unlike the Allies, the Germans had few reasons to cling to the past or outdated methods. The Reichswehr was also fortunate in having a forward-looking and modern-style commander in General Hans von Seeckt. "The whole future of warfare appears to me to be the employment of mobile armies, relatively small but of high quality, and rendered distinctly more effective by the addition of aircraft," Seeckt wrote in the 1920s.[27] A greater contrast to the views of French generals Pétain and Gamelin, or Britain's Haig, could hardly have been imagined.

Seeckt was determined to create out of the small but high-quality cadres of the Reichswehr the most modern and aggressively minded army in Europe. Like most of his colleagues, he wanted to take revenge for the humiliations heaped upon Germany after World War I – and the only way to do so was to modernize the German armed forces. Seeckt therefore retained only the best of the available officer material, such as Rommel and Guderian. The "old wood" was removed.

As for tanks, Seeckt endorsed any scheme, however dubious, whereby his army could acquire them. One was for Krupp industries to build "tractors" at its Ruhr plants once the French had departed. But this was slow and ineffective. Another was for Seeckt to use Germany's new-found friendship

Above: The armoured units then spread out, avoiding large concentrations of enemy trrops and fortified positions. The panzers swept around key logistical points, such as road and rail junctions, attempting to cripple enemy reserve, supply and command-and-control elements.

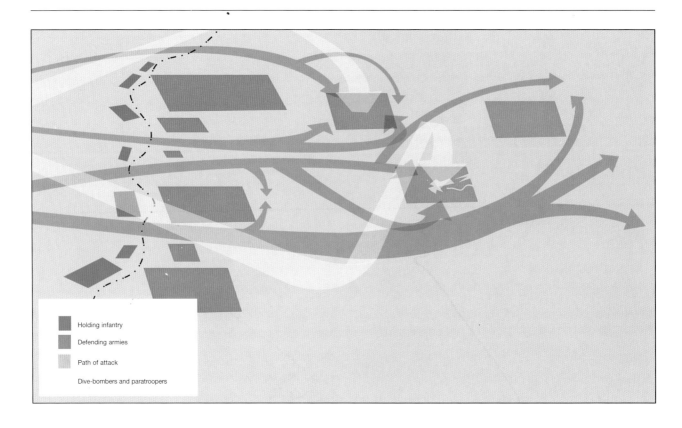

Above: Finally, armoured spearheads then drove deep into enemy held territory, as supporting infantry mopped up any remaining pockets of resistance. The attack then rolled on to the next contact.

Holding infantry

Defending armies

Path of attack

Dive-bombers and paratroopers

with that other international outcast, the USSR, to assist the Reichswehr. In deepest secret, a Soviet-German tank school was established at Kama, near Kazan, on the Volga River. The Soviets, not restricted in buying or producing tanks, bought Western models and the Germans trained their own and Soviet crews in handling them. At Lipetsk, a secret munitions factory and pilot school were established which laid the foundations for Hermann Göring's Luftwaffe (Air Force).[28]

Despite Seeckt's influence and enthusiasm for the tank, this was not true for the rest of the Reichswehr, where there were plenty of reactionary and obstructionist elements to impede progress towards a mechanized army dominated by tanks. The inspector-general of transport troops, General Otto von Stülpnagel, did his worst to prevent the creation of panzer divisions which he viewed as a utopian dream. Believing, like many other officers of the old school, that the tank was a mere auxiliary to infantry and cavalry, Stülpnagel forbade the employment of tanks above regimental size. Many shared his aversion and contempt for the cardboard and wooden vehicles the Reichswehr used in its exercises. It all changed in early 1931 when Stülpnagel was replaced by General Oswald Lutz as inspector-general.

Lutz made an inspired choice as his chief of staff when he selected Guderian for the post. Guderian was then a youngish and dynamic colonel who believed strongly in the future and potential of the tank. Although technically competent, Guderian had never been inside a tank before his appointment. In spite of, or probably because of, this lack of experience, Guderian did not feel bound by established conventions concerning the employment of tanks. [29]

Guderian and Lutz faced an uphill struggle to convince the rest of the Reichswehr that the tank was the future. When they advocated the building of heavy tanks with 50mm guns, the head of the Ordnance Office and the general-inspector of artillery offered them light tanks and 37mm guns instead. One victory was scored during the summer exercises at Jüterbog in 1932, when armoured cars were deployed for the first time and converted many younger cavalry officers to the concept of mechanization. [30]

In January 1933, these moves towards modernization were given a massive boost when Hitler came to power. The new chancellor purged the army of conservatives and replaced them with reformers. General Werner Freiherr von Fritsch became commander-in-chief of the army, and General Werner von Blomberg became minister of war. Both were supportive of modernization, mechanization and the creation of a panzer force as part of the new German armed forces named the Wehrmacht. The following spring, Lutz – again with Guderian as his chief of staff – was made the head of Kommando der Panzertruppen. The important post of chief of the general staff was filled by General Ludwig Beck who, unfortunately, opposed the tanks as much as Stülpnagel and refused to heed Lutz's call for the establishment of any panzer unit larger than a brigade. [31] Beck persisted in viewing the tank, based on the experience of the French, as a minor supportive weapon. [32]

The panzer divisions

Nevertheless, Hitler, Blomberg and Fritsch lent their powerful support to the creation of the panzer arm, and by October 1935 three panzer divisions had been created. Guderian took command of the 2nd Panzer Division at Würzburg. These units may have looked impressive on paper but, due to the demilitarization of German industry, production remained sluggish. There was simply not enough heavy steel being produced in Germany to build the required number of tanks (some 500 per division) to make these formations more than paper tigers. [33]

Guderian, planning ahead, favoured the manufacture of medium and heavy tanks, viewing light tanks as more of a nuisance than an asset in modern warfare. He also insisted on the tanks being adequately crewed so that no single crew member would feel overworked or exhausted. This had been a

Above: German infantry were equipped with their own instant fire support to overcome enemy resistance. This is a 150mm s IG 33 infantry gun.

problem with tanks during the last war, and Guderian insisted on handpicking the crews as carefully as the Luftwaffe selected its pilots. The Allies, by contrast, showed no such concern for their crews, which were left isolated and overworked because of inadequate staffing levels.

Guderian had his way with the recruitment of the crews, but saw himself defeated by the needs of the new Nazi government for propaganda. Hitler wanted the world to believe that he had a huge fleet of tanks. He opted therefore to mass-produce light and cheap machines. They may have been impressive on parades, but these tin-plated boxes were of little use against a real enemy. The Panzer I (PzKpfw I)[34] was a thinly armoured, poorly armed (it had only two machine guns), light (5.7 tonnes or six tons) tankette that could hold its own only against armoured cars. Despite these huge flaws, 1500 of the machines were produced by 1939. The Panzer I's successor, the Panzer II (PzKpfw II), a stop-gap model, weighed 9.8 tonnes (10 tons), but had only a puny 20mm gun as its sole armament.

Left: The panzer division was provided with motorized infantry equipped with MG34 machine guns, mortars and light anti-tank guns to give added support against especially stubborn resistance. This is the 37mm Pak 36 anti-tank gun.

Main picture: Belgium, May 1940. German artillery crew in action. The 150mm s FH 18 was the backbone of German medium artillery in World War II.

There was no justification for producing 1400 of these unimpressive machines, of which 1095 were still in service with the army in May 1940. At least the Panzer I had been phased out by this time. By contrast with these vast numbers of light tanks, there were only 211 Panzer IV and even fewer Panzer III tanks in service by September 1939. [35]

In May 1940 the Panzer III (PzKpfw III), with a crew of five, a 50mm gun, two machine guns and a road speed of 40km/h (25mph), was the mainstay of the German tank forces facing the French. Although it was a fairly good machine, the Panzer IV was far more impressive since it was as fast as the Panzer III but had thicker armour (30mm, or 1.2in) and a far heavier gun (75mm). The Panzer IV was the only German tank that could match the French Char-B. That said, the Germans had a more modern approach to tank armour-plating, which varied in thickness from place to place and was sloped to ensure that Allied anti-tank guns could not penetrate it. [36] The main problem for the Germans was that they did not have enough tanks.

In May 1940, Germany had 388 Panzer IIIs and 278 Panzer IVs. This shortfall was filled by the Allies' short-sighted betrayal of Czechoslovakia in October 1938. Among the vast booty from the conquest of this country was not only a huge armaments industry, including the Skoda and Bren works, but also more than 1000 modern Czech tanks. The T-35 and T-38 models were as good as the Panzer III. Both had 50mm (2in) armour, a 37mm gun, a machine gun and could achieve a road speed of 56km/h (26mph). Thanks to the Allies, Hitler could field 410 T-38 and 829 T-35 tanks. These vehicles made up half of the tanks in Rommel's 7th Panzer Division in 1940. [37]

Blitzkrieg: equipment and theory

Tanks were the mainstay of Germany's Blitzkrieg (Lightning War) tactics, but this approach required supporting weapons either around them or, in the case of Stukas, above them. Between 1939 and the summer of 1942, both on the Eastern Front and in North Africa, the combination of Panzer IVs and Stukas in close cooperation was deadly. The Stuka was Germany's most effective weapon of mobile war, since this dive-bomber was used as flying artillery against enemy lines of communications and strongpoints. With a crew of two, the Stuka would attack from 3050m (10,000ft) at an angle of between 70 and 80 degrees and drop its bomb load at below 984m (3000ft). The delivered load was deadly and remarkably accurate. [38]

The Stukas were controlled by Germany's Luftwaffe and were therefore not under direct panzer command. This made cooperation difficult and, as the war progressed, less reliable. The panzer division had therefore three battalions of artillery ("Panzerattellerie") to accompany and support the tank advance. One battalion consisted of 12 big 150mm s FH 18 howitzers, and the remaining two of 105mm howitzers towed by large halftrack vehicles. This towed artillery was faster than horse-drawn artillery, but slower than SP (self-propelled) guns, of which the panzer divisions were woefully short in 1940.[39]

Thus the tank, the Stuka and the motorized artillery were the core of the panzer division – but it needed further troops to support its advance. It also had motorized infantry equipped with MG34s, mortars and light anti-tank guns to give added support against especially stubborn resistance. None of the infantry units were more important than the pioneer ("Pioniere") troops equipped to build bridges, cross rivers and lay minefields. They had varied tasks that were reflected in their equipment, such as flamethrowers, explosives, smoke units, mine detectors, inflatable boats (to carry tanks across rivers) and pontoons. The pioneers were very much a core unit in the panzer division,[40] as were the motorcycle (MC) battalions in the infantry brigades, which drove to the front and then dismounted to fight. In France and Poland, during summer campaigns and with good roads, the MC units did excellent work for the panzers. However, in bad weather or on poor roads the MC units were redundant and a liability.[41]

Above: Commander-in-chief of the German Army, General von Brauchitsch, turned down Rommel's request for command of a panzer division, but was overruled by Hitler.

All this hardware aside, the big question was whether the theories of mobile, lightning war would work in practice. For most of the nineteenth century the dictum had been that to achieve victory a lot of blood had to be expended to crush the enemy. "Blood is the price of victory. Philanthropists may imagine that there is a skilful method of disarming and overcoming the enemy without great bloodshed, and that this is the proper tendency of the Art of War. That is an error which must be extirpated."[42] The experiences of World War I, especially the bloodbath on the Western Front, seemed to confirm the truth of Clausewitz's dictum.

During much of the interwar period, the former combatant nations of the Great War sought to find solutions to the problem of a war of attrition. The French did so by building the Maginot Line to keep the war out of France,

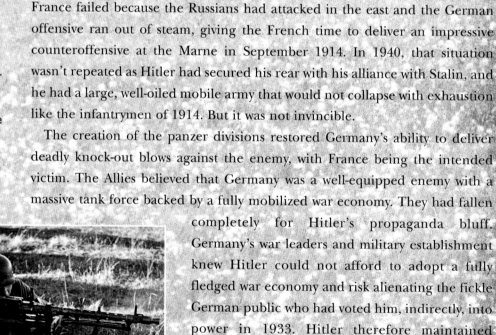

Main picture: Hitler was fortunate that his conquest of Czechoslovakia in 1938–39 yielded much military equipment. This material included T-38 and T-35 (seen here) tanks, both of which played a crucial part in the 1940 campaign in France.

Below: German infantry prepare to use the fearsome MG34 general purpose machine gun.

while Germany sought the solution, as before, in mobile and offensive war. The Prussian tradition, during the Bismarck era, had been to isolate one's enemies and then, with one deadly blow, to destroy each enemy's field armies. This had worked well against Denmark in 1864. It had been even more effective against Austria, at Königgrätz, in 1866. Four years later the armies of Napoleon III were destroyed at Sedan. A similar attempt in 1914 to knock out France failed because the Russians had attacked in the east and the German offensive ran out of steam, giving the French time to deliver an impressive counteroffensive at the Marne in September 1914. In 1940, that situation wasn't repeated as Hitler had secured his rear with his alliance with Stalin, and he had a large, well-oiled mobile army that would not collapse with exhaustion like the infantrymen of 1914. But it was not invincible.

The creation of the panzer divisions restored Germany's ability to deliver deadly knock-out blows against the enemy, with France being the intended victim. The Allies believed that Germany was a well-equipped enemy with a massive tank force backed by a fully mobilized war economy. They had fallen completely for Hitler's propaganda bluff. Germany's war leaders and military establishment knew Hitler could not afford to adopt a fully fledged war economy and risk alienating the fickle German public who had voted him, indirectly, into power in 1933. Hitler therefore maintained something like a peacetime economy until 1942 to keep consumption and living standards up to a "peacetime" level. Hence, for both strategic and political reasons, Hitler and his regime needed a swift, inexpensive war that would prove popular with the public. His alliance with Stalin not only

removed the nightmare of a two-front war, which assisted him in the crushing of Poland, but removed the threat of an Allied blockade starving him of much-needed strategic raw materials such as oil, grain, rubber and minerals. These were delivered cheaply and promptly by his new ally, the USSR. Germany could not afford a war of attrition or a lengthy conflict.

Guderian and his tank theorists had developed the new model of lightning war gradually during the 1930s in the light of their own experiences, as well as taking on board the Soviet and British theories of tank warfare. A mere accumulation of panzers would not in itself be the key to victory, but rather their organization in divisions, corps and even armies. These formations, whatever their size, had to be integrated fully into a combined-arms war machine. The panzers had to be the core of this machine. Airpower, closely combined with the panzers and their support services, was the key to the achievement of victory in the theory of the Blitzkrieg. The enemy was not to be destroyed by the sheer application of raw power, but overwhelmed by a series of enveloping movements and the paralysis of its war-making infrastructure. The strategy was to make the enemy lose the ability and will to fight so much that it would capitulate, as happened in Poland, France and later in Yugoslavia.

The panzers, in combination with motorized infantry, artillery and engineers, were to attack the enemy on a narrow section of front. They would punch a hole, pour through and drive deep into the enemy's rear, enveloping its frontline formations and destroying lines of communications, depots and troop reserves.

Once knocked off-balance, the enemy was to be pursued relentlessly until its forces were either destroyed or had capitulated. Here, tanks and armoured cars could be used to maximum effect. However, the key was the use of airpower in combination with the massed columns of tanks.

High-altitude bombing was to target and wreak havoc on the enemy's railway lines, junctions, stations and bridges. This would prevent troops and supplies reaching the front. Similarly, roads filled with refugees and troops were to be bombed to spread panic, confusion and further demoralize the enemy. The Stukas could be used for precision-bombing of nests or pockets of enemy resistance that proved tough to overcome. Through a series of such continuous blows the enemy, off-balance

Below: The Spanish Civil War was a proving ground for German strategy and weapons. Here, General Franco (left) discusses tactics with Italy's General Berti (centre) and the war minister General Davila (right).

and unable to rally its defences, would be forced to surrender. Perhaps, as in France, the demoralization of the civilian population would spread to the military and political leaders. Then capitulation would prove inevitable and Germany would be victorious.

Blitzkrieg put into practice in Spain and Poland (1936–39)

In April 1936, General Franco led the Spanish Nationalists against the defunct Spanish Republic that had been established only five years earlier. Hitler chose to intervene on Franco's side. Not only were German aircraft instrumental in transporting Franco's feared Foreign Legion across the Straits of Gibraltar, but Hitler also sent a small panzer force (25 Panzer I tanks) under the command of Lieutenant-Colonel Wilhelm von Thoma – later to be one of Rommel's foremost commanders in the desert.

On 6 December, Thoma could report that these light tanks were completely useless in modern warfare and should be phased out as quickly as possible and

Below: German panzers roll into Poland in 1939, demonstrating the effectiveness of Germany's Blitzkrieg strategy. Germany struck with 53 divisions, attacking an enemy with fewer than half that number.

replaced by gunned tanks. Thoma's conclusions coincided entirely with Guderian's, and contradicted the conservatives in the high command. Thoma pointed out that tanks should be used in large and mobile units, preferably divisions, if they were to have a decisive impact on the battle front.[43]

Three years later it was Poland's turn to be invaded and destroyed by Hitler's new military might. Poland would not take sides in the conflict between Hitler and Stalin, and ended up being the victim of the unscrupulous policies of both. In August 1939 the USSR and Germany signed a non-aggression pact, and on 1 September the Germans invaded Poland. Rommel, despite every evidence to the contrary, believed the war was justified and that the Poles would be crushed in less than two weeks. It took twice that time despite Germany's complete superiority in the air and on the ground.

The Germans struck with 53 divisions against fewer than half that number of poorly equipped and led Polish divisions. The Polish Army launched a brave but futile counterattack at Bzura that cost 19 divisions trapped in a huge pocket. On 17 September both the Poles and Germans were stunned when Stalin invaded eastern Poland. By 6 October all Polish resistance had come to an end. As the head of Hitler's personal security, Rommel played no active part in the Polish campaign but he was a keen and impressed observer of the progress of the panzers. It seemed the theory of Blitzkrieg had worked, and that the tank was the weapon of the future.

That same month Rommel, ambitious as ever, hinted to Hitler that he would like to command a panzer division. Hitler, a shrewd judge of character, supported his request with enthusiasm. The army's commander-in-chief, General von Brauchitsch, turned down the request and instead offered

Below: Germans troops in Poland in September 1939. Rommel believed that the Poles would be crushed in less than two weeks. It took twice that time despite Germany's complete superiority in the air and on the ground. By 6 October all Polish resistance had come to an end.

Above: Poland did have tanks with which to oppose the German invasion. However, the quality of Polish troops, equipment and tactics, coupled with limited quantities, meant that there was little effective opposition. This is a knocked-out Polish 7TP light tank.

Rommel a mountain division, arguing that he had no experience of tanks. Rommel's leadership in World War I should have made it obvious that he was the right man to command a panzer division. Hitler realized this, ignored Brauchitsch's petty objections,[44] and on 6 February 1940 Rommel received new orders that made him commander of the 7th Panzer Division.

His appointment no doubt irritated Brauchitsch, the other top brass and more experienced panzer commanders, who persisted in viewing Rommel as Hitler's personal protégé. Four days later Rommel arrived at Bad Godesberg to take charge of the division, whose officers he found flabby and living under peacetime conditions. Rommel always believed that rigorous and frequent training would keep the troops not only out of mischief but also reduce wartime casualties. Instead of the four panzer regiments it should have had, the 7th Panzer Division had only two. Rommel was lucky in that one of these, the 25th Panzer Regiment, had an exceptional commander in Colonel Karl Rothenberg. Like Rommel, he had been decorated with the "Blue Max" during World War I.

Half of Rommel's division was made up of Panzer III and IV tanks; the other half was made up of lighter Czech T-38s that were both faster and more heavily armed than the German Panzer I and II models. It says something for Rommel's intelligence and abilities that he mastered in three months the intricacies of commanding a panzer division. By April 1940 Rommel was steeped in the role of a panzer general and about to be the spearhead of Hitler's next Blitzkrieg.[45]

Chapter notes

1 Irving, pp.19-22. At Stuttgart, his old bugbear and thorn in the flesh, Ferdinand Schörner, played clumsy and irritating practical jokes at Rommel's expense. Rommel did not appreciate Schörner's sense of "humour"; neither had he forgotten this unscrupulous and ambitious officer's tricks during the Italian campaign.

2 Ibid, p.23.

3 Ibid, pp.24-27.

4 Ibid, pp.28-30.

5 Christer Jorgensen and Chris Mann, *Tank Warfare* (London, 2001), pp.9, 10, 12, 19.

6 See H. Reid, *J.F.C. Fuller: Military Thinker* (London, 1987), and J.F.C. Fuller, *Tanks in the Great War, 1914-1918* (London, 1920).

7 Jörgensen & Mann, p.20.

8 Heinz Guderian, *Achtung Panzer! The Development of tank warfare* (London, 1999), p.142. Original publication in German (Berlin, 1937).

9 Jörgensen & Mann, p.21. See chapter four of this book for Hobart's Egyptian misadventures.

10 Ibid, pp.21-22.

11 Deighton, p.167.

12 Guderian, p.143.

13 Aidan Crawley, *De Gaulle* (London, 1969), p.71.

14 Len Deighton, *Blitzkrieg*, p.235. The Line took its name from the Minister of War (1930-32) André Maginot, who died before May 1940 and was thus spared the humiliation of seeing his vaunted line failing to protect France.

15 John Williams, *France: Summer 1940* (London, 1940), p.12.

16 William Shirer, *The Collapse of the Third Republic: an inquiry into the Fall of France in 1940* (London, 1940), p.167.

17 Guderian, p.145; Deighton, p.234.

18 Guderian, p.146.

19 Deighton, p.231.

20 Williams, pp.62-63. Deighton describes the Somua as the best tank in the world in 1940.

21 Ibid. The British tanks were as follows: 75 Matilda Mark IIs (A12), 126 A10s and 30 A13s.

22 Williams, p.17.

23 Deighton, p.224.

24 Ibid, p.221.

25 Guderian, p.133; Thomas L. Jentz, *Panzertruppen* (Atglen, 1996), p.8.

26 Deighton, p.179.

27 Ibid, p.221.

28 Jentz, p.8; R.R.`Abramovitch, *The Soviet Revolution* (London, 1962), p.254.

29 Guderian, *Panzer Leader*, pp.23-25.

30 Ibid, pp.27-28.

31 Ibid, p.32.

32 Jentz, pp.24, 30.

33 Guderian, *Panzer Leader*, pp.31, 36; Deighton, p.179.

34 PzKpfw stood for Panzerkampfwagen or armoured fighting vehicle.

35 Deighton, pp.186-188.

36 Williams, pp.50-51.

37 Williams, p.51; Deighton, pp.232-233.

38 Deighton, p.224.

39 Ibid, p.194.

40 Ibid, pp.200-201.

41 Ibid, p.202.

42 Purnell's, Vol.1, Barrie Pitt, *Blitzkrieg!*, p.11.

43 Jentz, pp.45-46.

44 Irving, p.36.

45 Ibid, pp.38-40.

CHAPTER 3

The Ghost Division

Rommel's panzer spearhead and the Blitzkrieg against France *(May–June 1940)*

The French had been instrumental in the development of motorized transport, the tank and other devices of modern war, but had gone back to relying on the horse, artillery and fortifications. They trusted that the Maginot Line (built during the early 1930s) would keep the Germans at bay. The French high command did not trust the tank, and by May 1940 France had a mere three tank divisions facing 10 panzer divisions. The French military leaders had rejected Colonel Charles de Gaulle's call for the building of six such divisions since it would have cost £85 million. These generals clearly hadn't stopped to count the massive cost of the Maginot Line.[1]

Nevertheless, the French had an impressive number of tanks, and many of them were better than their German counterparts. In May 1940, the French and her allies had 3600 tanks facing 3000 German panzers.[2] This French numerical superiority was squandered by flawed tactics, a lack of vision and a shortage of tank officers able to handle large formations in a real battle situation. Colonel de Gaulle was one of the very few French officers capable of commanding an armoured brigade or division in combat. But it was mainly the French conviction, shared by Great Britain, that the tank was a supportive, rather than an independent, arm that doomed the French tanks. Deployed in penny packets, they were cut to shreds by the German Stukas, anti-tank guns and the panzers during the coming battle that would decide France's fate for the next four years.

Left: Rommel, shown here after the campaign in 1940, had every reason to be proud with his own and his division's role in the defeat of France. This was, from a strategic point of view, his most brilliant all-round performance. He and the 7th Panzer Division had been instrumental in France's stunningly rapid downfall.

Yellow versus Sickelschnitt: planning the defeat of France

The German planners sat down in late 1939 to plan the invasion and defeat of France. The best they could come up with was a modernized version of the Schlieffen Plan. As in 1914, the Germans would invade the Low Countries in a broad, sweeping front stretching from the North Sea to the southern tip of Luxembourg. Having captured Belgium, the Germans hoped to trap the French Army and the British Expeditionary Force (BEF) somewhere in central or eastern

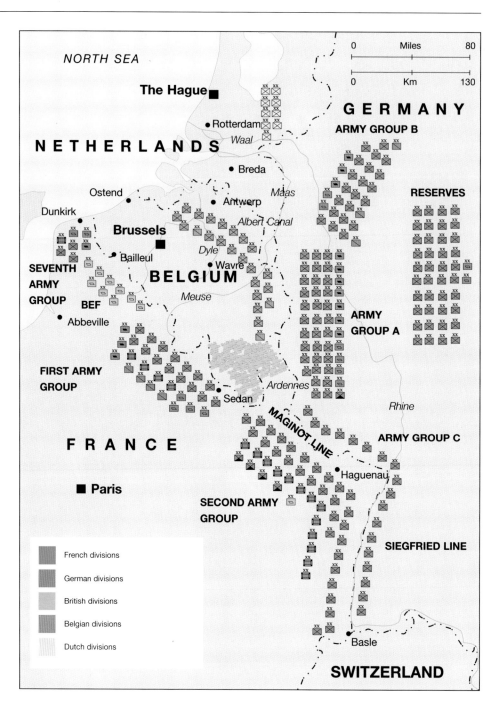

NORTH SEA

GERMANY

ARMY GROUP B

The Hague

Rotterdam

NETHERLANDS

Waal

Breda

Ostend

Maas

Antwerp

RESERVES

Dunkirk

Albert Canal

Brussels

Dyle

Bailleul

Wavre

SEVENTH

BELGIUM

ARMY

Meuse

GROUP

BEF

ARMY

GROUP A

Abbeville

FIRST ARMY

GROUP

Sedan

Ardennes

Rhine

FRANCE

MAGINOT LINE

ARMY GROUP C

Haguenau

Paris

SECOND ARMY

SIEGFRIED LINE

GROUP

French divisions

German divisions

British divisions

Belgian divisions

Basle

Dutch divisions

SWITZERLAND

Right: The disposition of German
and Allied forces at the beginning
of May 1940.

France between themselves and the Maginot Line.[3] This plan, named Yellow, was
unimaginative and potentially disastrous in that it was merely a replica of the
familiar Schlieffen Plan.

The Allies had done much to block a potential German advance through the Low
Countries, with fortifications along the Dyle River, at Eben Emael and in the
Netherlands – Fortress Holland. Furthermore, they had planned, in the so-called
Dyle manoeuvre, to advance into Belgium and southern Holland with the entire

BEF and 33 of the best French divisions to block just such a German advance. Had Yellow been acted upon, the result could have been a total disaster for the Germans that might have led to a repeat of the stalemate reached during World War I.

The Germans were spared this by Hitler's objections to Yellow, and by the existence of another option. A brilliant officer, Erich von Manstein, had come up with Sickelschnitt (Sweep of the Scythe). Instead of a north–south sweep into the interior of France, the Germans would strike through the Ardennes, cut France in two, trap the bulk of the Allied forces in Belgium and then roll up the entire enemy front. Manstein called for the concentration of Germany's entire armoured might opposite the Ardennes. The panzer divisions, closely supported by the Stukas and motorized infantry, would attack with full force. This sector should be attacked, argued Manstein convincingly, since the French believed the Ardennes to be impassable to tanks and therefore did not expect an attack there.

Instead of being delighted with such a brilliant plan, the generals were furious that Manstein had the affront to present it without their authorization. As a "reward" he was stationed in Poland and forgotten until 10 January 1940, when a German Storch light aircraft force-landed in Belgium and the Yellow plan fell into Allied hands. Hitler recalled Manstein, and forced the high command to adopt Sickelschnitt.[4]

According to the plan, Army Group B (General von Bock) was to invade the Low Countries as a diversion to lure the Allies into Belgium where they were to be trapped. It was Army Group A (General Gerd von Rundstedt) that was to carry out the main attack with five armies comprising 44 divisions (including seven out of Germany's 10 panzer divisions) through the Ardennes. Rundstedt's thrust was to be supported by General Hugo Sperrle's 3rd Air

Below: The German plan to punch through the weakly held French centre with a concentrated strike was a brilliant choice. It meant that if French forces moved north to protect Belgium and Holland, the main thrust could trap the Allies. To convince them to move north the Germans launched a large diversionary attack through the Low Countries, and whilst this decption focused the Allied attention, the main thrust burst through the Ardennes.

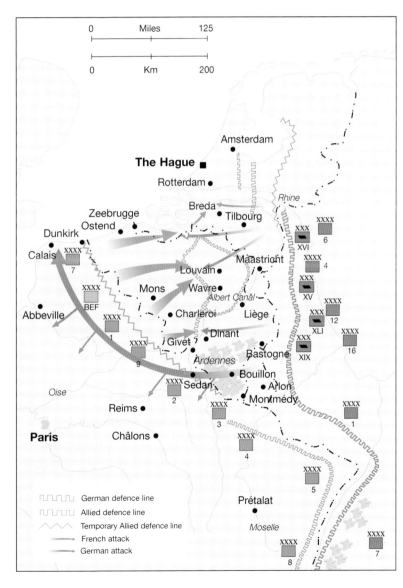

Fleet with 2000 aircraft, including the feared Stukas. General von Kluge's Fourth Army was to spearhead the offensive, with General Hermann Hoth's XV Panzer Corps at the head. Hoth's corps comprised General Hartlieb's 5th Panzer Division and Rommel's 7th Panzer Division.[5]

Invasion: the battle for the Meuse (10–15 May)

At 48 years of age, Rommel was about to become famous as the commander of the panzer assault that defeated France in one of World War II's most brilliantly executed campaigns. At 13:45 hours on 9 May, the codeword Dortmund reached Rommel's headquarters. This meant that the invasion of Belgium would commence at dawn the next day.[6] At 04:30 hours on 10 May Rommel's advance guard crossed the frontier into Belgium, finding the bridges blown and the roads blocked. This slowed the division's advance. But the Belgians, like the French, had committed a fatal error in not keeping the bridges manned against the attackers. This allowed the Germans to rebuild them or set up pontoon bridges in safety. The following morning Rommel

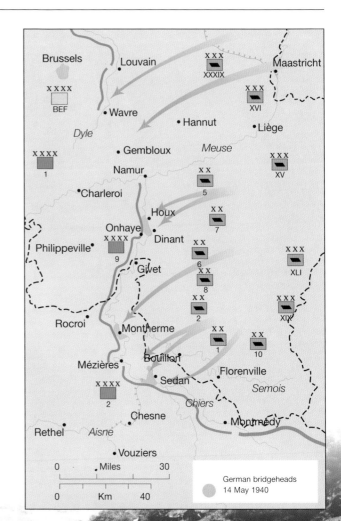

Above: This Belgian fort, like the fortifications of the French Maginot Line, failed to stop the German advance in 1940.

Above left: Rommel's panzer attack into France was one of the most brilliant and daring campaigns of the entire war. As his forces swept across the River Meuse, beleaguered French units tried in vain to halt his advance.

Left: Rommel (on the left, in peaked cap) and motorized infantry cross the Moselle River in 1940 during a training exercise. To his troops and subordinates, Rommel was everywhere at the same time, always urging them to keep up the advance.

broke the resistance of the Belgian "Chasseurs Ardennes" at Chabrehez, and by noon his advance guard had reached the Ourthe River. As the French had abandoned the river, Rommel's sappers swiftly built a pontoon bridge across it. The advance guards subsequently defeated the inferior French Renault and Hotchkiss tanks in the first armoured encounter at Marche. Rommel noted how victory on the battlefield belonged to the side that struck first, and how "those that lie low and await developments usually come off second best".[7] During this campaign he was to prove beyond any doubt how true this was.

For Rommel, these were his Romanian and Italian exploits played out on a larger stage and with far more formidable weapons.[8] To keep up the momentum, he concentrated on the next objective and deliberately ignored his flanks, using his division's greater firepower to subdue pockets of French resistance. By the evening of 11 May, Rommel admitted in a letter to his wife that he was hoarse from shouting orders, but confident of victory.

Hoth, who recognized that Rommel's advance needed support, transferred Colonel Werner's 31st Panzer Regiment from the more ponderous 5th Panzer Division to Rommel's 7th. Werner was ahead of the rest of Rommel's tanks, and his armoured cars had reached the bridge across the Meuse at Yvoir. An attempt by the commander of the advance guard to rush the bridge failed when a Belgian lieutenant, De Wispeleare, sacrificed his life to blow up the bridge. The Germans would have to cross in rubber dinghies. Nevertheless, Rommel's Motorized Infantry Brigade held the entire eastern bank of the Meuse, between Dinant and Houx, by nightfall on 12 May.[9]

That same day Rommel had a stroke of good fortune when one of the motorized brigade's patrols found an abandoned, but intact, weir across the river at Houx island. The patrol crossed the spine of the weir on foot and occupied the tiny river island. In their hurry to retreat, the French had left one of the lock gates undamaged.[10] The German troops crossed to the west bank and established a precarious foothold in the face of withering French fire. By midnight on 12 May, Rommel had, for the loss of 27 men, established a small bridgehead on the west bank of the Meuse. Due to poor lines of communication and a cumbersome command structure, the French Ninth Army's commander, General Corap, was not aware of this until the following day.[11]

Elsewhere, Rommel was not having the best of the fighting. At Dinant, the 6th Rifle Regiment was trying to cross the river, but the infantry were pinned down by deadly fire from the French side. Rommel, who came to inspect the scene, ordered that several houses on the east bank be torched to give smoke cover for the crossing. Under battalion commander Colonel Steinkeller, the regiment finally crossed and captured the village of La Grange.

Rommel was still unhappy with the division's lack of progress and drove south to Bouvignes, where Colonel von Bismarck (7th Rifle Regiment) had one company across but could not reinforce it since his dinghies were destroyed. It was the same story at Leffé, where one company was across, but the rest of the troops refused to risk a crossing in broad daylight and under deadly French artillery and rifle fire.[12]

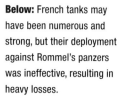

Below: French tanks may have been numerous and strong, but their deployment against Rommel's panzers was ineffective, resulting in heavy losses.

Breakthrough: 14–15 May

To his troops and subordinates, Rommel was everywhere at the same time, with the constant risk that he would be wounded or killed. He took personal command of the 7th Rifle Regiment to get it over the river, and crossed with the first wave. They were attacked by French tanks but Rommel, ever prepared to use bluff, ordered flares to be shot at the tanks in the hope of fooling the French into believing that the Germans had anti-tank guns. The bluff worked and the French withdrew. Rommel then returned to the other bank and cajoled the pioneers into building an 17.7-tonne (18-ton) pontoon bridge so that he could get his tanks onto the west bank of the river and begin the attack proper.

On 14 May, Bismarck marched on Onhaye, while Rothenburg, one of his commanders, got 30 panzers to the west bank. Rommel was almost killed and captured by French colonial troops that offered the toughest resistance to the Germans, but by the evening the village of Onhaye was in German hands.[13] Rommel had consolidated a bridgehead 11.2km (7 miles) deep, and he was one jump ahead of Guderian at Sedan. At 02:00 hours on 15 May, Corap ordered the Ninth Army to retire from the Meuse while Rommel, leaving Major Heidkämper in charge, raced ahead with Rothenburg and Werner's panzers.

Above: Gun emplacements of the Maginot Line. This elaborate defence system certainly deterred a German attack across the Franco-German border, but was successfully outflanked by the Wehrmacht in the north.

Rommel brushed aside the feeble French counterattack by General Bruneau's 1st Armoured Division.[14] That same morning, French Prime Minister Paul Reynaud phoned his counterpart in London, Winston Churchill, with a dramatic message. He told him that the German panzers were pouring across the Meuse like an irresistible torrent and that all attempts to stem the tide had failed. Reynaud admitted, when Churchill tried to remonstrate with the Frenchman: "We are beaten. We have lost the war." Churchill could not believe that Hitler had managed to defeat France in a matter of five days when the Kaiser had not been able to do so in four years.[15]

Rommel and his panzer crews would have been delighted to know this, but they were aware only of progress in their own sector. The Ninth Army, softened up by Stuka attacks, was now retreating in confusion towards the French frontier. Rommel's advance was playing havoc with the rear areas, but his infantry was 16km (10 miles) behind the panzers, whose crews were completely exhausted.[16] That

Below: The Blitzkrieg in action. German tanks, self-propelled guns and armoured cars race across France in May 1940.

afternoon, Churchill flew to Paris and the meeting with the French cabinet shook him since the ministers were completely defeatist. He asked Reynaud when the reserves could be thrown into a French counterattack. The French premier replied that there were none left. Churchill, previously a great believer in French military power, was shocked by the premier's reply.[17] By the evening, Rommel had advanced 27.2km (17 miles) and broken the Ninth Army, all for the loss of 15 men.[18]

As Rommel advanced east, he encountered the extension of the Maginot Line stretching from Longwy to the Channel. Although not as strong as the main fortifications (especially the stretch from the Rhine to Longwy), it was still a problem. The bunkers were of heavy, steel-reinforced concrete, protected by anti-tank ditches and thick, barbed-wire entanglements. Rommel's troops, supported by mortar fire, flamethrowers and artillery, broke through to capture or destroy the bunkers.[19] He was delighted to have penetrated the vaunted Maginot Line.[20]

During 16 May Rommel reached the Cerfontaine woods and tricked the French into letting him through without a fight. He placed troops waving white flags on the outside of his tanks, and the enemy was so astonished that it let them through without a shot being fired. By this time Rommel's advance was accelerating at such speed that the enemy seemed to be paralyzed.[21] That day Rommel's panzers beat and destroyed the French 1st Armoured Division at Avesnes; its commander, General Bruneau, was captured.[22] The French lost 100 tanks, and the only unit that could have halted Rommel's advance had been destroyed.[23]

By the morning of 17 May, the 7th Panzer Division had captured 10,000 French troops.[24] Rommel appeared to lead a charmed life since several officers around him had been killed. His fame back in Germany was on the rise. Journalists showed great interest in him, and he told them: "In this war the commander's place is here, right out in front! I don't believe in armchair strategy. Let's leave that to the gentlemen of the General Staff. This is the age of Seydlitz and Ziethen all over again. We've got to look at this war like a cavalry action. We've got to throw in tank divisions like cavalry squadrons, and that means issuing orders from a moving tank just as generals once used to do from the saddle."[25]

The dash to the sea (18–20 May)

After midnight on 18 May Rommel received orders that the division was to advance from Le Cateau to Cambrai. But at 06:00 hours, Rothenburg's aide arrived to report that the 25th Panzer Regiment was low on ammunition, fuel and was in danger of being cut off. Rommel set out to find and assist Rothenburg, leaving Major Heidkämper, his chief of staff, in charge. Rommel reached Rothenburg, whose predicament was not as bad as he had thought. The French tank attacks were mere pinpricks, but the supply situation was a serious impediment to a fast advance on

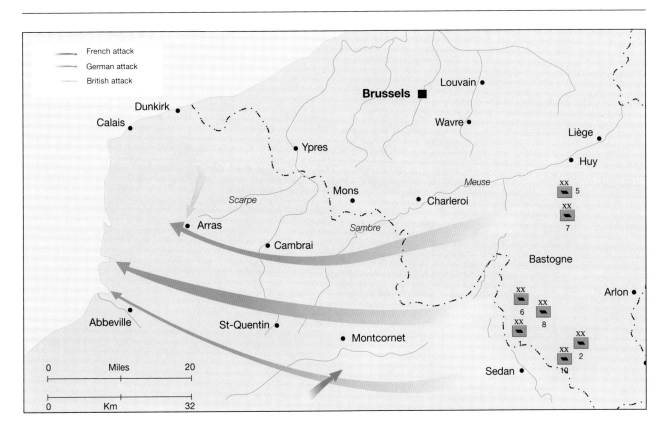

Legend:
→ French attack
→ German attack
→ British attack

Dunkirk
Calais
Ypres
Brussels
Louvain
Wavre
Liège
Huy
Mons
Charleroi
Meuse
Scarpe
Arras
Cambrai
Sambre
Bastogne
Arlon
Abbeville
St-Quentin
Montcornet
Sedan

XX 5
XX 7
XX 6
XX 8
XX
XX 2
XX 10

0   Miles   20
0   Km   32

Cambrai. Again Rommel took a calculated risk that succeeded when he sent a composite battalion made up of motorized infantry (in soft-skinned vehicles) accompanied by a few tanks and self-propelled (SP) guns towards Cambrai. Without investigating properly, the French, in a state of exhaustion and near panic, assumed that the dust cloud advancing so rapidly was composed of tanks. They offered scant opposition, and by nightfall Cambrai – the city where the first tank battle of all time had been fought – was in Rommel's hands.[26]

Meanwhile, there had been a major crisis of confidence back at division HQ because Heidkämper seemed to have lost his head. Rothenburg had been given no fuel because Heidkämper had assumed, completely erroneously, that Rommel, Rothenburg and the entire 25th Panzer Regiment were lost. Hitler claimed that he lost a good night's sleep due to the news of the loss of Rommel and Rothenburg (his best panzer generals). When Rommel heard of Heidkämper's panic he was infuriated and determined to sack this product of general staff training.[27] Rommel eventually accepted Heidkämper's excuses, and was reconciled with an officer whom some have described as competent.[28]

What remained of the French Army was by now in a poor state. Of the 70,000-strong Ninth Army, less than 7000 remained effectives. Meanwhile, Rommel, like Guderian determined to cut France in two, was continuing his inexorable advance to the Channel. On 19 May, Hoth made an impromptu visit to Rommel's HQ and

Above: As German forces successfully burst out from the Meuse bridgeheads, they swept west in a lightning assault. The battered French forces began to disintegrate, and only a few scattered reserves stood between the advancing German Army and the sea.

agreed with his policy of night-time advances to cut German casualties and keep the French off-balance. At nightfall, Rommel's advance guard captured Marquin, where the strategic Canal du Nord crossed the Arras road. By the following morning, at 05:00 hours, the troops had taken the village of Beaurains only 4km (2.5 miles) from Arras. Rommel was, however, stalled and held by the British garrison under Major-General R.L. Petrie. That day Guderian's panzers had reached the Channel at Noyelles.[29] France was scythed in half and her best troops, including the BEF, were north of the German frontline.

There was now a change of French command that the Allies hoped would turn the tide in their favour. Gamelin, having forfeited Reynaud's confidence, was replaced by General Maxim Weygand, a sprightly 73-year-old fighting general who devised a new plan to break the Germans.[30] He wanted the British, with their armoured brigades, to attack at Arras while the French mounted an offensive from the south. If it succeeded, the German funnel-shaped advance to the Channel would be cut in two, and those panzers that had reached the Channel would be cut off from the main force.

The Battle of Arras (20–21 May)

At Arras the largest and most impressive collection of Allied tanks in a single formation was assembled for Weygand's counteroffensive. "Frankforce" was under the command of the British tank expert and 50th Division commander Major-General de Martel. Martel, like Rommel, led his tanks from the front in a command car, and was an aggressive commander of the cavalry school.

Below: Tanks from the 25th Panzer Regiment take a rest before moving to cross the Somme. On 5 June, Rommel opened the attack. Crossing via two abandoned railway bridges, he established, despite fierce French fire, a small bridgehead south of the river.

Frankforce comprised 58 Mk Is and 16 Mk IIs (Matildas), which were impervious to the light German anti-tank guns. The British armour attacked unexpectedly and, for once, the hunter became the quarry as the German crews found their shots bouncing off these monsters. As on later occasions, Rommel was elsewhere when the British attacked and had to rush to take command.

Martel's Matildas left Rommel, for the only time during this otherwise meticulous campaign, momentarily lost for a solution. His answer was to turn Germany's famous 88mm anti-aircraft guns on the Matildas along a defence line running from Beaurains to Agny. By the end of the day's fighting, the Germans had knocked out nine Matildas but had sustained the heaviest tank losses during the entire campaign. The British had the satisfaction of putting a temporary halt to Rommel's runaway advance. They gave him a serious scare and, at the same time, subjected the SS-*Totenkopf* Division to a thrashing.[31] After Arras, Rommel came to view the British officers and men with deep respect. It was only the improvised use of the 88mm guns and the sheer determination of his troops, after a hard fight, that forced the determined British attack to end in bloody stalemate.[32] This temporary halt in his advance taught Rommel

Above: Rommel (right) and other German officers take stock as the lightning-fast invasion of France continues.

Above: General Maxim Weygand of France devised the British armoured attack at Arras, backed by a French offensive from the south. If it had succeeded, the German advance would have been cut in two. However, it failed.

Below: Belgium, May 1940. A tank of the 36th Panzer Regiment moves into a combat position during the opening stages of the invasion that prompted the early fall of France.

some valuable lessons about the quality of both British tanks and their crews. He later put this information to good use in the desert.

After the shock of Arras, Rommel regrouped and then used his favourite tactical feint. While his panzers outflanked the enemy, the infantry overran the British anti-tank guns. This temporary halt and slower pace of advance allowed the 5th Panzer Division to catch up with the 7th. By evening, Werner's regiment held the Lorette Heights outside Arras, where a French monument had been erected with the ominous text: "Who holds Lorette Heights holds France". Rommel's advance guard threatened the Lens road and therefore Frankforce's access to Arras, which was occupied by German motorized infantry.[33] Rommel was exultant, telling Lucie: "My division has had a blazing success capturing Dinant, breaking through the Maginot, capturing Cambrai and then Arras." Some 60 of the best Allied divisions were trapped in northern France, and Rommel concluded, "As I see it the war in France may be over in a fortnight".[34]

The Battle of Lille and the end of the northern campaign (26–29 May)

Rommel now took the opportunity to rest his exhausted crews and their equally worn-out tanks while he prepared a new and final stage in this campaign: the battle of Flanders. Stationed around Béthune, Rommel was in splendid form, while the weather was warm and sunny.[35] Two days of much-needed rest and recuperation did wonders for the division, which had lost 1500 men and 60 officers (12 percent of its manpower) during the campaign. Rommel concluded that these sacrifices were "very little compared with what's been achieved". He added that "the worst is now well over" since the French, in his view, were beaten.[36] By this time Rommel had a mere 86 tanks left, of which only four were the heavier Panzer IV models. However, he now had control not only of the 7th, but also of the

5th Panzer Division. This gave him the mechanical muscle to continue the advance. The most immediate task was to break the British lines along the La Bassée Canal east of Béthune.[37]

On 26 May, with the short rest period over, Rommel ordered the canal to be crossed by the infantry and machine-gun battalions. Well-aimed British sniper fire prevented the Germans from crossing, and Rommel was forced to direct in person the counter-fire required to drive away the British. By the afternoon, Rommel had established two makeshift pontoon bridges across the canal, and was no doubt delighted to receive much-needed reinforcements in the shape of two additional armoured regiments – equipped with Panzer III and IV tanks.

That same day, Lieutenant Hanke, on behalf of a proud and pleased Führer, pinned the Knight's Cross on Rommel's already well-decorated chest.[38] As his adjutant wrote to Lucie, the decoration was well-deserved: "Every man of the division ... knows that nobody has deserved it more than your husband. He has led the division to success which must, I imagine, be unique."[39] Rommel was more concerned about advancing and encircling the Anglo-French forces holding Lille, and he intended to attack the fortress city from the southwest.[40] At 18:00 hours, led by Rommel himself, the division pressed on towards Lille and again, due to his boldness, he was almost captured by the French.[41]

By midnight, the advance guard was on the western outskirts of Lille where fresh supplies of petrol and ammunition reached the division.[42] It was the German infantry that had finally caught up with the runaway "Ghost Division". Rommel noted with great pride in his reports that his division had captured 6900 prisoners and 49 tanks, "not bad for Thuringians".[43]

Final thrust: the battle for France (5–22 June)

Rommel, brimming with pride, was the only divisional commander invited to a Führer conference at Charlesville on 2 June.[44] The discussion concerned Operation Red, the attack across the Somme and the invasion of the rest of France south of the river. Hitler radiated warmth and gratitude. He had every reason to be pleased with Rommel's outstanding and brilliant performance, especially since he had handpicked

Below: The British Matilda tanks used against Rommel in the Battle of Arras provided one of the few setbacks for the German general. His inspired use of 88mm anti-aircraft guns destroyed the Matilda threat, though.

"his" general for the command of one of the key panzer divisions. Rommel was both flattered and pleased that Hitler had marked him out for special treatment.[45]

The general returned to his division, which by now had moved south to the Somme, well pleased that six days of rest and recuperation had done wonders for its effectiveness. With the equipment in good repair and his troops rested, Rommel, facing the southern frontline, believed it was time to attack the French again before they had time to recover.[46] Time was of the essence in this campaign, and Rommel's hunch was correct. The French, once over the shock of aerial Stuka attacks combined with massed tank formations, were regaining their customary fighting élan. During the next phase of the campaign, aptly named the Battle of France by Weygand, the French showed much greater fighting spirit and some of the dogged determination of the previous war. With their backs against the wall, as at the Marne in September 1914, it was possible that the French might spring a surprise on their attackers. However, this seemed a forlorn hope since the BEF had been evacuated, the French had lost all their mechanized and armoured divisions, and the best 24 of their infantry divisions had also been lost in the battles for Belgium and Sedan. This left Weygand to command some 50 battered and over-stretched divisions to hold more than 322km (200 miles) of frontline against the Germans.

Weygand realized that he could not hold a continuous frontline; he therefore opted for an entirely different strategy. His troops were instructed to hold at all cost fortified positions (nicknamed hedgehogs), which bristled with anti-tank guns, artillery and machine guns, even if the enemy surrounded them. There was to be no retreat, and the troops were exhorted to fight to the death against the invaders.

Rommel was not going to give the French the satisfaction of fighting him the way Weygand wanted, since he would avoid the hedgehogs altogether. At 16:00 hours on 5 June, Rommel opened the attack across a narrow stretch of the Somme. Crossing via two abandoned railway bridges, and despite fierce French fire, he established a

Below: Rommel and trusted officer Rothenburg (second from right), June 1940. Rothenburg's 25th Panzer Regiment spearheaded the 7th Panzer Division's drive through France, reaching the Channel on 10 June.

small bridgehead south of the river. Rommel advanced across the open countryside to avoid the French hedgehogs in so-called formation drive (Flächemarsch), whereby the panzer regiments advanced in a box formation.

The front and sides of the formation were made up of the tank battalions, the rear comprised anti-tank and reconnaissance battalions, while motorized infantry was located in the centre. In this fashion, the division advanced at an average of 64km to 80km (40 to 50 miles) per day. Rommel's advance was so fast that the French civilian population, like their military, could not keep pace. At Elbeuf, a confused and slightly myopic Frenchwoman came up, grabbed Rommel's arm and asked: "Are you English?" Rommel shook his head, whereby the woman, shocked at realizing who she was dealing with, screamed in terror, "Oh les barbares!", and promptly disappeared back inside her house. Rommel's reaction was a mixture of bemused surprise and pity for the French population.

Above: With a stranglehold on much of northern France, the German Army launched Operation Red, the conquest of the rest of France. This second onslaught against the remaining French units did encounter some stiff resistance from the defenders, but ultimately Weygand could not muster enough strength to push back the Wehrmacht. A strategic withdrawal across the entire front was ordered, and France signed an armistice days later. The solid purple line represents the demarcation line; the broken purple line shows the limit of the German advance when the truce was signed.

The battle for France

The 7th Panzer Division was the first to reach the Seine at Sotteville, by midnight on 8 June. In a nearby chateau, Rommel snatched two hours of sleep.[47] After their initially fierce and brave show of resistance, the French frontline troops were running out of supplies and hope in equal measure. They were beginning to disintegrate.[48] Rommel, repeating his dash to the sea, was once again pushing to trap the Allies in a large pocket around Dieppe.[49] Covering 96km (60 miles), Rommel managed to reach the Channel west of Dieppe and thereby trap several French divisions and one British – General Victor Fortune's 51st (Highland) Division.[50]

Rommel's advance was so rapid and unexpected that the confused and bewildered French population often cheered his tanks in the mistaken belief that they were British. Rommel, in his own command tank, led the advance from the front. Rothenburg's 25th Panzer Regiment as usual headed the drive, and on 10 June it had reached the Channel. Rothenburg was so exhausted that he drove his tank through a wall on the sea front. Rommel reached Saint-Valéry on 11 June.

The proud Highlanders put up fierce resistance against the advancing Germans, but the combination of artillery and tank fire, backed by waves of Stuka dive-bombers, broke their will to resist. This time there was no armada of small ships to

Above: One of the effective Czech T-38 tanks acquired by the Germans and forming almost half of Rommel's tank force of the 7th Panzer Division during the invasion of France.

take them home to Great Britain (unlike at Dunkirk). The following morning, the French Ninth Army capitulated to Rommel and he drove into the town in triumph. The French generals accepted their fate with good grace, and one even congratulated Rommel on his feat in command of the Ghost Division. Fortune did not join in the bonhomie of his allies, and was infuriated that he had been forced to capitulate without a proper fight to such a young and junior general.[51]

All in all, Rommel had captured a total of 46,000 enemy troops, including 8000 British soldiers. Once the shock of fighting had worn off, he was surprised at the British officers' sang-froid. But their good humour did not extend to accepting an invitation from Rommel to an alfresco lunch with him and his officers.[52] "The battle is over," wrote Rommel to Lucie on 12 May. "Today one corps commander and four division commanders presented themselves before me in the market square of Saint-Valéry, having been forced by my division to surrender. Wonderful moments."[53] He was especially pleased to have captured a British general and his division, and to have occupied Le Havre without resistance.[54]

Meanwhile, on 10 June, the French Government had retreated in great haste to Bordeaux (a sure sign that France was falling apart). Weygand moved his headquarters to Briane, and Italy's Mussolini finally dared to declare war on a collapsing France. His invasion of the French Riviera, however, turned into a military farce when the French not only halted his advance but threw his Fascist legionnaires back across the frontier.

By 11 June, the Germans had established three bridgeheads across the Seine, and at 11:00 hours Paris was declared an open city. Three days later the cocky Germans, accompanied by a military band, could begin the occupation of what singer Maurice Chevalier called the city of light and the "the most beautiful girl in the world". The French Army, now reduced to 30 full-strength divisions, could at least be proud of the fact that it had, unlike during the battle for the Meuse, done its very best to try to stem the German flood.[55] Even Weygand was rapidly losing heart. More and more strident voices were heard both at his HQ and inside the government that "we cannot go on like this. We have to sign an armistice."[56]

Unaware of these fatal developments for France, Rommel and his tired troops enjoyed four days of sun, bathing in the sea, good French wine and food.[57] Then they had to continue the advance. On 16 June Rommel's tanks crossed the Seine while Paris had fallen and General Leeb's inactive Army Group C finally broke through the Maginot Line at Saarbrücken. Rommel's advance had been transformed into almost a peaceful occupation of the French countryside that seemed virtually untouched by war.[58] The 7th Panzer Division covered some 322km (200 miles) in two days (by 17 June).

Under orders from Hitler, who wanted to occupy as much of France as possible before the French asked for armistice terms, Rommel turned his tanks towards Cherbourg. This was a strategic and heavily fortified port at the northern end of the Contentin Peninsula.[59] On 18 June, Rommel attacked and captured Cherbourg with its 30 forts ringing the city. The large garrison put up scant resistance.[60] Rommel took 30,000 French prisoners. This meant that his division had captured 97,000 Allied troops during its six-week advance.[61]

By this time France was mortally wounded and her army bleeding to death. The German advance could not be stopped. Having brought back Marshal Pétain[62] to provide some starch to his wavering cabinet, Reynaud was shocked to find that the old marshal was an arch defeatist. Reynaud wanted to continue the fight at the side of Great Britain and evacuate the remainder of France's armed forces to North

Below: During his drive through France, Rommel's 7th Panzer Division alone captured 97,000 Allied troops, with up to 30,000 French prisoners taken during the capture of Cherbourg. These are some of the French prisoners.

Above: Humiliation for France. On 22 June 1940, General Huntziger, head of the French armistice delegation, and General Keitel, representing Hitler, signed the instrument of the armistice. France had fallen, and Rommel and his division had been instrumental in the great victory.

Africa. His brave suggestions were ignored by the majority in the cabinet, and by 17 June Reynaud had been replaced by Pétain.

The French held only the Loire front against the Germans. On 22 June General Condé, whose army group (Third, Fifth and Eighth Armies) held the Maginot Line, capitulated. This followed a move by Guderian's panzers to reach the Swiss frontier and cut him off from the rest of France. A staggering 400,000 French troops became German prisoners, and by this act the French Army ceased to exist as a coherent fighting force.[63]

That same day, at 06:30 hours, General Huntziger, head of the French armistice delegation, and General Keitel, representing Hitler, signed the instrument of the armistice. France was totally crushed. Alsace and Lorraine in eastern France were annexed by the Reich. Some 60 percent of the remainder would be under direct German military occupation for the next four years. The south would be ruled by Pétain's collaborationist Vichy Government. Never before had the French been forced to endure such a draconian and harsh defeat at the hands of Germany.

Three days later Rommel wrote that he was fewer than 322km (200 miles) from the Spanish frontier, after advancing down the Atlantic coast. "How wonderful it's all been," concluded Rommel.[64] He had every reason to be proud and contented with his own and his division's role in the defeat of France. This was, from a strategic point of view, Rommel's most brilliant all-round performance. He and the 7th Panzer Division had been instrumental in France's stunningly rapid downfall.

Hoth, while praising Rommel in public, criticised the general behind his back as being too impulsive, needing greater experience and better judgement. Kluge complained that Rommel was too apt to grab all the glory for himself at the expense of others, such as the Stuka crews and the infantry troops, while he simply took material, troops and tanks from Hartlieb's 5th Panzer Division. Rommel was also accused of being too positive towards the Nazis and their stooges, such as Hanke, and other political officers.[65]

Some of this criticism had a grain of truth but seemed, on the whole, to have been the gripes and moans of jealous men. Rommel had stolen the limelight because he was a better soldier and commander. He wasn't shy about flaunting his abilities or pride in his achievements. However, this campaign of jealousy and sniping was to continue during his two years in the desert.

Chapter notes

1 Aidan Crawley, *De Gaulle* (Collins, London, 1969), pp.70-76. Like Guderian, de Gaulle had made himself very unpopular with the French high command and ossified top brass by advocating the use of tanks in his 1934 book *L'Armée de Métier*.

2 Purnell's, Vol. 2, Major-General R.H. Barry, *The Military Balance*, pp.95-103.

3 British Expeditionary Force.

4 Purnell's, Vol. 2, Alistair Horne, *Breakthrough at Sedan, 10–20 May 1940*, pp.113-114.

5 Shirer, p.587.

6 Irving, p.40.

7 Horne, *To Lose a Battle*, pp.246-270.

8 Ibid, p.311.

9 Ibid, pp.271, 295-296.

10 The French had left it intact because they feared the water level of the Meuse would fall too low and allow the Germans to cross. However, they failed to place troops in this vital sector to prevent a German capture of the weir and the lock.

11 Horne, pp.297-299, 311. Corap was a brave but out-of-date French colonial officer with no experience of tanks and completely wedded to the past. He was, unfortunately for the French, the rule rather than the exception among its army commanders in May 1940.

12 Ibid, pp.312-315.

13 Ibid, pp.316-317, 361-363.

14 Ibid, pp.368-369, 394-396.

15 Williams, *The Fall of France*, p.56.

16 Horne, pp.398-399.

17 Horne, *Breakthrough at Sedan*, p.123.

18 Horne, *To Lose a Battle*, p.400.

19 Ibid, pp.460-463.

20 RP.34, Rommel to wife, 23 May 1940.

21 Irving, p.42.

22 Horne, *To Lose a Battle*, p.465.

23 Horne, *Breakthrough at Sedan*, p.120.

24 Horne, *To Lose a Battle*, pp.468, 498.

25 Irving, p.45. Rommel was never to better this statement as the very essence of his style of war.

26 Horne, *To Lose a Battle*, pp.501-503.

27 Irving, p.46.

28 Horne, *To Lose a Battle*, p.502, footnote 2.

29 Ibid, pp.530, 549-550.

30 Horne, *Breakthrough at Sedan*, Purnell's, Vol. 2, p.124.

31 Horne, *To Lose a Battle*, pp.562-565, 567-569.

32 Irving, pp.46-47.

33 Horne, *To Lose a Battle*, pp.586-587.

34 RP.34, Rommel to Lucie, 23 May 1940.

35 RP.34, Rommel to Lucie, 24 May 1940.

36 Ibid, Rommel to Lucie, 26 May 1940. See Horne, *To Lose a Battle*, p.604, Footnote 2.

37 Horne, *To Lose a Battle*, p.604.

38 Irving, p.47.

39 RP.39, Schraepler to Frau Rommel, 27 May 1940.

40 RP.39, Rommel to Lucie, 27 May 1940.

41 Irving, p.48.

42 RP.42-43, Rommel to Lucie, 29 May 1940.

43 Irving, p.48. Thuringians had a reputation – probably undeserved – among their fellow Germans for being unmilitary and most lacklustre soldiers.

44 Ibid.

45 RP.43, Rommel to Lucie, 3 June 1940.

46 RP.43, Rommel to Lucie, 4 June 1940.

47 Irving, p.49.

48 RP.53, Rommel to Lucie, 7 June 1940.

49 RP.53, Rommel to Lucie, 10 June 1940, at 05:00 hours.

50 RP.62, Rommel to Lucie, 11 June 1940.

51 Irving, p.50.

52 RP.66, Rommel's notes.

53 RP.66, Rommel to Lucie, 12 June 1940.

54 RP.66, Rommel to Lucie, 14 June 1940.

55 Purnell's, Vol. 2, pp.173-174, Colonel Adolphe Goutard, *The Fall of France, 20 May-25 June 1940*. Born in 1893, Goutard took part in the campaign of 1940 and had the sweet revenge of fighting Rommel's men in Tunisia three years later.

56 "World at War" (BBC series, Vol. 2), interview in the 1970s with Colonel Beaufre of the French GHQ staff.

57 Irving, p.51.

58 RP.66, Rommel to Lucie, 16 June 1940.

59 Irving, p.51.

60 RP.66, Rommel to Lucie, 20 June 1940.

61 Irving, p.51.

62 Philippe Pétain (1856–1951) had led the defence of Verdun in 1916 with dogged determination, and had restored the French Army's morale through necessary reforms a year later. He was known as a careful and considerate commander, but by 1940 Pétain was a complete defeatist who blamed his country's defeat on the influence of the left. He became yet another tired, old voice that called for an armistice even at the price of humiliation and despair at the hands of the "Boche".

63 Goutard, p.175.

64 RP.85, Rommel to Lucie, 25 June 1940.

65 Irving, p.52.

CHAPTER 4

The Desert Whirlwind

The arrival of Rommel in North Africa and his first desert offensive *(March–April 1941)*

Mussolini, Italy's fascist dictator since 1924, was ambitious for himself and his country. He desired above all else to expand Italy's African empire at the expense of the British territories of Egypt and Sudan. Mussolini wanted desperately to link his East African empire[1] through a victory over the British in Egypt.[2] To the over-confident Italians, that seemed an easy enough task since the tiny British forces in the Middle East had a huge area to cover. The British had only 36,000 troops to defend Egypt. The Italians had some 250–300,000 soldiers in Libya under the command of Mussolini's best offensive general, Marshal Rudolfo Graziani, whose military reputation was built on the crushing of the Libyan nationalists led by Umar al Mukhtar. Graziani had conquered the interior of Tripolitania in 1922–23, and marched an army to Kufra. Despite these bold campaigns, the Italians did not manage to capture and execute Mukhtar until 1932 – bringing a 20-year colonial war to an end.[3]

Mussolini on the march (June–September 1940)

Given Italy's problems in crushing the poorly equipped Libyans and Ethiopians, the British seemed to pose a bigger problem for Mussolini's troops. However, Mussolini was adamant that his Libyan army was capable of conquering Egypt on its own. He gave repeated orders between June and August for Graziani to attack.[4] Graziani pointed out that his colonial army was equipped and trained to fight native insurgents, not a modern and well-equipped European foe. The Army of Libya, significant in numbers, wasn't impressive in any other way. It was woefully short of armour and mobility. Armoured warfare was a complete mystery to its troops and their officers, and Graziani kept postponing an attack. A skirmish on the Egyptian border during June 1940 saw the British easily defeat the Italians, whose armour was so poor that the British could shoot the Italian tankettes (Ansaldo) to pieces with their heavy machine guns. It was only in September that Graziani finally acted and ordered General Berti's Italian Tenth

Left: Rommel (left) in Tripoli, 1941. Nicknamed the Desert Fox, Rommel made the desert his own through a mixture of cunning and high-speed manoeuvres that proved extremely effective. However, he was plagued by supply difficulties throughout the campaign.

Army to invade Egypt – which it did after some delays. But the offensive during 13–16 September was a cautious affair. Berti's army only reached Sidi Barrani, a few miles inside the border known to the British as the "wire".[5]

General O'Connor's lightning offensive and conquest of Cyrenaica (December 1940–February 1941)

The British command structure was cumbersome. General Sir Archibald Wavell was Commander-in-Chief Middle East; under him was Lieutenant-General Maitland "Jumbo" Wilson (in charge of Egypt). Finally, detached to defend Egypt from an Italian invasion was the Western Desert Force (WDF) under General Richard O'Connor – a tough, energetic and aggressive Irishman eminently suited to give the fascists a run for their money. Although the WDF was vastly outnumbered by the Italians, it was well-equipped with tanks – 200 light, 75 medium and 45 heavy. The Italians had 240 light, 60 medium and no heavy tanks, but had far more aircraft and field guns than the British. The crucial difference between Graziani's army and O'Connor's was that the British knew how to use their armour.

What was to become the desert war's most famous British unit, the 7th Armoured Division, had been created at Mersa Matruh in 1936. In September 1936 the renamed Mobile Division Egypt received a new commander in the form of Major-General Percy Hobart, along with Martel one of the few brilliant tank commanders in the British Army. Hobart was devoted to the idea that tanks were the future of modern warfare and, like most messiahs, he made more enemies than converts. He trained his formation to fight in the desert and as a modern, swift-moving armoured division. Unfortunately, Hobart had an argument with Wilson in September 1939. "Jumbo", irritated by the erratic, if brilliant, Hobart, had him shipped back to Great Britain.[6]

We will never know what Hobart could have achieved in the desert had he not been fired. However, Wilson found a good replacement in General O'Connor, who proved to be a master of mobile and mechanized war in the desert. After months of preparations, the British attacked the Italians. On 6 December 1940, while the Royal Air Force (RAF) tackled the Italian airfields, British armour advanced on the Italian frontline. The Italians found, like the Germans six months earlier, that their puny anti-tank guns were hopeless against the Matildas. The shells simply bounced off the armour plating. The British had

Far right: The Italians had 240 light, 60 medium and no heavy tanks. Their enemy, the British Western Desert Force, had 200 light tanks, 75 medium and 45 heavy ones. This is a column of M 11/39 medium tanks.

Below: The Italian army in North Africa was numerically strong, but had only a modest fleet of light and medium tanks – and little understanding of how to use armour.

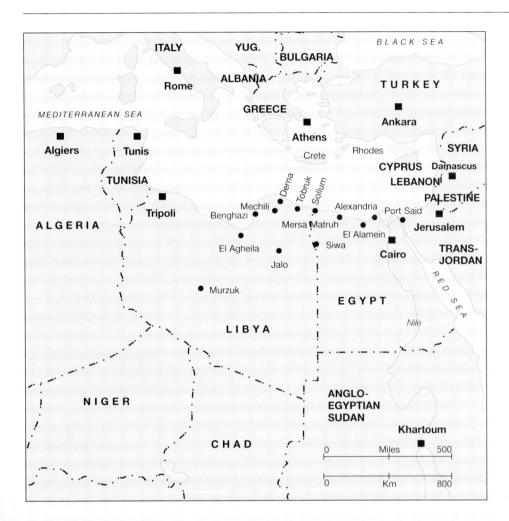

Above: Mussolini's best offensive general, Marshal Rudolfo Graziani. His military reputation was built on the crushing of Libyan nationalists. Graziani had conquered the interior of Tripolitania in 1922–23, and marched an army to Kufra.

Left: An overview of the North African theatre of operations.

Above: General Sir Archibald Wavell (centre) was the British Commander-in-Chief, Middle East.

Below: Italy's army in the desert war was totally outclassed by the British, and vast numbers of prisoners were taken. Often, as shown here, they were marched away from defeat with just one guard.

good co-ordination between their tanks and their artillery. The Italian gun crews, by contrast, either stood their ground (even if crushed by the British tanks) or surrendered, since retreat was impossible due to their lack of mobility.

On 16 December, the 7th Armoured Division (70 cruisers and 120 light tanks) was preparing to cross into Cyrenaica, and that same day Sidi Omar fell to the British. The 16th Armoured Brigade, led by the Matildas, overran Bardia on 16 January 1941 and took 40,000 prisoners. Tobruk, held by 25,000 Italians, was reached by Australian troops on 21 January. By this time, Graziani was left with a field army of 40,000 soldiers. The following day, Tobruk fell to the British with its entire garrison, 200 guns and 70 tanks. The Italians did learn from their previous mistakes, and once the troops' fear of tanks wore off they began to fight back. On the morning of 24 January, for example, the Italian *Babini* Armoured Brigade, equipped with 120 obsolete M-13 tanks, managed to chase off the 7th Armoured Brigade. It was only with artillery support and reinforcements that the British defeated the Italians.[7]

Operation Sunflower (November 1940–March 1941)

On 29 January Derna fell to the Australians as the Italians continued their retreat. The British, showing great persistence, pursued their enemy without respite. By 15 February, the whole of Cyrenaica was in the hands of the British, who had scored a great triumph at the Battle of Beda Fomm (3–5 February), and had captured in total some 130,000 Italian troops, 850 guns, 400 tanks and 1000 lorries.[8] This was a massive haul for an army that was only the size of an Italian army corps and heavily outnumbered by its enemy. After a six-week offensive and having covered 322km (200 miles), the British, ably led by O'Connor, seemed

poised to take Tripoli and end the desert war before it had really begun.[9]

The Germans were growing increasingly worried about the North African situation. Earlier, Hitler, preparing to assist Mussolini, had sent General Wilhelm von Thoma to study the conduct of the Italian Army in the desert.[10] Thoma was unimpressed, and viewed an intervention by Germany as imperative if the whole of North Africa was not to be lost to the enemy. Hitler offered the 3rd Panzer Division to the Italians in November 1940. This offer was first accepted, then declined by Rome.[11] Rommel, as yet completely unconnected with the desert war, wrote to Lucie on 8 January: "I'm not surprised that our allies aren't having things all their own way in North Africa. They probably thought war was easy, and now they've got to show what they can do. They began just the same in Spain, but fought very well later."[12]

The main reason for German lack of interest in Italy's North African misfortunes was due to Berlin's preoccupation with plans for the invasion of Great Britain. If Operation Sea Lion succeeded, then North Africa would become an irrelevance. The invasion was cancelled (ensuring Great Britain's survival) in favour of an invasion of the USSR a year later. Rommel believed the invasion of Great Britain should have been attempted despite the risks.[13]

Above: Thick black smoke drifts over the port of Tobruk following its capture by the British in January 1941. In the foreground can be seen several captured Italian armoured fighting vehicles.

Above: A British Mk IV light tank serving as part of the Western Desert Force during the Italian invasion of Egypt.

This did not mean that Hitler could abandon Mussolini to his fate. On 1 February 1941, the Italian Government officially asked for German assistance, and four days later Hitler offered them a panzer division in return for holding Tripolitania at all costs. The following day, Hitler met Rommel in Berlin to tell him that he had been appointed to command the Deutsche Afrika Korps (DAK), made up of one panzer division and one light division that would be sent forthwith to Africa. Rommel was to be under the nominal command of the Italians, but he would have direct access to Hitler.[11]

Overall the Führer was not having a very good time with his allies in the south. As part of his plan to weaken Great Britain, Hitler had been hoping to get Franco's Spain on his side. In November 1940, Hitler had a meeting at Henday, on the border of Spain, with the *Caudillo*[15] to try to persuade him to become, like Italy, a fully fledged ally of Germany against Great Britain. What Hitler had in mind was an attack on Gibraltar (Operation Felix)[16], and then for Spain to help shut off Great Britain from the Mediterranean. Franco, who came late to the meeting, insisted on his siesta and proved completely intractable on every point. After the meeting, Hitler complained that he would rather pull out several of his teeth than have another meeting with the obstinate Spaniard.

On 11 February 1941, Rommel arrived in Rome to a less than enthusiastic reception from Italy's Commando Supremo (CS), which nevertheless gave its half-hearted approval to Rommel's suggestion of shifting Tripoli's forces to Sirte. When Rommel heard that the British might advance on Tripoli, he asked General Geissler (commander of Luftflotte 10 – X Air Corp) to shift his bombing campaign to the port of Benghazi. The following day, Rommel flew to Tripoli where he met with Lieutenant Heggenreiner, the German liaison officer, who told Rommel that the Italian Army was very close to collapse. Afterwards, Rommel went to see his nominal superior General Gariboldi, who had replaced the disgraced Graziani as commander-in-chief of the Italian Army of Africa.

Below: Rommel's Tripoli headquarters, 1941.

Gariboldi disapproved of Rommel's idea of a stand at Sirte as being too far forward. Rommel simply ignored Gariboldi and flew southeast towards Sirte that same afternoon. He was to pay scant regard to the Italian generals and the high command. Having completed his tour, Rommel ordered the Italian X Corps (*Brescia* and *Pavia* Divisions) to Sirte.[17]

Two days later, the first elements of the DAK – namely one battalion of light infantry and another of anti-tank guns – began to arrive at Tripoli.[18] Eventually, Rommel would have the 5th Light

Division (later renamed 21st Panzer Division) and 15th Panzer Division. Rommel, who wanted his forces to be moved swiftly into battle, was impatient and risked a British air-raid attack to continue unloading the ships during the night, with the whole scene lit up like a Christmas tree by strong searchlights. One DAK veteran, Winrich Behr (only 21 years old at the time), remembers that few of the troops had any experience of war, let alone of the desert. Many, including himself, treated this as the beginning of a marvellous adventure. To most of them, Rommel was just another general.[19] Typical of Rommel, as he got the first tanks ashore he decided to boost his troops' morale while deceiving enemy agents (whom Rommel was sure were lurking around in Tripoli) with a splendid parade. To exaggerate his strength, he sent his tanks around the block several times in a sort of military carousel. Deception and bluff were to be the hallmarks of Rommel's desert campaign.

But what campaign? Hitler, planning his invasion of the USSR, needed to have his hands free elsewhere and therefore did not want a major role for his forces in North Africa. This was to continue to be Hitler's firm conviction until it was

Top: The Afrika Korps arrives in Tripoli during February 1941. Rommel went to great efforts to convince Britain that he had landed a far stronger force in North Africa. The panzers drove round the block several times.

Above: Rommel wasted little time after arriving at his Tripoli HQ in organizing the first attacks on British positions.

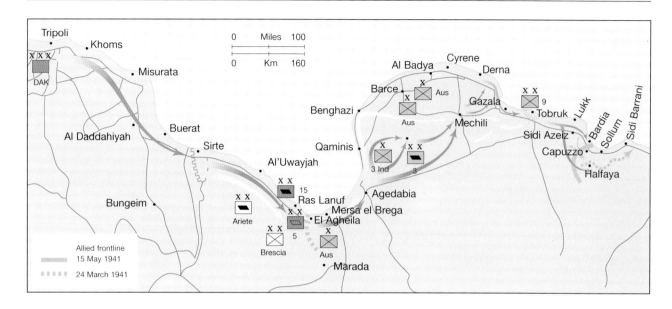

Above: With their supply lines stretched, the Allies were forced into retreat after retreat as Rommel's panzers drove the Commomwealth forces back during their first offensive.

Below: Rommel's (left) first offensive saw his men advance 563km (352 miles) east without resistance. In March 1941, after he realized that the British would not attack, he got Hitler's permission to invade Cyrenaica.

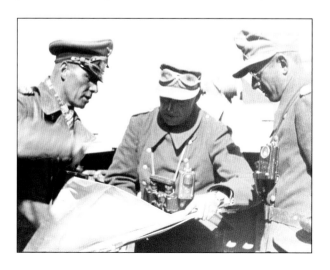

too late and the battle for North Africa was already lost. For the Germans, the desert campaign was always a sideshow, however spectacular Rommel's later victories were. As a result, his campaigns were always hampered by the lack of German support and the lack of supplies. For Rommel, the next two years would be a campaign on a shoestring budget of tanks, fuel and men.

By the time of Rommel's arrival in Africa the Axis situation seemed most precarious, and a lesser man would probably have given up. By 15 February, the day after his arrival, the British were in control of Cyrenaica after a brilliant and furious offensive operation that saw the two divisions of the WDF take 130,000 Italian prisoners, 850 guns, 400 tanks and thousands of other motorized vehicles.[20] For all practical purposes, Italy's African army had ceased to exist, and the road to Tripoli lay open to a British advance.

That month, the Axis suffered yet another major, and permanently disabling, setback when the Free French took Kufra, a strategically placed oasis town in the southeastern corner of Libya. In 1940, most French colonies remained loyal to the new Vichy regime. Prominent exceptions were the Central African colonies, including the Congo. In early February 1941, a small French unit of 100 French and 300 French-African troops, led by General Jacques-Philippe Leclerc (real name Viscount de Haute Coque), marched on Kufra from the French colony of Chad. The advance guard attacked Kufra on 7 February and pinned down the Italian garrison (64 Italians and 352 Libyans) until the main force arrived 10 days later. The garrison had plenty of ammunition, artillery and machine guns but, as usual, the Italians were deficient in morale. They were terrified of the French colonial troops, who were reputed to be ruthless and murderous African savages. The Italians therefore chose to capitulate. A decade of Italian colonial rule was at an end, and the Allies – thanks to French audacity in crossing the Sahara – had gained a crucial base of operations for deep raids and attacks behind Axis lines. Without Kufra, the Long Range Desert Group (LRDG) and the Special Air Service (SAS) would never have been able to stage such daring raids against Axis lines of communications.[21] The Italian performance at Kufra did not bode well for Rommel's use of these often unreliable troops during the coming campaign.

It seemed likely that Rommel and his tiny army would be swept out of North Africa if and when O'Connor renewed his offensive. When he had won the victory of Beda Fomm, O'Connor signalled, "The Fox killed in the open". In fact, the Fox had just arrived, and he was very much alive. The British halted their advance on 12 February at Sirte. Had they pressed on towards Tripoli, the city would probably have fallen into their hands. The British intervention in Greece, to support it and Yugoslavia against a German invasion, put paid to the proud Irish general's hopes to take the Libyan capital. By not doing so he prolonged the desert war by two long, bloody and agonizing years.

Unbelievably, the British were not aware that Rommel had been made commander of the German expeditionary force to North Africa until 8 March.[22] The two antagonists had as yet not made contact. This took place on 27 February when a German patrol along the Via Balbia driving east and a British one driving in the opposite direction encountered each other. The convoys of armoured cars

Below: Panzer II tanks of the Afrika Korps begin Rommel's first and unexpected offensive in March/April 1941.

passed each other without recognition. Probably wondering why these "Italians" wore such strange uniforms, the British commander finally woke up and shouted: "My God, did you see who they were? Germans!" With that realization, the British turned and so did the Germans, driving at full speed towards each other. Only the command vehicles opened fire, while the other vehicles swerved and struck the sand dunes on either side of the road. There were no casualties, and both protagonists could withdraw with their dignity intact.[23]

Dust, sand and lots of it: the Western Desert as an arena of war

Only the Arctic[24] could compete with the North African desert as a more unpleasant and hostile environment in which to fight a modern war. The British called the region of desert west of the Nile, which stretches all the way to French North Africa, the "Western Desert". Measuring two-and-a-half million square kilometres (one million square miles), it is an area the size of continental India and is 1930km (1200 miles) in length from the River Nile to Tunisia. From the Mediterranean to the African savannahs in the south is a distance of more than 1600km (1000 miles).

From Cyrenaica (western Libya) to Alexandria (at the mouth of the Nile) there stretches a 64km- (40-mile-) wide coastal strip of land that is higher in altitude than the more southerly desert. The strip is made up of limestone sands with clumps of bushes, palms and occasional small pockets of cultivated land. While south of Cyrenaica and Tobruk the accessible desert through which mechanized vehicles could travel was wide, this was not true elsewhere. Rommel's see-saw campaigns during three years of war were fought in the area between two crucial bottlenecks, which meant the normal sweeping operations south of enemy held positions could not be conducted.

The first and most westerly was at El Agheila, where the Great Sand Sea, 966km (600 miles) long and 241km (150 miles) wide, almost reached the shores

Below: Captured British troops near the port of Benghazi.

of the Mediterranean. It also reduced the border between Egypt and Libya to a mere 322km (200 miles) in length from the Mediterranean Sea to the Great Sand Sea. The other, easterly, bottleneck was at El Alamein, where the coastal strip narrowed into a funnel-shaped corridor between the sea and the Qattara Depression.

The Depression was feared as an area of treacherous soft, wet sand and salt marshes. It was therefore impassable for motorized vehicles and tanks. Those who tried to cross it by vehicle said it was like driving on top of the crust of a rice

pudding. Hence the war would rotate around these two points and focus on the mid-point: the excellent and well-fortified port of Tobruk. Hard-surfaced roads and railways, crucial for the conduct of modern war, were in short supply. The British had built a railroad from Alexandria but only to Mersa Matruh, some 241km (150 miles) short of the Libyan border. The coastal road was only a single, thin layer of tarmac that could not withstand continuous heavy traffic, while the Via Balbia in Libya, stretching from Tripoli to the Egyptian border, was a real feat of Italian engineering. Other routes were mere tracks which, during the rare heavy rains, turned to quagmires. Rain would turn the wadis into torrential channels of water and mud. And as the desert sand was like powdered clay, any movement would create clouds of white, choking dust that could indicate the presence of troops on foot for miles around.[25]

Above: Even during war there is time for humour. As this sign indicates, Rommel's rapid progress left the Germans in charge of former British-held territory.

Rommel's first offensive and the conquest of Cyrenaica (March–May 1941)

In short, this was a challenging environment that would make huge demands on every man who fought there. Troops had to acclimatize to dry, hot, unfriendly conditions or face the real possibility of perishing at the hands of nature itself. No one summed it up better than Rommel when he said that "the desert is a tactician's paradise and a quartermaster's hell".[26] Ultimately, his campaign's initial brilliant success, built on his tactical genius and bold leadership, could not compensate for his own negligence of the supply situation and the huge problems with which his overworked and unappreciated quartermaster had to grapple. It was these problems that resulted in his ultimate failure to win the campaign in October 1942.

Rommel's men had advanced some 563km (350 miles) east without encountering any resistance.[27] On 19 March, after he realized that the British would not attack, Rommel flew back to Germany to get Hitler's permission to invade Cyrenaica. This was given, but Brauchitsch told Rommel that he could advance only as far as El Agheila as he would not receive any reinforcements. Brauchitsch omitted to tell Rommel about Hitler's intention to invade the Balkans and later the USSR. By 11 March, the entire 5th Panzer Regiment (105 medium and 51 light tanks) would arrive. The Luftwaffe had some 50 Stukas and 20 fighter planes, but coordination was not as good as Rommel would have liked since the Luftwaffe squadron in North Africa remained outside his control.[28]

The British were having problems of their own. The command structure was tortuous since Wavell had appointed General Wilson as Military Governor of Cyrenaica, while the WDF was under the command of General Philip Neame. The WDF had lost its best units to the BEF being sent to Greece. The 2nd Armoured Division was very weak, as was the RAF. Wavell was not impressed with Neame, whose ideas he disliked and whose pessimism was a constant source of irritation. There seemed to be no threat of a German attack since Wilson had estimated that it would take Rommel until May to be ready for an offensive. His argument hinged on the fact that the 5th Light Division would complete its transfer to Tripoli by mid-April, and that the 15th Panzer Division would arrive by May.[29]

Wilson's argument might have held true had he been dealing with an ordinary German general, but Rommel was too impatient and struck before the British were prepared. On 24 March, Rommel took El Agheila in a lightning strike that left the British shocked.[30] Two days later, Churchill telegraphed Wavell to say "we are naturally concerned at the rapid German advance to Agheila. It is their habit to push on wherever they are not resisted. I presume you are only waiting for the tortoise to stick his head out far enough before chopping it off. It seems extremely important to give them an early taste of our quality."[31] What Churchill could not have realized at the time was that Wavell's enemy was not a slow-moving, cautious tortoise but a fast-moving fox.

Above: Panzer III and SdKfz 251 halftrack outside Tobuk. In spite of his tanks, motorized infantry and experience, Rommel could not find a way past the Australians into Tobruk.

On 31 March the 21st Panzer Division beat the 2nd Armoured Division at Mersa Brega, which gave the Germans a morale booster, since it showed how weak the WDF had become. The following day, the DAK attacked in three directions, like a fan, across Cyrenaica, and on 1 April Rommel had taken Agedabia. At this stage of the desert war, Rommel hadn't managed to mould the DAK into a new 7th Panzer Division, or into the kind of fighting force that he wanted. Flying his Storch light aircraft above the whirling dust clouds of the advancing German columns, Rommel constantly urged his commanders to attack and exhorted them to move faster. He lost patience with Streich, commander of the 5th Light Division, when he asked for four days to refuel and refit his tanks. Rommel replied brusquely: "You have 24 hours."

Above: An SdKfz 251 of the Africa Korps during the advance to Tobruk. Each vehicle could carry 12 troops.

On 3 April the British abandoned Benghazi, but not before they had destroyed the supply dumps there. Rommel, writing to Lucie that same day, was pleased at the DAK's "dazzling success" which probably had led to German high command and Italian CS consternation. "The British are falling over each other to get away. Our casualties are small. Booty can't be estimated."[32] No doubt Rommel felt that this was France all over again and that the British, like the French, would need only a few hard punches to be broken. When the Luftwaffe reported that the road to Mechili was open, Rommel ordered Colonel Schwerin, leading a composite force of Germans and Italians to "make for it. Drive fast."[33] This order was typical of Rommel, whose style of command was direct, simple and aggressive. When in doubt, attack and drive hard.

Below: The desert threw up plenty of challenges of its own, in addition to those resulting from fighting a mechanized war.

The following day, Streich ran out of fuel halfway to Mechili; General Kirchheim's column was checked by the Australians (whose tough fighting prowess was to be respected by the Germans); and Colonel Olbricht's column had not even left Antelat. Rommel was infuriated at the incompetence and

Above: The Australian "bush artillery" in action at Tobruk in April 1941. Their rugged resistance continually frustrated Rommel's efforts to take the key port and fortress.

slowness of his subordinates. On 5 April he took personal command of Streich's unit and ordered Ponath's machine-gun battalion to unite with Olbricht's panzer battalion, and advance on Derna.[34] Nevertheless, Rommel was delighted with his progress so far, but he believed that the success of the DAK depended completely on his personal leadership and presence at the very tip of the advance.[35] He was right.

On 5 April, Schwerin's column (to which Streich belonged) captured Tengeder, and the following day (6 April) Mechili fell to the Germans. By this time O'Connor, who should have replaced Neame, had become an advisor to the general. This confused the British command structure still further. The 2nd Armoured Division had lost all of its armour, and only the 7th Australian Division was fighting back with determination.

Around Derna, a British staff car was captured, and inside were both generals – Neame and O'Connor.[36] The capture of the latter was an unmitigated disaster. He was the only British desert general who had the competence and experience of mobile warfare to give Rommel a serious run for his money. Wavell was shocked at the loss of his right-hand man, and was desperate enough to suggest that they exchange O'Connor for six or more Italian generals. Whitehall turned down Wavell's request.[37] That was a serious mistake since O'Connor was worth at least 10 times that number of Italian generals. The fighting Irishman remained in an Italian prisoner-of-war (POW) camp until he could escape in 1943. He returned to defeat Rommel's panzers in Normandy.

Rommel, too, had a close escape during the advance. Flying in his Storch, he saw the familiar dustbowl of an advancing column that had to be Olbricht's, and he ordered his pilot to land. As they descended, they saw, to their horror, that the troops were wearing the characteristic British soup-plate helmets. They made a rapid ascent but the tail of the aircraft was shot through.[38] On 7 April Derna fell, and the day after General Gambier-Perry, commander of the 2nd Armoured Division, was captured. Rommel was photographed in conversation with the British officer.[39]

Wavell must have begun to wonder if, at this rate, he would have any generals left to command a faltering WDF. He was willing to lose the whole of Cyrenaica, including the strongpoint of Tobruk, in order to save his army from Rommel's whirlwind advance. Rommel, for his part, was probably a bit disappointed that the British did not try to hold the Cyrenaican bulge. He was confident, however, that he could break the WDF if he kept up a relentless attack. The ultimate aim, he believed, had to be the Suez Canal. Ignoring CS orders and Gariboldi's lame objections, Rommel did not halt on the Derna-Mechili line, but swept on towards Tobruk. Meanwhile, von Wechmar's 3rd Reconnaissance Unit was advancing on Bardia, while Lieutenant-Colonel Knabe's motorized infantry approached Sollum and Mersa Matruh.[10] On 12 April, the DAK had taken Bardia and reached the Egyptian frontier.[11]

A thorn in Rommel's side: Tobruk (1941)

In two weeks the British had retreated more than 640km (400 miles), leaving most of Cyrenaica to be re-occupied by the Germans. The port, and fortress, of Tobruk was still held by the Australians, led by General Morshead, known to his troops as "Ming the Merciless" for his reputation as a no-nonsense commander of the old school. The town's garrison consisted of the 9th Australian Division and 18th Infantry Brigade.[12] On 7 April, Churchill sent a message to Wavell that could not be misunderstood. "Tobruk, therefore, seems to be a place to be held to the death, without thought of retirement." Wavell had wanted to construct his defence line some 322km (200 miles) farther east at Mersa Matruh, but now he was forced to change his plans due to Churchill's orders.[13]

To put confidence and fighting spirit back into the Australians, Wavell flew to Tobruk for talks with Morshead. He was reassured by the Australians' toughness

Below: Tobruk proved relatively easy to defend if the troops had the courage and determination of these Australians. Dugouts led to a series of interconnected natural caves such as this, where the Australians lived and worked.

and by Morshead's steely resolve, especially as the garrison had plenty of water, food, ammunition and strong defences which were continuously being reinforced. If the Australians and the British understood the vital importance of Tobruk, so did Rommel, who told his commanders, "we must attack Tobruk with everything we have, immediately your panzers have taken up positions, and before Tommy has time to dig in".[44]

What was it that made Tobruk so important to Rommel and Churchill? The town, with a population of only 4000, was hardly important in itself, but it was the only decent port between Tripoli and Alexandria. Benghazi had a port, but it was only half the size of Tobruk; and Rommel, if he was to continue his advance eastwards, needed a port large enough to supply his troops closer to Egypt than either Benghazi or Tripoli. Furthermore, Tobruk had a desalination plant that produced 182,000 litres (40,000 gallons) of water a day. Its stores held a wealth of supplies the DAK could use. Finally, in the hands of an aggressive and able commander, such as Morshead, Tobruk was a constant threat to Rommel's flanks and lines of communications. But Tobruk would be a difficult nut to crack, even for a deadly combination of Stukas, heavy artillery and German tanks.

Tobruk was surrounded by a line of heavy concrete dugouts inside natural caves, each interconnected by a series of trenches with firing points for mortars and machine guns. The dugouts could each house 30–40 men. In front of the dugouts was a line of barbed wire, and in front of this a deep and wide anti-tank ditch. This formidable line of defence was additionally supported by a second line, some 1830–2740m (6000–9000ft) behind the first. This second line was made up of the same kind of defences but without the benefit of an anti-tank ditch. In every way Tobruk was a formidable fortress city held by the British Empire's élite troops – the Australians.[45]

Below: In hot and dusty conditions, soldiers of Rommel's legendary Afrika Korps march through the North African desert in April 1941. Three men are carrying bipod-equipped MG34 machine guns.

Rommel, whose self-confidence had soared with the desert dash, was sure that he could take Tobruk without much ado. But he was not the same man when he was up against an enemy that was well dug-in and determined to fight it out to the bitter end. Frankly, Rommel was not a good commander in a war of attrition and had little experience of positional warfare. Schwerin's initial probe against the perimeter on 11–12 April failed to make an impression, and the following day Rommel ordered Streich, in whom he had no confidence, to prove himself by personally leading an attack against El Adem along the Tobruk road.

Meanwhile, Ponath's 8th Machine-Gun Battalion made a night attack which breached the anti-tank ditch and allowed the 5th Panzer Regiment to crash through. While the infantry held the frontline, the Australian artillery skilfully poured fire on the advancing German tanks. A combination of infantry, artillery and Cruiser tank fire stopped the German attack. Rommel noted: "I was furious, particularly as the tanks had left the infantry in the lurch," and the *Ariete* Division broke and fled after only light artillery fire from Tobruk. Rommel ordered the Luftwaffe to drop leaflets with a call to surrender, which drew an angry Australian reply that they had no white hankies since all had been used as lavatory paper. Thanks to Rommel, they now had a nice bunch of white printed leaflets to use in the "Dunny" (toilet).

Above: German Chief of Staff General Franz Halder, whose dislike of Rommel was due to his impression that the general was Hitler's protégé and a rank outsider. Halder was dismissed by Hitler in September 1942.

Frustration before Tobruk

Rommel led the next attack during 16–17 April in person, but to no avail. He blamed the poor equipment and training of the Italians for the failure.[16] Little reliance could be placed on the Italians and their fighting resilience as they feared British tanks and artillery fire. Rommel noted glumly how the Italians, as in 1917, were "quick to throw up the sponge".[17]

Rommel's criticism of the Italians was somewhat unfair since it was the tougher-than-expected resistance of the Australians that halted his improvised attacks. The Australians, unlike their enemy, were used to the dust, heat and discomfort of the desert. They were tough troops in open warfare, but even more determined when behind concrete and barbed wire. Unlike other troops, the Australians did not buckle under the combination of artillery, Stuka and panzer attacks but fought back with every available weapon.[18] Rommel, like other German soldiers, came to admire these tall, bronzed and tough soldiers who displayed such cold-blooded courage even under the fiercest fire. One day during the siege, Rommel's driver, Heinz Schmidt, was amazed to see one Australian climb out of his trench, sit down on the parapet, take off his characteristic slouch hat and wave cheerfully at the Germans. All this was going on while the bullets whizzed and buzzed past him like angry bees.[19]

Rommel's first serious setback in the campaign gave his critics in the German high command a god-given opportunity to carp about his risky African adventure and intervene to halt his runaway career. None proved more vitriolic than Chief of Staff General Franz Halder, whose dislike of Rommel was due to his impression that the general was Hitler's protégé and a rank outsider – not part of the establishment. Halder now wanted to "to head off this soldier gone stark mad". He intended to send a dependable officer, General Friedrich Paulus, to North Africa to assess the situation and report back to Berlin.[50] Paulus arrived on 26 April to a less than warm welcome from the DAK commander. With some justification, Rommel viewed the arrival of Paulus as high command interference and the harbinger of his eventual dismissal from command.[51]

Paulus was critical of the attacks against Tobruk, but soon came round to Rommel's views on how the campaign should be conducted. But he recommended that the DAK end the pointless siege of Tobruk, which could be conducted by the Italians instead, and fall back on Gazala.[52] Rommel (in private) complained about his troops outside Tobruk being thin on the ground when the end of the Greek campaign might see increased British reinforcements reaching Egypt.[53]

On 30–31 April Rommel made one final attack, and broke the southwestern corner of the perimeter – for the loss of 35 tanks.[54] But there seemed no point in making unsuccessful attacks when his supplies and reserves were dwindling. By 6 May Rommel was reduced to hoping that the continuous Stuka attacks and the shortage of water inside Tobruk would break Allied morale.[55] That proved a forlorn hope, as Rommel probably realized, and the British were soon attacking his main front in the east. This gave him the excuse to disengage from a hopeless situation and return to what he excelled at, the cut and thrust of mobile war.

Below: Soldiers and vehicles of Rommel's Afrika Korps at the end of April 1941. They and their commander had performed well in their first campaign against the British in the desert.

Chapter notes

1 Eritrea, Ethiopia (Abyssinian Empire), conquered by the Italians during the invasion of 1935–36, and Italian Somaliland.

2 In 1882 the British had invaded and occupied Egypt, which until 1914 was formally part of the Ottoman (Turkish) Empire. After World War I, while Egypt was technically "independent", the British had both a military presence in, and political predominance over, the country. Egypt, with the naval base of Alexandria and the Suez Canal, was a crucial piece in Great Britain's Middle Eastern jigsaw puzzle. As for Sudan, it was an Anglo-Egyptian condominium on paper but in reality was ruled, since its conquest in 1898–1901, by the British – like any other colony.

3 General History of Africa, Vol. VII (ed. A. Adu Boahen), pp.51-53.

4 Dennis Mack-Smith, Mussolini (London,1993), p.255.

5 Jörgensen & Mann, pp.71-72.

6 Kenneth Macksey, Beda Fomm (London, 1972), pp.26-28.

7 Ibid, pp.63, 71, 73-74, 78-79, 90, 94,106,109, 121, 123.

8 Salmaggi & Pallavisini, p.104.

9 Jörgensen & Mann, p.73.

10 Macksey, p.47.

11 Fraser, p.217.

12 RP.87, Rommel to Lucie, 8 Jan. 1941.

13 Fraser, p.214.

14 Ibid, p.217.

15 The equivalent to Führer in Spanish, meaning leader.

16 Ian Kershaw, Hitler, Vol. 2 (London, 2000), p.348.

17 Purnell's, Vol. 4, Liddell Hart, The Rommel Papers, p.354.

18 Salmaggi & Pallavisini, p.104.

19 Channel 4 documentary, 2002, "The Real Rommel", interview with Rommel's ADC, Winrich Behr.

20 Salmaggi & Pallavisini, p.104.

21 Arthur Swinson, The Raiders, p.32-37.

22 Jackson, The North African Campaign, pp.69, 89, 91.

23 Alan Moorehead, African Trilogy, p.140.

24 See Chris Mann and Christer Jörgensen, Hitler's Arctic War: the German Campaigns in Norway, Finland and the USSR (Hersham, 2002).

25 Deighton, Blood, Tears and Folly, pp.244, 246.

26 Ibid, p.244.

27 RP.103, Rommel to Lucie, 17 Feb. 1941.

28 Purnell's, Vol. 4, p.357, Kenneth Macksey, Rommel's first attack. Cyrenaica (March–April 1941).

29 Ibid, pp.357-358.

30 Ibid, p.360. Wilson's view was shared by Brauchitsch. At Agheila, Rommel had a natural defence line since he could hold the line between the sea and the inland salt marshes.

31 Liddell Hart, History of the Second World War, p.179.

32 RP.111, Rommel to Lucie, 3 Apr. 1941.

33 RP.113, Rommel's diary.

34 Jackson, pp.101, 103-105.

35 RP.104, Rommel to Lucie, 5 Mar. 1941.

36 Macksey, p.363. With Neame and O'Connor were also Brigadiers Coombe and Rimington; Salmaggi & Pallavisini, p.116.

37 Jackson, p.106.

38 RP.115, Rommel's diary.

39 Ibid.

40 Ibid.

41 Salmaggi & Pallavisini, p.120.

42 Liddell Hart, p.180.

43 Ibid.

44 Schmidt, p.37.

45 Purnell's, Vol. 5, p.537. John Foley, Cyrenaica, April–November 1941, Tobruk survives.

46 Jackson, p.108.

47 RP.131, Rommel to Lucie, 23 Apr. 1941.

48 Jackson, p.114.

49 Schmidt, p.45.

50 Liddell Hart, p.181.

51 Schmidt, p.55.

52 Ibid, p.60.

53 RP.131, Rommel to Lucie, 25 Apr. 1941.

54 Liddell Hart, p.181.

55 RP.133, Rommel to Lucie, 6 May 1941.

CHAPTER 5

Our Stubborn Friends

Rommel's defeat of the British offensives
(May 1941–January 1942)

Rommel had won a splendid victory. He believed that no offensive had been launched with less preparation, which had placed a great demand on the commander's ability to improvise. Rommel was annoyed that his subordinate commanders had spent too much time in refuelling and refitting tanks and vehicles. Those who criticized him seemed to have forgotten that in a real war situation it was the commander's drive and determination that mattered more than his intellect. Rommel was convinced that the momentum of an offensive had to be kept up at all times. He therefore felt that the demands he had placed on his subordinate commanders during this first offensive weren't unrealistic.[1] Unfortunately, the German high command saw North Africa as nothing but a sideshow, whereas Rommel believed that the main effort in the Mediterranean should be on his front and not in the Balkans. What could he have achieved with the resources poured into the bloody battle of Crete?[2]

Operation Brevity: the first battle of Hellfire Pass (14–27 May 1941)
Rommel's obsession with Tobruk was a serious mistake since it allowed the disorganized British to get their act together and plan a counterattack. Wavell was determined to do so if he got more supplies, troops and tanks. By early May Wavell had come up with a new plan, Brevity, that aimed to push Rommel back and relieve Tobruk by attacking the German positions at Sollum and Fort Capuzzo.[3] On 12 May, the crucial Tiger Convoy arrived in Alexandria with vital supplies for the Eighth Army (formerly the WDF). These supplies included 135 Matilda tanks, 82 Crusader tanks and 21 light tanks. The Crusaders were good, fast tanks but, like many other machines of the early years of the war, were seriously undergunned and mechanically unreliable.[4]

On 25 April, Colonel Herff had occupied Halfaya Pass – better known by its British nickname of Hellfire Pass – while Rommel had pulled the DAK out from the Tobruk Front and concentrated his army around Sollum instead. This was on

Left: Rommel (centre) in May 1941, still fixated by Tobruk but about to be the target of counterattacks by the well-supplied British forces.

Above: A British plan, Brevity, aimed to push Rommel back and relieve Tobruk by attacking the German positions at Sollum and Fort Capuzzo (shown above).

Below: DAK officers near Fort Capuzzo in May 1941. By the look of the officer on the right, these men have seen recent combat.

the direct orders of Halder, who worried inordinately about casualties and wanted to leave any siege warfare to the Italians. Wavell had given command of the 7th Armoured Division to Brigadier Straffer Gott, known as Gentleman Gott. His spearhead, the 4th Royal Tank Regiment (RTR), was equipped with Matildas. On 14 May, the 4th RTR and 32nd Guards Brigade attacked Hellfire Pass. The Italian gunners put up stiff resistance, which alerted the garrison of Fort Capuzzo. The Durham Light Infantry (DLI) then attacked Capuzzo, which fell after some heavy fighting. Rommel was by now quite worried about the deteriorating situation, and believed that this was the harbinger of a full-scale British attack.[5]

Worried about Herff's heavy losses at Hellfire Pass, Rommel sent Lieutenant-Colonel Cramer (8th Panzer Regiment) and the ubiquitous 88mm Flak guns to shore up a crumbling front. Herff managed to retake Capuzzo, but a British raid on the coast captured 100 troops and confused the Germans into thinking that the British might attack in this sector instead. Rommel, though, was more worried about the pass. In British hands it could be used by Wavell to relieve

Tobruk, or even retake Cyrenaica. Gott recalled his forces but left the 3rd Coldstream Guards to hold the pass. Rommel viewed the Pass as crucial, and on 26 May he ordered Herff to retake it with 160 panzers. The German plan was quite simple: while Bach's Light Infantry Regiment made a frontal attack from the west upon the pass, Cramer would attack from the south and below the pass. Thus the Coldstream Guards would be encircled unless they were withdrawn in time. Gott had no intention of allowing the Coldstream Guards to be destroyed, though, and ordered them to retire. The British had lost six tanks, artillery and 150 troops in a relatively minor battle. Rommel had once more shown his tactical superiority over the British, and was now free to reinforce and fortify the Libyan frontier with minefields covered by 88mm guns.[6]

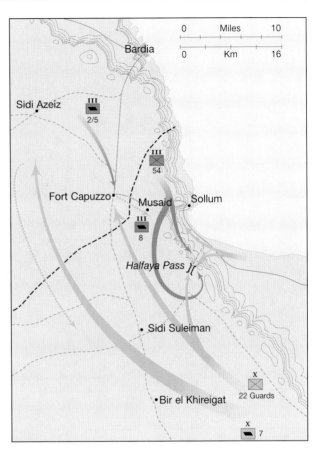

Operation Battleaxe: the second battle of Hellfire Pass (15–17 June)

Rommel was convinced that the British would strike soon. He was right, but it would take a few weeks. Wavell had more pressing problems in May 1941 than even Rommel, since the Iraqi military (with pro-Nazi views) had seized power in Baghdad and thereby threatened British airbases and oilfields. Furthermore, the Vichy French in Syria were showing dangerous pro-German tendencies that could be cured only with some cold British steel.[7]

Above: Trying to prevent the capture of Tobruk, Commonwealth troops launched Operation Battleaxe, attacking Rommel's formations at the Halfaya Pass in May 1941.

The arrival of the Tiger Convoy reinforced the British tank formations, which allowed Wavell to plan the next attack with some hope of success. His new plan, Operation Battleaxe, was a most ambitious affair. Wavell hoped not only to relieve Tobruk but to defeat Rommel decisively. This he would do by defeating the DAK on the frontier before Rommel had a chance to shift his forces from Tobruk. Wavell estimated that Rommel had 25,000 troops and 200 tanks along the Tobruk Front, and 13,000 troops and 100 tanks along the border.[8] In fact, Rommel had 200 panzers by mid-June and had fortified the Sollum area, which included the battle area of Hellfire Pass and Hafid Ridge. The 15th Panzer Division held the frontier, and the 5th Light Division was outside Tobruk.

Wavell had a considerable tank advantage (300 tanks) against Rommel (170 panzers) in the immediate battle area. That suited the British fine, since they wanted a tank-only battle, without interference from other arms. This was to prove a fatal error, since the Germans were fighting a combined-arms battle, where artillery and infantry supported the tanks. The difference in tank strength would be more than made up for by Rommel's brilliant use of the 88mm guns – the secret, and deadliest, ingredient in Rommel's tank-killing techniques.[9]

Day one

At dawn on 15 June, the British offensive began with a three-pronged attack against Hellfire Pass where Rommel had placed his well-concealed 88s. C Squadron of the 4th RTR, supported by the Cameron Highlanders, was shot to pieces by these gun emplacements. By 10:00 hours the squadron had only two tanks left, and the Highlanders had to retreat because of German infantry counterattacks. Meanwhile, the 7th RTR captured Capuzzo (which after a few hours of battle was a smouldering ruin), while the 7th Armoured Brigade, with its brand-new Crusaders, attacked as well. To keep this new tank secret from the Germans, the 2nd RTR (with A9 and A10 tanks) spearheaded the attack that was aimed at sending a hook around the Germans' southern flank while the Crusaders were kept to the rear. During their attack on the Hafid Ridge, the 2nd RTR lost all but two of its tanks.[10]

Bottom: Tanks, troops and armoured personnel carriers of the German 5th Light Division in mid-1941.

Below: A surprise and a disappointment, the British Crusader tank made its first appearance at Hellfire Pass. It had an alarming tendency to break down on the battlefield.

At Hellfire Pass, the Matildas were pounded by the 88s, whose shells penetrated their thick armour with ease. This ended the tank's reputation as Queen of the Desert. Map point 206 saw the heaviest fighting between the Crusaders, German infantry and anti-tank gunners.[11] The Crusaders had a tendency to break down due to mechanical failure and catch fire when hit by enemy shells. The 6th RTR lost 17 Crusaders when it engaged Panzer IIIs and IVs, the latter with their superior 75mm guns. The failure of the Crusader as a battle tank was also due to the crews not having enough time to train with the machines before battle. By the end of the first day, Rommel's panzers were more or less intact, and he could be reinforced by the 5th Light Division and anti-tank guns from Tobruk.[12]

Day two

The British by this point had only 100 tanks spread thinly along the front. The British tank commander, Lieutenant-General Noel Beresford-

Peirse, compounded British problems by ordering that the tanks be repaired on the spot to save time. It may have saved time, but it made the tanks and their repair crews sitting ducks for deadly, roving German patrols. By the morning of 16 June, Rommel's tank force was not only larger than that of the British, but his crews were far more rested. Furthermore, Rommel had an excellent overview of what "our stubborn friends" were up to due to the British habit of talking freely on the radio. This was translated and immediately transmitted to the German HQ.[13] This allowed Rommel to anticipate his enemy's every move.

General Creagh had decided that the 7th Armoured Division was to have another crack at the Hafid Ridge, spearheaded by the 4th Armoured Brigade (with Matildas) supported by artillery. Meanwhile, the 7th Armoured Brigade would either support the 4th Armoured Brigade, or block the panzers should they attempt to outflank the British lines around Sidi Omar. Unfortunately, Rommel put paid to these plans by striking first. The 15th Panzer Division attacked Capuzzo. The 5th Light outflanked the British left with the aim of cutting off the 4th Indian Division, whose commander, General Messervy, was forced to retain the 4th Armoured Brigade to hold Capuzzo itself.[14] A fierce tank battle then developed between Sidi Omar and Capuzzo, waged by the 5th Light Division and the 4th Armoured Brigade, which lost 50 out of its 80 tanks in a five-and-a-half-hour-long battle. But at least the panzer attack against Sidi Omar was halted.[15]

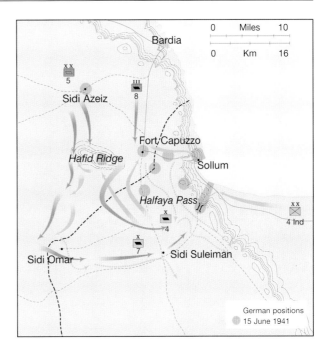

Above: As Commonwealth forces thrusted towards Sollum and Fort Capuzzo, German units swept around their exposed flanks and attacked the Allied lines of communication.

Below: British prisoners taken at Hellfire pass. Rommel's troops could afford to be cheerful, while the British had good reason to be glum after Hellfire Pass. The British had lost half their tanks and 900 men.

Day three

During the night Rommel was convinced, judging from the frantic and often confused British radio messages, that his enemy was in complete disarray. When his radio listeners intercepted a message from Creagh calling for Beresford-Peirse to come up to the

front, Rommel's hunch was reinforced. It seemed that Creagh had lost control of the situation. He therefore decided to hurl all his panzers against the left flank of the 7th Armoured Division. Thus the panzers shifted north, captured Sidi Omar, and went through the enemy tank division – the British were now forced to flee. Rommel's plan to trap the British west of the pass had succeeded; he had run rings around them. But for the rearguard actions of Brigadier Alec Gatehouse's Matildas (4th Armoured Brigade), a British retreat would have turned into a complete rout.[16]

Above: Rommel's "secret weapon", the 88mm anti-aircraft gun. It was used with great effect against British tanks.

The reckoning

When the fighting was over the British had good reason to be glum. They had lost half their tanks and 900 men. Rommel's losses were 25 panzers and 700 dead.[17] The main reason for the debacle was that the British kept the tank battle separate from the rest of the army, thereby weakening their military resources. There was poor coordination between the regiments and other units of the army, exacerbated by the number of Commonwealth and Empire units involved. In addition, the British commanders had an unfortunate and often fatal habit of fighting by committee.[18] As for more specific causes, the British had not expected that Rommel could make such good use of the bulky 88mm guns, built originally for anti-aircraft use. The British tanks and infantry were also mauled by his low-profile and easily concealed 50mm anti-tank guns. Believing all this firepower to be coming from German panzers, the British overestimated the enemy's tank strength, which proved detrimental to troop morale.[19]

Like Rommel himself, the 88mm gun was to take on a dangerous glamour and reputation as a wonder weapon. A captured British captain told his captors that it wasn't fair or sporting of them to use the 88. Well then, replied the Germans jovially, why build tanks whose armour is so thick that we have to use it? Rommel's driver, Schmidt, who witnessed the episode, found the whole situation ridiculous – like a bunch of school boys after a football match.[20]

Rommel, now established as a hero among his men, praised his troops, both German and Italian, who had displayed unaccustomed nerve and resolve under fire in a brilliantly fought battle.[21] The British, by contrast, had nothing to be proud of, except the bravery and toughness of their troops. One historian concluded that Battleaxe (a battle that most DAK veterans forgot, according to Schmidt[22]) showed all the weaknesses in the British mode of operation. "As the story of the

North African campaign unfolds, British amateurism stands out in harsh contrast to German professionalism, in which Rommel's men showed an uncanny sense in devising new tactics in close cooperation with each other to meet the changing circumstances of the desert war. Rommel himself demonstrated the advantage of single-minded command, and was not to be stopped until the British found a military dictator of their own."[23]

Above: The Panzer III was Rommel's most numerous tank in 1941, although not as heavy and powerful as the scarcer Panzer IV.

Wavell, who had found himself pushed and cajoled by the bullying of Churchill, was relieved of his command on 21 June, and went east to become the new British military commander in India and the Far East.[24] Churchill had lost confidence in the bookish and taciturn Wavell. His low opinion of this intellectual and outstanding soldier was not shared by Rommel. In his opinion, Wavell was definitely several cuts above most British commanders, since he combined excellent strategic planning, strategic sense and balanced courage. Rommel admired Wavell's simple and clear-cut plan that was let down by the poor quality of the tanks, especially the Crusaders, and by his subordinate commanders' mistakes.[25]

Flies, disease and Asinus Mussolini: a desert soldier's life

For an army renowned for its smart turnout and parade image, the DAK veterans soon took on a more down-to-earth appearance. Their tunic jackets were quickly bleached by the unrelenting sun, as was their hair. Most of the time the troops walked around in shirt sleeves (unheard of back in the Fatherland). Long trousers were also discarded in favour of shorts, and instead of the notorious German jackboot the DAK wore soft, easy and practical lace-up shoes with green, knee-length stockings. The troops lived in tents which had to be covered by sand on the sides and on top for camouflage and for stability. In daytime, the tents were "only really useful ... for hatching eggs". [26]

Below: Rommel's Afrika Korps on the desert battlefield in 1941. A British tank burns in the background.

According to Lieutenant Ralph Ringler, there were dangers and annoyances lurking everywhere. Every morning one had to shake one's boots free of sand and of the odd scorpion since these insects, whose sting could kill a man, had a habit of nesting in them. There were also leeches that could be nasty for an unwary washer who used the water in wells or cisterns. Every night

Above: Water that one did not drink was used to shave or wash in. Troops would use sand to rub and clean their clothes.

Above: A light four-wheeled vehicle of Rommel's 5th Light Division in the Halfaya Pass area in 1941.

mosquito nets had to be erected to keep out the bloodsucking vermin that bred in their millions in the salt swamps and putrid salt lakes that dotted the coastal desert region. The only good thing about being close to the sea was the ability to take a morning bath in the cool, clear salt water of the Mediterranean.[27] The following advice was given to the troops: "Wear strong shoes and never go barefoot in the sand. After a bite [from a horned viper or other poisonous snake] immediately tie off the wound and later open it again so that the poison will be washed out with the blood." As for scorpions: "After a sting, tie off wound immediately, then enlarge it. The only antidote is an injected serum. If possible get remedial medical assistance."[28]

The great Napoleon had stated that an army marches on its stomach, and he was right. In the desert, with no women, little alcohol and no other forms of entertainment, the soldiers' only abiding pleasure was food. The German troops grumbled a lot about their atrociously stodgy and unvaried diet. The troops ate sardines in oil, bulky tinned meat sausages (Bierwurst) and what some German wit called either "Alter Mann" (Old Man) or "Asinus Mussolini"[29]. These were small round tins filled with

tough and sinewy beef marked AM in Italian.[30] With such a one-sided and dull diet, it was little wonder that the Germans took every opportunity to pilfer and raid British supply dumps. After the fall of Tobruk in 1942, the Germans were delighted to capture an intact NAAFI kitchen which contained unheard-of delicacies, such as tinned South African pineapples, Irish potatoes, canned beer, British pork sausages, cigarettes and fried potatoes. The Germans even found Australian bully beef a luxurious delicacy after AM[31] – a view probably not shared by Australians tired of eating "bloody bully beef" all the time.

Above: Troops of the 15th Panzer Division with locals in mid-1941. The Germans quickly discovered that wheeled vehicles had difficulties traversing sand dunes and steep slopes in the desert.

Ensuring the supply of fresh and safe water was a constant headache. Here the Germans, unlike their enemy, were at least blessed with the jerry can which the British either stole or copied for their own use. A sturdy and well-built metal container, this was used for transporting either petrol or water to the frontline. Water had to be drunk in large amounts due to the constant and profuse sweating caused by the desert heat. Water that one did not drink or spat out into a container was later used to shave or wash in. Instead of scarce water and soap, the troops would use sand to rub and clean their clothes, or a small amount of petrol (also scarce) to keep bugs and vermin out.

Unlike the luxury-loving Italian officer corps and some of his own German colleagues, Rommel shared his soldiers' discomforts. He ate, slept and lived under the same conditions as his troops. This was both a personal choice and a deliberate personnel policy. Rommel was frugal, indifferent to most material things, and was of the opinion that he did not need the comforts that others

Below: Fuel was probably even more important to Rommel than water. He faced persistent supply problems. Pictured here is a fuel depot with the precious commodity stacked in German jerry cans.

Above: DAF personnel just before Operation Crusader, November 1941, where the British attempted to use some of Rommel's tactics against him.

believed were so essential. By eating little, sleeping in a simple military bed and keeping fit, Rommel believed he would remain in better physical and mental shape than if his quarters were more comfortable and his food richer (a view not shared by the Italian high command). This was also a clever leadership ploy on his part. By sharing his troops' many and varied discomforts, Rommel showed that he would not ask them to endure conditions that he was not willing to put up with himself, and he knew that this would boost their morale. No doubt the enormous respect the troops felt for Rommel was built partly on the fact that he was willing, despite being quite a bit older than his soldiers and most of his officers, to live with the almost inhuman conditions of the desert war.

Rommel's own method of getting rid of persistent bedbugs was to remove the mattress and bed clothing, douse the iron bedstead with petrol and then set fire to it.[32] As for his food (a sore point for a man with frequent stomach pains), he ate the same fare that his troops had to put up with. On 6 October 1941, Rommel complained that the chicken they had eaten must have come from the chicken coop of Pharaoh Ramses II, since it was so old and bad that it was inedible even after six hours of cooking.[33]

Rommel relaxed by making energetic and murderous use of his flyswatter. When his mobile HQ was close to the sea, he and his staff would always take the opportunity for a sea bath and swim. But his favourite pastime (when his hectic campaigning allowed) was to go hunting gazelles.[34] Again, this was combining relaxation, exercise and honing Rommel's superb hunting skills on the battlefield. Rommel, it seems, did not care if he hunted gazelles or the British, as long as he was hunting a quarry of some sort.

Operation Crusader (November 1941–January 1942)

Obviously the stalemate in the desert would not persist. Sooner or later it would be broken by the side that was strong and bold enough to strike first. None was more aware of this fact than Rommel himself, and he realized that the British were up to something. With Stalin's Russia in dire straits, the British would be obliged to come to the USSR's rescue, and since a landing on the continent was too dangerous a venture when Germany ruled the roost, there was only one place left for the British to attack: North Africa.[35]

Rommel's hunch was right, although it would not have taken a genius to figure out that the British would have to make an attack in North Africa since this was the only active front she had against Germany. This was a major advantage to the British. They could concentrate all their attentions on one single front, and supply the Eighth Army on a scale that was lavish by comparison with the DAK.

Hitler's entire attention was on the Eastern Front where things were about to go horribly wrong for Germany, and which rebounded badly on Rommel's chances of winning the desert war. Furthermore, while the British could, in relative safety, ship supplies and reinforcements around the Cape, Rommel's supply routes, although shorter, were exposed to British air attacks from Malta.[36]

The supply problem

Unlike his enemy, Rommel was facing a dwindling supply of troops, tanks and victuals of every kind. Worst of all was the sharply reduced number and quality of his tanks. He had in total some 174 German models, mainly Mark IIIs, and 146 obsolete Italian machines.[37] The Italian tanks were completely unfit for modern war since they dated from the late 1930s. They were built as a support weapon for infantry. They were not only slow, but under-gunned, poorly powered and had very thin armour. Although the Panzer IIIs were far superior to any Italian model, they were inferior to the far more powerful and heavier Panzer IVs. These excellent machines were shipped to the Eastern Front at a time when Rommel, with no more than a handful, could have made very good use of them to inflict a decisive defeat on the British.

Below: Rommel (left) prior to Operation Crusader, in which he was obliged to confront the British with considerably smaller numbers of tanks and aircraft.

As if this were not enough, the Germans were far outnumbered in the air by the RAF's Desert Air Force (DAF), which could muster 700 machines. To face this aerial armada, Rommel had only 320 aircraft, many of them the slower and older Stukas that could not compete in a dogfight with Spitfires and Hawker Hurricanes.

In total, Rommel had six Italian divisions and three German ones. At least with the arrival of more Panzer IIIs he was able to upgrade the 5th Light Division to full panzer division status, as the 21st.[38]

By contrast, the British Eighth Army was lavishly supplied and equipped. Auchinleck had 150,000 troops and a powerful strike force in the form of three armoured divisions.[39] These had a combined strength of 700 tanks and a further 500

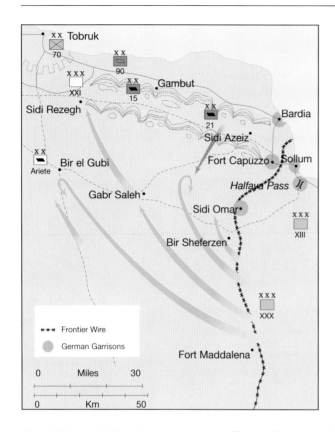

Tobruk
70
90
XXI
15
Gambut
Sidi Rezegh
21
Bardia
Sidi Azeiz
Fort Capuzzo
Sollum
Bir el Gubi
Ariete
Halfaya Pass
Gabr Saleh
Sidi Omar
XIII
Bir Sheferzen
XXX
Frontier Wire
German Garrisons
Fort Maddalena
0   Miles   30
0   Km   50

Above: Following the failure of Battleaxe, Churchill pushed Auchinleck to mount a fresh offensive against the Halfaya Pass. Operation Crusader was the codename for this new assault.

Below: The RAF's Spitfires (shown here) and Hurricanes provided Britain with air superiority over the desert, and found rich pickings among the German Stukas.

machines being repaired or on their way to the front.[40] The quality of the British tanks was also getting better. The Valentine, an improvement on the A10, was under-gunned with only a puny 2pdr (40mm) gun in its turret. To compensate for this less-than-impressive tank, the Americans, whose neutrality was wearing dangerously thin, had supplied their unofficial ally with the Stuart Light Tank, which the British called the Honey. With a top speed of 58km/h (36mph) and a high-velocity 37mm gun, the Honey was fast and hard-hitting enough to equal the medium Panzer III. These impressive machines, and a large supply of 37mm anti-tank guns, began to arrive in North Africa during October.[41]

The British had a major numerical advantage that they could put to good use, and Churchill was pressing for Auchinleck to exploit his position. As he had removed Auchinleck's predecessor for his supposedly ponderous style of command, the Commander-in-Chief Middle East was under great and growing pressure from London to get on with the task of defeating Rommel. But the "Auch" would not be rushed by Churchill or anyone else in London. Both men and machines were unseasoned, and had not had time to acclimatize to the often atrocious conditions of desert combat.

Auchinleck would not make a move until he and the army were ready to attack, and only after he had found the right general to command the Eighth Army.[42] He felt that he had found the right man for the task in Lieutenant-General Sir Alan Cunningham, the conqueror of Italian East Africa.[43] Although very successful against Mussolini's isolated and poorly led forces in Ethiopia, Cunningham wasn't ideal due to his lack of experience with tanks and the conduct of a modern, fast-moving and mechanized campaign. Nevertheless,

Cunningham had an impressive array of units. He had two army corps at his command – Lieutenant-General Godwin-Austen's XIII Corps, and Lieutenant-General Norrie's XXX Corps. As with the DAK, the core of the Eighth Army was its armoured units, and in particular three armoured brigades, each with a tank strength far greater than any of Rommel's panzer divisions. The brigades were the 4th, with 166 tanks; the 7th, with 129; and the 22nd, with 158 machines.[44]

Auchinleck's plans

Auchinleck's plan of attack was brutally simple. Had his troops and subordinate commanders been more experienced, and the latter bolder, it might have worked. The Auch had taken a leaf out of Rommel's book. While Godwin-Austen's XIII Corps kept the Germans occupied along the border, with an implied threat to the Axis forces besieging Tobruk, XXX Corps would stage a flanking hook to the south through the desert. XXX Corps was to outflank the DAK and sweep the Germans out of eastern Cyrenaica.[45] The plan's simplicity was its strength but also its weakness, since it seems incredible that the British thought Rommel would not recognize his own tactics. That is exactly what happened, and the plan failed.

To begin with, Rommel was preoccupied with his fatal obsession of taking Tobruk. He was underestimating the British, and hadn't noticed the build-up.[46] Rommel was more worried about being trapped between the British frontline and the Allied garrison of Tobruk, as well as being concerned about his supply situation. He simply did not believe that the British were bold enough to launch an all-out offensive against his frontline.[47] The British had not only picked up their tactics from Rommel, but also copied his clever tricks with camouflage and concealment. A heavy sandstorm just before the offensive aided this, and ensured that the Germans did not send out the necessary aerial reconnaissance.[48]

Below: General Gott, on the right, is seen here inspecting his lines. His 7th Armoured Division was the most famous of the Eighth Army's armoured units, spearheading the Operation Crusader attack.

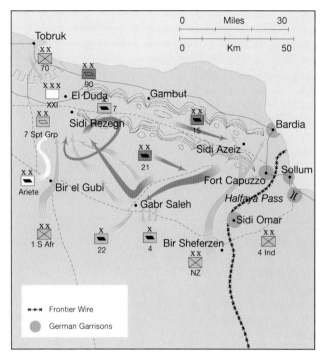
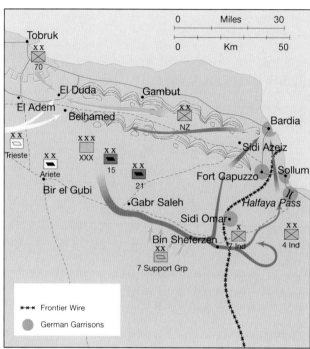

Above: 20-22 November 1941. As the British advanced on Tobruk, the Germans counterattacked with the Afrika Korps, inflicting serious losses on the 7th Armoured Brigade.

Above right: 24-28 November 1941. The New Zealand division drove on regardless towards Tobruk, and briefly relieved the city. However, Rommel's men pushed the Allies right back to the frontier wire.

At 06:00 hours on 18 November, the British offensive began. It was spearheaded by Major-General Gott's 7th Armoured Division (with 450 tanks), the most famous of the Eighth Army's armoured units, smashing its way through the Axis lines of defence. Rommel returned to his much-neglected HQ where he announced that this could only be a British feint! General Ludwig Cruewell, commander of the DAK, believing that the British meant business, convinced Rommel that this was an all-out offensive to crush the DAK. By the afternoon, the British attack, cutting deep and hard into the Axis lines, had achieved its initial objectives.[49]

The battle raged with continued ferocity during the next day, and on the morning of 20 November Rommel, back to his former self, had brought his deadly anti-tank guns into action. What helped him was the better-than-expected performance of the Italians, who put up an impressive defence of their position at Bir el Gubi. This gave Rommel time to prepare his defences.[50] The British were saved by Cruewell's mistaken orders which sent the 15th and 21st Panzer Divisions against Capuzzo. They soon ran out of fuel and got stranded in the middle of the desert. Only the 15th managed to return to maul the 4th Armoured Brigade at Gabr Saleh.[51]

Meanwhile, in the Tobruk sector, the British 70th Division made a serious dent in the Axis lines, which could have proved a potential threat to Rommel's entire position and his plans for a counterattack at Sidi Rezegh.[52] The two panzer divisions found their way back, combined, and during a fierce night battle defeated the 4th Armoured Brigade. Cruewell proved to be an impressive commander, and his leadership during this fight was, according to one authority, nothing short of inspired. During his attack against Bir el Gubi, Cruewell reduced the 7th Armoured Division to a mere 70 tanks.[53]

"Sunday of the Dead": the height of the battle (23 November)

There followed a few days of fierce but confused fighting. The climax came on Sunday 23 November. In Germany, this day is called "Tottensonntag" – Sunday of the Dead. Early in the day, the New Zealanders, admired as tough and fearless soldiers, captured Capuzzo and almost took Cruewell prisoner when they stormed DAK headquarters. The Germans counterattacked. They captured 3000 Allied troops, but lost 70 tanks out of some 160 remaining. This was a tactical success but a pyrrhic victory, since Rommel's slender panzer forces could not afford such losses in tanks, even if it led to victory.

It also showed clearly what a gambler Rommel was. He had little choice, however, since he was conducting a campaign on a supply shoestring and on a front being ignored by his superiors back in Berlin. Rommel showed a predator's instinct for the right moment to strike and secure a kill. General Cunningham was, by now, deeply depressed at how the battle was developing; and the British, having fought well but failing to secure a victory, were off-balance. Rommel decided to attack: after five hours of fierce fighting he had advanced 96km (60 miles), and by 16:00 hours his forces had reached the border.

Meanwhile, Cruewell, whom Rommel feared had been captured, had escaped from his pursuers by driving off at breakneck speed in a captured British staff car. Rommel sent a forward unit to try to capture the enemy's supply dumps, but had to drop the ambitious idea of advancing to the British-held railhead of Habata and the Jarabub Oasis. He blamed this failure on the slowness of the Italian advance and the 15th Panzer Division. Luckily for the British, Rommel's reconnaissance patrols advanced eastwards at too northerly a point and failed to locate and capture two British supply dumps south of Trigh el Abd.[54]

Without captured British petrol, Rommel's tanks were running out of fuel. This reduced their speed and range, undermining the whole concept of Rommel's fast cut, thrust and parry style of mobile war. It was also claimed that he was reckless and that his absence from his HQ had confused his command of the battle. According to

Below: One of Rommel's Panzer III tanks during Operation Crusader, which was fought from November 1941 to January 1942.

Above: Italy's General Bastico, shown here decorating a blackshirt volunteer, to whom Rommel played reluctant host prior to his orderly retreat after Operation Crusader.

Rommel himself, and to historians such as Liddell Hart, this was the sniping of his detractors back in Germany. After all, as Liddell Hart pointed out, this approach of leading from the front had secured Rommel's great victories earlier in the year, as his swift and deadly thrusts kept the British on their toes and ensured their eventual defeat.[55] Rommel himself, writing home on 30 November, was most pleased about the way the fighting was going.[56]

The fighting continued with uninterrupted intensity and ferocity, as neither side was willing to yield the battlefield. As it was, Rommel and the Germans, despite their inferior strength, had the better of the fighting – and the British had yet again showed their inferiority in handling large armoured formations. Fritz Bayerlein, Cruewell's chief of staff, criticized the British for spreading their tanks too thinly on the ground, and for making a completely unnecessary attack against Sollum, when they should have concentrated their massive armoured might against Acroma and Sidi Rezegh.

German evaluation of British tactics

The Germans, whose style of command in the desert was one of improvisation and local initiative, were appalled at the British rigidity in adhering to a strict plan, even when reality told them to change their methods and style. To fight by the rule book was bad enough in Europe, but in the desert it was an unmitigated disaster. Bayerlein concluded that, to the Germans, "the main thing in the open desert is to bring the enemy under effective fire and start hitting him before he is in a position to hit back".[57]

There was also a major difference in the way the Germans and British viewed tank warfare. The Germans, with their Blitzkrieg doctrine, saw the tanks as an integrated part of a well-oiled machinery of war that included every other service including engineers, infantry, artillery and the air force. The British, whose tank forces were often led by former infantry or cavalry commanders (such as Norrie), did not possess this experience and understanding of the true nature of mobile tank warfare. They attacked in a dispersed fashion and often with small groups of tanks, which allowed the Germans, combining minefields, artillery and tanks, to crush the British regiments and brigades piecemeal. The British wasted their heavy tanks (Matildas and Valentines) in attacks that lost momentum as the unnerved Axis troops quickly regained their composure. Trying to

Below: While the Stuka dive-bomber still provided effective support for Rommel's tanks, it was vulnerable to the RAF's Spitfires and Hurricanes.

pin down and destroy Rommel's panzers was like trying to catch a fox with a net. The panzers were too elusive, mobile and well-led to fall for this clumsy tactic.[58]

The fighting continued, as each side rolled with the punches during the period from 29 November to 1 December. Rommel, despite his slender tank forces and precarious fuel situation, persisted in thinking in terms of an offensive that would snatch the initiative from the British and allow him to push them back across the wire. Rommel wanted to relieve his hard-pressed garrisons along the frontier and prevent the British from concentrating their forces at Bir el Gubi. But on 5 December his attack against El Duda failed. An earlier attack against Sidi Omar had suffered at the hands of dug-in élite Indian (Sikh) infantry, supported by British artillery – they had wreaked havoc among the German panzers. Rommel cancelled a planned offensive against Bir el Gubi.[59]

Two days later, finally accepting that his forces were too weak, Rommel ordered them back to Gazala.

By 11 December his forces were back in good order, without the British being able to prevent their retreat.[60] Despite his obsession with Tobruk, Rommel faced the fact that his troops were exhausted and should be pulled out of the line. He still hoped and believed he could escape what he saw as the enemy's pincers, and hold Cyrenaica.[61]

The mere hint of Cyrenaica falling to the British brought Italy's Commando Supremo back to life, and at his HQ in the Bay of Ain al-Gazala Rommel played reluctant host to General Bastico. Rommel, who

Above: Rommel and his staff in early 1942. His achievements during Operation Crusader were hardly a victory, but his retreat was successful and he saved a large part of his army.

called the Italian general "Bombastico" (to the amusement of his staff), was treated to a torrent of Italian "bombast". This amounted to a threat on Bastico's part that the Italians were removed from Rommel's command and would be used to block the British advance at Agedabia. For political reasons of prestige, the Italians could not accept that Cyrenaica would fall into British hands yet again. Rommel threatened to leave the Italians to their fate should he be forced to retreat. Bastico withdrew his threat and accepted, ungraciously, Rommel's decision.[62]

Meanwhile, the British continued to attack but the 4th Armoured Brigade failed to capture Gazala between 14 and 16 December. General Ritchie's 15 December offensive on the right flank and in the centre of the frontline had more success, though.[63] That day Rommel's panzer forces were reduced to a mere 30 tanks compared with the British, who had 200 left.[64]

On 20 December, Rommel gave the order to retreat.[65.] Two days later, without an air umbrella, his army began the doleful march westwards without

Rommel having any clue where he would make a stand.[66] Rommel's swift decision and rapid retreat from the frontier caught the British off-guard. They had to improvise a hasty advance (they had expected a drawn-out battle in a constricted area), and so Ritchie detached a large number of troops to take Beda Fomm and thus cut off Rommel's escape westwards.[67] Rommel, determined that the British should pay for every inch of territory they captured, decided to abandon the entire Benghazi bulge in favour of a fast retreat and making a stand at Mersa Brega.[68] He was confident that he could escape Ritchie's trap only if the Italian formations didn't collapse.[69]

The results of Operation Crusader

Rommel's main consolation was that the British had found Benghazi empty of loot; and that Cruewell, whom Rommel had given up hope of seeing alive, had returned safely.[70] He gave the British a bloody nose at El Haseiat,[71] giving his army time to escape. A jubilant Rommel noted on 30 December that his army had escaped destruction at the hands of the advancing British. Ritchie had failed to trap the DAK between the Eighth Army and the Mediterranean coast.[72] Modestly, and accurately, Rommel attributed the escape of his army to the endurance and superhuman efforts of his troops.[73]

This successful retreat was hardly a victory, and it came at great cost. Not only had the whole of Cyrenaica fallen to the British, but Rommel had abandoned the border garrisons deep behind British lines. Bardia was held by Major-General Schmitt with 8800 Axis troops, while Sollum and Halfaya Pass were held by 6300 troops under the Italian Major-General de Giorgi. On New Year's Eve, Bardia was pounded from the air, the sea and land by the British. By 2 January, the Halfaya Pass/Sollum garrison was in British hands, and a fortnight later (17 January) Bardia capitulated.[74]

Operation Crusader had come to an end. It was, despite the earlier setbacks, a resounding success and almost comparable with O'Connor's victories a year earlier. The Axis forces had lost 33,000 troops (20,000 Italians and 13,000 Germans) compared with British and Commonwealth losses of 18,000.[75] Even worse for Rommel was the fact that he had lost 300 tanks against 278 for the British. These were losses that the British could replace with less trouble than Rommel.[76]

Below: Rommel's forces may have been forced to retreat after Operation Crusader, but this burning British Crusader tank shows that Great Britain paid a high price, losing almost 300 tanks to Rommel's panzers, artillery and troops.

Chapter notes

1 RP.119, Rommel's diary.
2 RP.120, Rommel's diary.
3 Robin Neillands, *Desert Rats*, p.71.
4 Ibid, p.72.
5 Purnell's, Vol. 4, p.544, Joachim Rösseler, *Operation Brevity: the Struggle for Halfaya (May 1941)*; Neillands, p.71.
6 Rösseler, p.545.
7 Purnell's, Vol. 4, p.548, Kenneth Macksey, *Operation Battleaxe: Wavell's last Offensive, May–June 1941.*
8 Neillands, p.72.
9 Ibid.
10 Ibid, pp.73-74.
11 Macksey, p.551.
12 Neillands, p.76.
13 Macksey, p.554.
14 Neillands, p.77.
15 Macksey, p.554.
16 Neillands, p.78.
17 Macksey, p.555.
18 Jackson, p.131.
19 Liddell Hart, p.188.
20 Schmidt, p.65.
21 RP.146, Rommel to Lucie, 18 June 1941.
22 Ibid, 64.

23 Jackson, pp.131-132.
24 Neillands, p.79.
25 RP, Rommel's notes, 146-147.
26 George Forty, *Afrika Korps at War*, Vol. 1, *The Road to Alexandria* (London, 1978).
27 Ibid, p.116.
28 Ibid, p.138.
29 Mussolini's bum.
30 Schmidt, p.60.
31 Ibid, p.150.
32 RP.150, Rommel to Lucie, 30 Aug. 1941.
33 RP.151, Rommel to Lucie, 6 Oct. 1941.
34 RP.150, Rommel to Lucie, 10 Sept. 1941.
35 RP.152, Rommel to Lucie, 12 Nov. 1941.
36 Neillands, p.80.
37 Liddell Hart, p.192.
38 Neillands, p.82.
39 Ibid, p.80.
40 Liddell Hart, p.191.
41 Neillands, p.81. The Americans also provided instructors to train the British crews in the use of the Honeys.
42 Auchinleck was

Commander-in-Chief Middle East and therefore not the direct commander of the Eighth Army.
43 Somalia, Eritrea and Ethiopia or Abyssinia. The last country had only been occupied by the Italians as late as 1936.
44 Neillands, p.82.
45 Liddell Hart, p.193.
46 Ibid, p.194.
47 Purnell's, Vol. VI, Geoffrey Evans, *Crusader: Auchinleck recovers Cyrenaica (November 1941–January 192)*, p.661.
48 Liddell Hart, pp.194-195; Purnell's, Vol. VII, Fritz Bayerlein, *War in the Desert: Winter 1941–42, Cyrenaica*, p.779.
49 Evans, p.662.
50 Liddell Hart, p.194.
51 Ibid.
52 Evans, p.662.
53 Ibid, p.665.
54 Liddell Hart, p.199.
55 Liddell Hart, pp.200-201; Evans, p.666.
56 RP.170, Rommel to

Lucie, 9 Dec. 1941.
57 Bayerlein, p.779.
58 Liddell Hart, pp.192-193.
59 Evans, p.668.
60 Liddell Hart, p.205.
61 RP.170, Rommel to Lucie, 9 Dec. 1941.
62 RP.173, Diary notes.
63 Evans, p.668; Liddell Hart, p.205.
64 Liddell Hart, p.206.
65 RP.175, Rommel to Lucie, 20 Dec. 1941.
66 RP.175, Rommel to Lucie, 22 Dec. 1941.
67 Purnell's, Vol. VI, Kenneth Macksey, *Crusader: the final stages*, p.671.
68 Ibid.
69 RP.176, Rommel to Lucie, 23 Dec. 1941.
70 RP.176, Rommel to Lucie, 25 Dec. 1941.
71 Liddell Hart, p.207.
72 RP.176, Rommel to Lucie, 30 Dec. 1941.
73 RP.176, Rommel to Lucie, 31 Dec. 1941.
74 Macksey, *Crusader*, p.672.
75 Liddell Hart, p.207.
76 Evans, p.669.

CHAPTER 6

High Tide

Rommel's masterpieces: the battles of Gazala, Tobruk and Mersa Matruh
(January–June 1942)

The British, by throwing Rommel out of Cyrenaica, had inflicted on the Fox his worst defeat so far in the desert war. This rankled enough, but was made worse by the Italian high command's gloating at the setback. Rommel was back to square one in this strange, see-saw war that flowed between El Agheila and the Egyptian frontier.

At El Agheila, Rommel had a natural defence line since the coastal road, the only supply route and avenue of advance for the British, had to pass through a narrow land corridor between the coastal sand dunes and the salt swamps of the interior. The other advantage of this position was that Rommel was now only two days away from his main supply base at Tripoli. This improved his supply situation, while the British, after a long advance, were running out of petrol, water, spares and reinforcements. It was time for the pendulum to swing back again. Rommel, not interested in waiting for the optimum time to strike, was about to spring an unpleasant surprise on the enemy.[1] A lesser general would probably have waited and rested his army on the El Agheila line before commencing with a counterattack.

The British, having won an apparent victory, had again become over-confident. Auchinleck was sure that Rommel had received a major setback and that he would not be in a position to launch a new offensive operation for a considerable period. Instead, the British occupied themselves with planning their own offensive, Operation Acrobat, set for February 1942. This promised to bring the desert war to a victorious conclusion by taking Tripoli.[2] Acrobat was an apt name for an operation that was never executed and saw the British, in Liddell Hart's words, make several long backward somersaults all the way to Gazala and beyond.[3]

Both sides received new tanks and units to replace previous losses. The battered and exhausted 7th Armoured Division had lost its commander, General

Left: Rommel began 1942 with the bitter taste of defeat in his mouth, but immediately began planning a series of aggressive moves that won him his most impressive victories over the British Eighth Army.

Campbell, whose death was a heavy blow to its morale. Campbell was succeeded by General Messervy, who had little experience of armoured warfare.

To replace the 7th Armoured Division, the British high command sent an entirely new formation, the 1st Armoured Division, to the desert with 150 brand-new Cruiser tanks. The problem was that the crews were composed of cavalry men, with little experience of tanks and mechanized warfare – and even less of desert conditions.

Rommel received no such largesse in tanks and crews. On 5 January, a convoy of six ships brought him 55 Panzer IIIs and IVs. Of these, 19 of the Panzer IIIs were J models with the long 55mm guns that gave 50 percent better armour penetration capacity than the short-barrelled version. Compared with the number of Auchinleck's reinforcements, this wasn't much, but it was enough for Rommel to plan a new offensive. By 12 January, Rommel had 111 panzers and was in a position to strike without warning.[4]

Rommel's surprise offensive

Below: Italy's General Cavallero (centre) was hardly a fan of Rommel. As the German's new offensive began, Cavallero ordered the Italian Mobile Corps to halt. Rommel made it quite clear that he would continue the advance with or without Italian support.

Less than three weeks after being thrown out of Cyrenaica, Rommel was ready to attack. At 08:30 hours on 21 January, his tanks assaulted[5] the British positions at Agedabia, catching them completely by surprise. The Eighth Army's commanders, officers and troops alike were all equally shocked by this unexpected move.[6] The 1st Armoured Division, supposedly the armoured spearhead of Operation Acrobat, was being refitted and was scattered across a huge stretch of desert.[7] It was therefore in no fit state to take on the full might of Rommel's panzers, and each of its brigades was defeated in turn. On 22 January, the 2nd Armoured Brigade lost half of its tanks, and the DAK defeated each of its tank regiments.[8] The 1st Armoured Division fared worse, as it lost 117 tanks, 33 guns and thousands of prisoners to Rommel, who put his success down to preserving complete secrecy. "We know from experience," noted Rommel in his diary, "that Italian headquarters cannot keep things to themselves and that everything they wireless to Rome gets round to British ears." Bastico exploded with rage that he, the nominal commander-in-chief, had been kept in the dark.[9] Rommel could not have cared less, and noted with delight that: "Our opponents are getting out as though they'd been stung. Prospects are good for the next few days."[10]

On 23 January, the DAK outflanked the British, and took Antelat and Saunnu.[11] The same day, Rommel received a most unwanted and angry guest in the shape of Italy's General Cavallero, whose task, he feared, was to stop his offensive. Indeed, Cavallero had ordered the Italian Mobile Corps (IMC) to halt. Rommel made it quite clear that he would continue the advance as long as possible, with or without the support of the Italians.[12] The German general seemingly had more trouble with his allies at this time than with the enemy.

Rommel's offensive towards Msus continued. Msus was where the British had planned to make a counterattack. Nothing came of it, and the German advance on Mechili and Benghazi continued without a break. On 25 January, after four days of successful fighting, Rommel concluded that, "Our blows struck home. And there's still one to come. Then we'll go all modest again and lie in wait for a bit". Meanwhile, Mussolini had intervened and given Rommel wide orders that allowed him to act independently of Cavallero.[13]

Having taken Msus, Rommel drove on and smashed through the 210th Guards Brigade on his way to Benghazi.[14] On 27 January, Rommel was delighted to have the Italians back in the race and he was delighted with the huge number

Above: Sunken ships in the harbour at Benghazi, December 1941. The port was taken by Rommel in January 1942.

Below: A Panzer III on the move. On 5 January 1942, a convoy of six ships brought Rommel 55 Panzer IIIs and IVs. This particular tank mounts a short-barrelled 50mm main gun.

Above: Members of the famous French Foreign Legion took part in the courageous defence of Bir Hacheim, which delayed Rommel's advance and won the Free French troops great respect.

of armoured cars, trucks, guns and tanks that were falling into his hands.[15] The following day, the Indians (the 4th Division) evacuated Benghazi, leaving huge amounts of petrol, oil, drums of water and other supplies stockpiled for Acrobat, to be devoured by the DAK. Italian and German troops took Er Regima, east of the town, to cut off the retreating British forces.[16] Rommel was thrilled with this bounty that his enemy had left behind, which would help him in the follow-up to the offensive. If the forces at Agedabia and Msus had advanced more quickly towards the coast then, at least according to Bayerlein, the Eighth Army might have been annihilated.[17]

The British had been dealt a massive blow. Auchinleck sent a flood of instructions and orders to the front. The result, as one British officer put it, was "orders, counter orders and disorder". This state of shock and panic in some units could account for the British abandoning the vital Benghazi depot[18] that should have been destroyed as soon as Rommel's tanks made an appearance. As if to compensate for these setbacks, the Royal Air Force (RAF) carried out a heavy raid against Tripoli and Misurata on 31 January. This failed to stop the victorious Axis offensive, since Barce fell that same day and the DAK pressed on towards Cyrene.

On 1 February, the British began to retire back to the Gazala line. Auchinleck ordered that Tobruk was to be held at all costs.[19] By 4 February, Rommel's army had pushed the Eighth Army some 240km (150 miles) eastwards, from Msus to Gazala.[20] "It went like greased lightning," wrote Rommel that same day.[21] On 5 February, the British left Mechili and the DAK took Tmimi. Two days later, Rommel's forces had reached the Gazala line where, in the face of the British defences, they halted.[22] Rommel had a 483km (300-mile) front that he hoped would stabilize, but at least he was in possession of Cyrenaica.[23] Only the jealous Italian high command wasn't happy, and "would be best pleased", claimed an irritated Rommel, "to see us get out of Cyrenaica again".[24]

On 14 February, after a pause of a week, Rommel ordered a new offensive to be launched, but it did not make much headway because of heavy rains. Operations were halted from 19 to 23 February, as the weather went from bad to worse.[25] There was now a long break in activity that lasted for the rest of March and April, except for air operations. While the Luftwaffe attacked Tobruk, the RAF pounded Tripoli in retaliation.[26]

Rommel was quite pleased at being close to the front, and during one of his many inspection tours he came across an abandoned house where the British, with their customary humour, had written on the wall: "Keep clean, we'll be back soon!" Rommel wrote: "We'll see about that!"[27] On 10 April, during a similar trip, Rommel had a lucky escape. A splinter struck him in the stomach, but hit him with its flat side and left only a purple bruise, the size of a soup plate, across his stomach. However, Rommel was shaken, and his terse comment was, "the luck of the devil".[28]

Meanwhile his supply situation and problems with Italian Army officers continued to plague him. Rommel, like most of his officers and men, realized they were unpopular with their allies since the Italians believed the Germans were insensitive about Italian pride, unappreciative of their military efforts and showed great arrogance towards them. Some of them went too far in their criticism of the Germans. General Gastone Gambara was fired when he told his officers in public that he lived for the day when he could lead the Italian Army against Germany. Rommel's only comment was: "What a fool!"[29] No doubt to soothe German feelings, and show his appreciation of Rommel, Bastico informed

Below: A hero in French, British and even German eyes, General Joseph Koenig was Commander-in-Chief of Fighting French Forces during the desert war, leading the resistance at Bir Hacheim.

Rommel that he would be given an Italian decoration. Rommel was not thrilled. "More troops would suit me better," he commented sourly.[30]

The delay in operations allowed the British to complete the construction of the Gazala defence line. Commenced in January, it was finished in May when Rommel launched his next offensive. The line comprised a belt of minefields extending from Gazala some 69km (43 miles) southwards into the desert. At regular intervals the line was strengthened by so-called boxes. At these points the minefields thickened, and were reinforced by fortified anti-tank ditches, machine-gun bunkers and thick layers of barbed wire. Each of these boxes was manned by an infantry brigade, including the 150th Infantry Brigade, the 201st Guards Brigade (in the Knightsbridge box), the 22nd Guards Brigade and the South Africans. Finally, the anchor of the whole line was the southernmost box at Bir Hacheim, which was held by the 1st Free French Brigade commanded by General Koenig.

A second defence line stretched 48km (30 miles) from El Adem to Sidi Muftah. On a map, and in theory, the Gazala line was a sort of desert Maginot, but its weaknesses were obvious. It was incomplete since it ended a bit south of Bir Hacheim which would allow Rommel, in his usual style, to outflank it through the desert. Furthermore, the boxes were placed too far apart. The British high command had hoped to overcome these weaknesses by stationing XXX Corps in the southern vicinity of Bir Hacheim.

Below: Afrika Korps officers survey the terrain prior to the assault on the Gazala line. As this picture illustrates, desert terrain offers excellent opportunities for long-range artillery and anti-tank guns.

The line served several purposes, but the main one was to defend the Egyptian frontier and Tobruk, while it also provided a jumping-off point for a British offensive. One couldn't but agree with historian David Chandler's conclusions, that the Gazala line was a white elephant and that the British defence line should have been constructed along the axis of Acroma, Tobruk, El Adem to Sidi Rezegh.[31]

Operation Theseus and Venezia

In mid-June 1942, the Axis had planned to strike against Malta, an irritating hornets' nest. In preparation, Italy's high command wanted Rommel to clear out the British from Gazala. Once Operation Hercules (the invasion of Malta) had been successful, Rommel could proceed to invade the Nile Delta (Operation Aida). On 1 May, he gave orders to attack the British. While Rommel with the tank forces swept around the south of the Gazala line, Cruewell would launch Operation Venezia, a frontal attack on the line that would serve as a diversion to keep the British occupied.

The British expected the Germans to strike frontally, at the centre of the line, and along the coastal road.[32] This served Rommel's purposes well, since he wanted to keep the British occupied in the north, while he struck with the 15th and 21st Panzer Divisions in the south. Having defeated the British at Gazala, which he called Marmarica, Rommel would finally capture Tobruk.[33]

Rommel had 332 German tanks, of which 240 were Panzer IIIs and only 38 were the superior Panzer IVs. He also had 228 Italian tanks, mainly obsolete

Above: Panzer General Cruewell (left, seen here with Bayerlein) was one of Rommel's most experienced and trusted subordinates.

M13s. Rommel faced 100,000 British troops and 849 tanks. The British had begun to receive new American material, of which the most important was the new Grant tank. This was the British production variant of the US M3 (medium) Lee tank. It weighed in at 28 tonnes (28.5 tons), had 57mm (2.2in) armour and two guns – a 37mm gun in the turret and a 75mm model in a sponson on the side of the hull. With the Grant, the British felt they finally had a tank that could take on the German panzers. It was only in the air that Rommel had a marked edge, as he had 700 Italian and German planes to pit against 200 RAF aircraft.[34]

Cruewell attacked in the early afternoon of 26 May. The British believed that this was the long-expected German assault, and concentrated the bulk of their forces against him. At 21:00 hours Rommel, leading in person the panzer divisions, advanced to the southwest straight into the Sahara. During the following morning Rommel's panzers scattered the 3rd Indian Brigade that had been caught unawares having breakfast. The 15th Panzer Division attacked the 4th Armoured Brigade, which was forced to retreat to El Adem.[35]

That same morning, the HQ of the 7th Armoured Division was captured by Rommel's advancing tanks. General Messervy – described by one British veteran as "a silly old man from the Indian Army" – tore off his epaulettes in time, pretended to be an old batman and then, accompanied by several other officers, managed to escape back to the British lines.[36] The rest of Messervy's division was scattered, and the 4th Armoured Brigade was committed piecemeal, which allowed Rommel to destroy it with ease. The British had no choice since Rommel's attack came so suddenly and unexpectedly.[37]

Ritchie believed that Rommel was reduced to 250 panzers while he still had 330 tanks, and that he therefore possessed a decided numerical advantage over Rommel. However, he chose not to launch a concentrated, massed attack against

Below: The Grant was the British production variant of the US M3 Lee tank. It had two main guns – a 37mm gun in the turret and a 75mm gun in a sponson on the side of the hull. With the Grant, the British felt they finally had a tank that could take on the German panzers.

Rommel's exposed position. Rommel's situation was truly precarious since the Italians (the *Pavia* and *Trieste* Divisions) were making only very slow and painful progress through the British minefields. Unless a viable corridor was created through the minefields, Rommel's forward forces would be cut off – and his panzer crews were already in desperate need of water and food. Taking personal charge of the battle, Rommel headed south to speed the convoys through the minefields and order his formation to concentrate for an all-out offensive.

On 29 May, the Italian *Sabratha* Division attacked and mauled the 1st South African Division. In this confused fighting, Cruewell was captured and General Alfred Gause, his chief of staff, wounded. Rommel was deprived of two of his most senior and most experienced subordinates just as he needed them most. Having tried, and failed, to concentrate his panzers southwest of the "Knightsbridge" position, Rommel, whose situation was worsening, went over to the defensive since the DAK could not reach Tobruk.[38]

Above: While the Ju 87 Stuka dive-bombers were vulnerable to attack by the RAF Spitfires and Hurricanes, they still played a devastating role in supporting Rommel's tanks during his 1942 desert offensive.

The battle of the Cauldron, part I: destruction of the 150th Brigade box

Rommel's new tactic was untried and ingenious. He created what he called a "cauldron", a defensive ring in which he sheltered his tanks and troops against the inevitable attack by Ritchie. The defences consisted of hastily laid minefields, anti-tank guns and the highly effective 88mm anti-aircraft guns. Rommel, who was in temporary command of Group Cruewell, was daring Ritchie to attack and waste his tanks against the cauldron's perimeter while he

turned his attentions to the boxes of the Gazala line. These boxes were situated in the middle of the cauldron – and would have to be disposed of.[39]

Rommel's first target was the box of the 150th Brigade, whose existence came as a nasty surprise. If the boxes could hold out long enough, then Ritchie hoped he would be able to crush Rommel's army between himself and the boxes until the Fox was forced to surrender. But, for this to work, Ritchie would have to concentrate enough armour and strike before Rommel had a chance to destroy the boxes. That meant Rommel would have to destroy the 150th Brigade before Ritchie could lumber into action.[40]

Inside the cauldron the situation was not pleasant; in fact, it was getting worse since Rommel and his men were running out of water – fast. A British major, Archer Shee, in command of the Indian prisoners, complained that his troops were not receiving enough water. Rommel snapped back: "You are getting exactly the same ration of water as the Afrika Korps and myself – half a cup. But I agree that we cannot go on like this. If we don't get a convoy through tonight I shall have to ask General Ritchie for terms."[41] Rommel wasn't exaggerating, and he would have to get cracking before it was too late.

The 150th Brigade box

The battle for the 150th Brigade box was one of the lesser-known episodes of the desert war, overshadowed by the more protracted and celebrated stand of the French at Bir Hacheim. The brigade was composed of troops from the north of England, and was under the command of Colonel C.W. Haydon. The brigade was now surrounded by the enemy, and quite isolated from the rest of the Eighth Army – a situation that all troops hate, and one that can prove deeply demoralizing. There was little hope of outside relief from the rest of the army, since Ritchie had decided that he could not launch an attack until 3 June, which would prove too late for the 150th. Neither was there any hope that Haydon could get relief from the more distant boxes. He was now quite alone and facing the full might and fury of the Afrika Korps.

By 30 May, German preparations for an attack were under way, as their sappers made numerous efforts to cut a hole in the British minefields but failed because of the defenders' withering fire. During the night, the British kept up an aggressive patrol activity that held the Germans at bay. At dawn the following day, wave upon wave of Stukas swept over the box, which was soon covered by thick layers of dust, sand and debris. This natural smokescreen gave the German sappers the cover they needed to penetrate the minefields. Then the panzers roared into action, assaulted the box and knocked out the British 25-pounder anti-tank guns. By the afternoon, despite desperate resistance by the defenders,

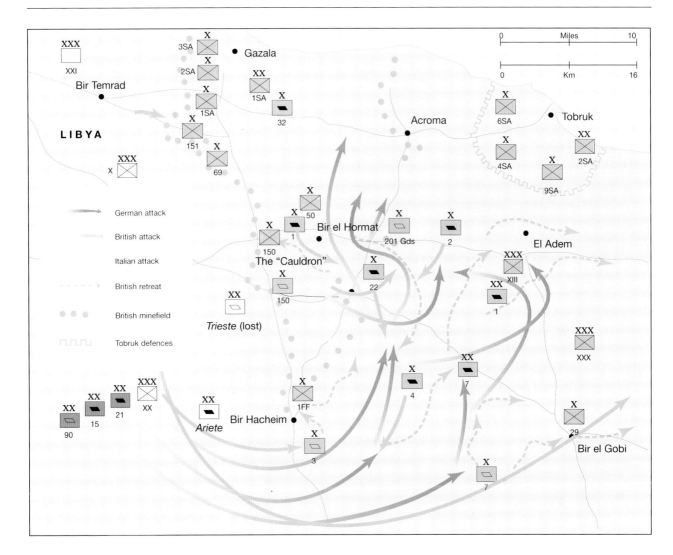

the box had fallen to the Germans, who captured 3000 prisoners, 124 guns and 101 tanks. Rommel's only disappointment was that he had not been able to congratulate the brave Colonel Haydon for a splendid defence. The colonel, like many of his men, was dead.

This was a critical victory that ensured the survival of the DAK in the face of formidable odds. Auchinleck, shocked that Ritchie had allowed an entire brigade to be destroyed without lifting a finger to save it, ordered him to attack. This he did, belatedly, on 2 June. In the face of Rommel's 88s and formidable anti-tank defences it was a slaughter, leaving heap upon heap of burning tanks. It was too little, too late.[12]

Rommel had breached the Gazala line, opened a lifeline to the west, and thus ensured that vital supplies of water, food, ammunition and petrol could reach him. He felt strong enough to send the 90th Light Division southwards, to Bir Hacheim, to support the *Ariete* Division.[13] Bir Hacheim, the anchor of the entire

Above: The British ought to have prevailed at the Battle of Gazala, 26 May–14 June 1942. That they did not, despite material advantages, is testament to the excellent training and motivation of the Axis units, and the textbook use of effective tactics by Rommel and his subordinate commanders.

Above: Rommel (centre) continued to lead from the front during his successful desert campaigns, risking his own life on numerous occasions. He believed close proximity to the frontline led to quicker reactions and better decisions – he was right.

line, was the key to the whole confrontation, and if it fell then Rommel would win the battle. Everything hinged on the fighting resolve and quality of the Free French Brigade and its commander, General Koenig, holding the Bir Hacheim box.

The troops, all of them denounced by the Vichy authorities as renegades, were a motley collection of former regular French Army, Foreign Legionnaires and volunteers. They were united in one single wish, to fight the hated "Boche" and redeem the tarnished reputation of their country. They also possessed another formidable asset in the tough, sallow-faced Koenig, who wore the Cross of Lorraine and his blue-red beret with pride. If ever there was a group of men determined to fight for their corner, it was this garrison.[11]

On 6 June, Rommel moved the 15th Panzer Division to give some muscle to the impending attack on the box. As ever, believing in bluff and tricks, he tested the waters first. Why storm a position if the defenders were willing to surrender? It had worked before during the invasion of France. Rommel sent the French a message: "To the troops of Bir Hacheim. Further resistance will only lead to unnecessary bloodshed. You will have the same fate as the two(!) English brigades which were wiped out two days ago at Got Valeb. We will stop firing as soon as you hoist the white flag and come out to us unarmed."[15] However, these French troops were not the demoralized hordes of 1940, but disciplined and determined soldiers led by a stubborn and proud general. Koenig's reply was characteristically short and rude: "Go to hell!"[16]

Rommel's response was as swift as it was violent. Shells from mortars, artillery, anti-tank guns and tanks, coupled with machine-gun fire and Stuka bombs, rained down upon the French. Koenig, worried about the demoralizing effect of this, radioed the RAF for assistance. The RAF, the only visible support the hard-pressed garrison had, adopted Bir Hacheim as its special mascot. The Spitfires had a turkey shoot at the expense of the slow-moving Stukas. The French were jubilant. Koenig radioed to the RAF, "*Merci pour le RAF*", which brought a characteristically British response from the boys in blue, "*Merci à vous pour le sport*".[17] The Germans failed to see the humour or sport in the slaughter of their air crews, and Field Marshal Kesselring, commander-in-chief of the Armed Forces South, disgusted with his losses at Bir Hacheim, insisted that Rommel attack the stubborn French with his tanks. For once it was Rommel who had to urge Kesselring to dampen his exuberance by pointing out the obvious truth that tanks were no good against prepared positions. The failure against Tobruk had clearly showed the folly of attacking fortified points with tanks.[18]

Rommel, not having been prepared for such stubborn and savage resistance, was deeply impressed with Koenig and his feisty garrison. He was especially impressed by their ability to withstand the tremendous around-the-clock pounding Bir Hacheim was taking. His sappers' valiant efforts were quite fruitless in the face of the withering and well-directed French fire.[19] Indeed, inside the Bar Hacheim box something of the stubborn and heroic spirit that had characterized the French defence at Verdun during the previous war had reappeared. Ritchie, anxious that the French might not be able to hold the box, radioed regularly to ask Koenig if his men would hold – to be told, by a calm and reassured Koenig, that they would.[50]

The fall of Bir Hacheim

This self-confidence and will to resist, characteristics the British admired more than any other, won Koenig's men the respect of the rest of the Eighth Army. At a time when nothing seemed to have gone well for their side, they were glad to have some heroes to celebrate.[51] If this continued long enough, then the British might simply wear down the DAK in a battle of attrition that the latter could not, unlike the British, afford. Rommel called Ritchie's passivity and failure to relieve Bir Hacheim "quite astonishing". After all, had the garrison been German, Rommel would have done everything to relieve it.[52]

This criticism, although valid, is not entirely correct. Ritchie made some half-hearted, but unsuccessful attempts to provide relief. He realized the enormous importance of not losing the Gazala line's anchor position to the enemy. On 5 June, as Rommel's vice around Bir Hacheim tightened, Ritchie launched his relief effort codenamed Aberdeen. In the face of the Axis

Below: Rommel's tanks kick up dust clouds as they advance to meet British armour at the Battle of Gazala in mid-1942.

Above: While they may have been designed as anti-aircraft weapons, the 88mm guns formed a vital part of Rommel's armoured assault force.

Below: Tanks, troops and artillery during the Battle of Gazala in June 1942 – Rommel's masterpiece.

minefields, artillery positions and mobile tank groups, Aberdeen was a slow, ponderous affair. British tanks were used in small numbers which were easy for the 88s to pick off. Aberdeen was a dismal failure that cost Ritchie two infantry brigades, four artillery regiments, 150 tanks and 6000 troops – 2000 dead and 4000 taken prisoner.[53]

After this catastrophic setback, there was little Ritchie could do, as he was left with only 170 working tanks and was inferior in numbers in the air. On 9 June, in a gesture of defiance, what was left of the 4th Armoured Brigade made a futile attempt to relieve Bir Hacheim.[54]

These attacks on the cauldron's outer perimeter could do nothing to interrupt or impede Rommel's meticulous preparations to crush Koenig. By the early morning of 7 June, the 90th Light Division finally managed, despite fierce French fire, to cut a sizeable hole through the minefields. Three days later, a massive Stuka attack was followed by a German assault group, led by Colonel Baade, that managed to break into the box and spread out to destroy any remaining French resistance.

Rommel had expected the French to stand and fight to the death. But Koenig was as daring and cunning as the Fox himself. He had already ordered his men to break out by attacking the German lines at a single point and making their way back to the British lines. Of the garrison's 3600 men, 2700 eventually reached the Eighth Army's main lines. Koenig escaped Rommel's trap in style by being driven though the German lines in a staff car driven by a British woman.

Some of the troops remained to give their comrades cover, and it was not until 11 June that the German flag had been planted in the box. Only some 100 wounded French troops remained to be taken prisoner. For two agonizing weeks, the French had held out and delayed Rommel's offensive in the process.

But with the fall of Bir Hacheim Rommel held half of the Gazala line, and he had won the battle of the Cauldron.[55] Rommel was delighted with his victory, but gave Koenig and his men well-deserved praise for a hard-fought battle by concluding, "Never in Africa was I given a stiffer fight than at Bir Hacheim".[56]

The Gazala gallop

The lessons of Bir Hacheim were not lost on Rommel as he prepared to march on Tobruk, the ultimate prize. However, before he could tackle the port he had to deal with the Eighth Army.

Churchill, frantic as ever about political prestige, put tremendous pressure on Auchinleck. This was transmitted down the chain of command to Ritchie, who was told that Tobruk was to be held at all costs. This meant holding what remained of the Gazala line as well. Ritchie could not therefore, as he should have done, pull back to a new defence line between Acroma and El Adem.

This gave Rommel the opportunity he had been looking for to use his remaining 120 German and 60 Italian tanks to destroy XXX Corps.[57] It is likely that any other general would have paused to rest and refit his tanks before taking on such an arduous task. It was typical of Rommel that he was confident, without being unrealistic or arrogant, that his panzer force could destroy an entire British corps. Rommel had the measure of his men who, he believed, had not been worn down excessively by Ritchie's attrition tactics or by the gruelling battle of Bir Hacheim.[58]

In fact it was imperative for Rommel to go over to the offensive before Ritchie had time to recover. He needed to keep the British off-balance. The ultimate aim was still to invade Egypt and race the British back to Cairo. On 11 June, Rommel sent the 21st Panzer Division against Sidra Ridge while the 15th Panzer Division, accompanied by the 90th Light Division, advanced on El Adem. By dusk,

Below: The 88, the most famous anti-tank gun of World War II. This gun is ready for action, with all four outriggers unfolded.

Above: A British 25lb field gun in action during Rommel's assault on the Gazala line around the Knightsbridge box.

the 90th Light had taken El Adem, which shattered Ritchie's plans for a counterattack. Messervy, the hapless commander of the 7th Armoured Division, was lost in the desert but eventually found his way back to the British lines.

During the night of 11–12 June, Rommel had yet again lured the British into an ambush, with their tanks advancing on his lines and being shot to pieces by the anti-tank guns. Once this had been accomplished, Rommel simply ordered his tanks to advance around the flanks and trap the British armour in a pincer attack. By dawn on 12 June, XXX Corps was left with 70 tanks – it had virtually ceased to be a proper fighting formation. Rommel had achieved his goal.

On 14 June, Ritchie, with Auchinleck's permission, abandoned the wreck of the Gazala line in spite of Churchill's shrill and insistent protests. Instead of abandoning Tobruk – after burning it to the ground and destroying its supplies – Auchinleck instructed Ritchie to hold the fortress town with a strong garrison, while the rest of the Eighth Army manned the Acroma–El Adem line.

It should have been obvious to both Ritchie and Auchinleck that this position, given the battered state of XXX Corps, could not be held. Norrie, the corps commander, was more realistic than his superiors, and he was not going to see XXX Corps wiped out. He therefore chose to abandon Gambut (site of the British HQ), El Adem (the cornerstone of Tobruk's defences) and the railhead at Belhamed (a vital communications centre). Henceforth, Tobruk was cut off and entirely bereft of support when Rommel, as expected, began to close in on the fortress. Meanwhile, the Eighth Army continued its retreat eastwards to the supposed sanctuary of Egypt. [59]

A wonderful battle: the fall of Tobruk

For more than a year the capture of Tobruk had been an overriding obsession with Rommel.[60] Now he had the golden opportunity to realize his ambition. Rommel's obsession was shared by his men, who had seen the port as a thorn in their flesh and a symbol of British defiance. This time, as they advanced on the town, there were encouraging signs that the enemy was close to collapse. The retreating forces had abandoned everything liable to slow them down. Those DAK soldiers who were veterans of the 1940 campaign in France had seen a similar scene on the road to Calais and Dunkirk. Obviously, the quarry was bleeding to death, and the Desert Fox was ready to strike.[61]

On 15 June, General Klopper of the 2nd South African Division was promoted to Garrison Commander of Tobruk.[62] Unfortunately for Klopper and his garrison, Churchill shared Rommel's unhealthy Tobruk obsession, and was now willing to sacrifice a huge number of troops to hold it. There is no doubt that Tobruk was a vital place with its depots, water desalination plant, modern port and proximity to the Belhamed railhead. However, it wasn't worth the price Churchill was willing to pay – especially as Auchinleck did not share his prime minister's views. Auchinleck was not prepared to sacrifice a good share of his army to hold Tobruk at all costs, and his naval colleagues did not relish another series of "milk rounds" between Alexandria and Tobruk, as in 1941.[63]

In the face of Churchillian obstinacy, there was little that Auchinleck or anyone else could do. The British were spared the burden of a second siege by Rommel, who shared his British colleagues' distaste for such a situation. Tobruk may have seemed a formidable fortress, as Klopper had 35,000 troops and stores to last for three months. This was deceptive, as disrepair, damage and apathy had led to the minefields not being maintained, with dangerous gaps through them. The concrete bunkers and fortresses built by Marshal Balbo in the 1930s were also in a state of disrepair. The town itself was one huge ruin.

But the real problem was the state of the garrison and its commander. Although the South Africans were as tough and determined as the Australians, they lacked experience in desert warfare – as did Klopper. Furthermore, Tobruk had no air support, since the nearest RAF-manned airfield was at Sidi Barrani, too far east to cover the Tobruk area. Tobruk was, therefore, at the mercy of Kesselring's air fleet. Thus, this inexperienced and demoralized garrison was lacking the most elementary support in the face of a formidable foe.

Below: Fast and furious, the Afrika Korps was the ultimate example of effective mobile mechanized warfare. Note the dust that affected engine pistons and cylinders.

Above: A German 20mm Flak gun on the outskirts of Tobruk, June 1942.

Below: The Afrika Korps on the way to Tobruk in June 1942.

Under these circumstances, it is no wonder that Tobruk fell to Rommel with surprising ease.[64]

Rommel, now quite experienced at taking fortified positions, swiftly closed the net around Tobruk. Given that Norrie had abandoned El Adem, the garrison had lost touch with the rest of the Eighth Army. The Germans had reached the Via Balbia (the coast road), thus cutting off Tobruk's land communications with Egypt; and on 18 June they occupied Gambut. The abandoned airfield there could now be used by the Luftwaffe to pound Tobruk – although this proved to be unnecessary. By 19 June, the Eighth Army had completed its withdrawal to the frontier, which allowed Rommel to attack Tobruk without much interference from the enemy.[65]

Given his previous experience, Rommel had every reason to treat Tobruk with due respect. However, he made the understandable mistake of overestimating the defences.[66] Working according to their standard formula, the Germans struck at dawn with a massive air raid comprising 150 aircraft, which attacked the perimeter zone with unheard-of force and violence. At 08:00 hours, following the bombing, Rommel's panzers attacked simultaneously XIII Corps (to keep it occupied) and pierced the British lines at Tobruk. By 16:00 hours, Rommel's troops had occupied all the airfields inside the pocket surrounding Tobruk. Three hours later, his panzers rumbled into the streets of the ruined town.

Klopper had been taken unawares and his morale – not high to begin with – collapsed. He gave orders that the fuel dumps in the western sector were to be destroyed, but that failed. At 02:00 hours on 21 June, Klopper issued orders that the garrison was to fight to the death. Four hours later, it seemed he had changed his mind and radioed for permission from Ritchie to capitulate. At 08:00 hours, with much of the Tobruk pocket in German hands, including the town, Klopper decided the battle was lost. He surrendered. At 09:40 hours he met Rommel on the Via Balbia and was driven back to the Tobruk Hotel by the triumphant German commander. As they drove, the road was lined with 10,000 glum British and Commonwealth troops.[67] This was the highlight of Rommel's desert war career, and the crowning moment of the entire campaign. The Battle of Marmarica (Gazala) was finally at an end. Great Britain had been humiliated.

In his triumphant Order of the Day, Rommel claimed to have captured 45,000 troops, 1000 armoured vehicles and 400 artillery pieces.[68] In this, Rommel was exaggerating. However, by any measure he had taken a huge number of troops, equipment and supplies. He had bagged 19,000 British, 9000 white South African and 9000 Indian and "native" South African troops. More importantly, he had captured a mountain of supplies that he could put to good use, including 1885 tonnes (2000 tons) of petrol, 4920 tonnes (5000 tons) of provisions and 2000 serviceable vehicles. Courtesy of the enemy, Rommel was now in a position to invade Egypt, and drive all the way to the Nile.

Rommel had losses of his own, though. These included 3400 German troops (13 percent of his total) and a catastrophic 70 percent of his officers (or 300 men). He, unlike his enemy, could not afford such casualties if he was to reach Egypt. But at least Tobruk, that British thorn in his flesh, had finally been removed. Rommel's official orders were terse: "Fortress Tobruk has capitulated. All units will reassemble and prepare for further advances."[69] That was the official view – correct, dry and unaffected. But with his wife there was no need for pretence. "Tobruk! It was a wonderful battle."[70]

The victory had far-reaching consequences both for the Axis and for the Allies. Churchill, who had placed such great emphasis on Tobruk being held, was in Washington for consultations with President Roosevelt when news broke of its fall. Adding insult to injury for Churchill was the fact that he was given the news not by the British Embassy in Washington but by Roosevelt himself. As if to soften the blow,

Below: A DAK soldier scans the horizon in the aftermath of the Gazala battles. The British were in full retreat, however.

Roosevelt offered to send 250 brand-new Sherman tanks to the desert forthwith, and all possible supplies the Americans could muster for her battered British ally. Churchill, although gratified by his ally's generous offer, continued to be downcast since "this was one of the heaviest blows I can recall during the war. Not only were the military effects grim, but it affected the reputation of British arms. Defeat is one thing; disgrace is another."[71]

The sombre mood on the Allied side was matched by the cries of jubilation in Rome and Berlin where, for once, Rommel's harping critics had been silenced by his spectacular success. Hitler was ecstatic with the news of his protégé's victory, and he rewarded Rommel with an equally spectacular promotion. He made Rommel Germany's youngest field marshal. Rommel was both stunned and gratified by Hitler's unexpected promotion. He noted, however, that he would have preferred to receive two or three divisions instead. This was not false modesty since he was in desperate need of reinforcements to replace his losses in both machines and men.[72]

Rommel as a leader of men and commander in war

Rommel had achieved a great victory which had established him, once and for all, as Germany's most famous military commander. How had this come about, and what were the secrets behind his phenomenal success? One major reason was that in the desert the mobile, offensive tactics of the panzer commander were ideal. North Africa

Below: Despite being outnumbered, Rommel's Afrika Korps overwhelmed its enemies and took large numbers of British prisoners at Tobruk.

was made for panzers, "for whose employment the flat and obstruction-free desert offered hitherto undreamed-of possibilities. It was the only theatre where the theory and principles of motorized and tank warfare could be applied fully and developed further. It was the only arena in which the pure tank battle between major formations could be fought."[73] In France, the infantry divisions were good at holding prepared positions, while in the desert they were more of a hindrance than an asset to the DAK. It was the mobile panzer forces that had saved the rest of the army from disaster. During the campaign of 1940, Graziani, despite his enormous numerical superiority, was at the mercy of the far smaller but more mobile British Army.[74]

Above: Rommel's drive towards Tobruk couldn't be stopped. The swiftness and fury of his attacks left the Allied troops with little choice but to surrender or die.

Mobility and the unfettered use of armour in an ideal tank country could account for much, but what was the essence of Rommel's own methods and ideas in the desert? Firstly, as he had proved time and again when fighting the British, it was essential to keep the DAK concentrated, while the British were divided and tended to attack in a piecemeal fashion. Then, it was important to threaten the enemy's supply lines, which might force him to break off an attack while one kept one's own supply lines secure at all costs. The panzers were the heart of the army, and the commander of this force had to keep very close to the front since "speed of reaction decides the battle". That meant he could take rapid decisions based on the actual frontline situation. Furthermore, Rommel believed firmly in the need for concealment to create the right conditions for seizing the element of surprise at the expense of the enemy. In conclusion, "speed is everything. The enemy must never be allowed time to reorganize. Lightning regrouping and reorganization of supplies for the pursuing forces are essential."[75]

Rommel also placed great emphasis on the intelligent use of artillery, especially in a mobile defensive role. Here, too, speed, mobility and long range were essential, since weight of armour

Above: Given the hopelessness of defending Tobruk, its valuable fuel and other supply depots should have been destroyed. Instead, Rommel was able to reap a harvest of valuable petrol and food for his army.

could not make up for lack of main gun power. In any case, tank firepower could only be delivered at the expense of speed and mobility. Rommel's artillery, therefore, needed to have plentiful supplies of ammunition, great range and great mobility, "for the side with the bigger gun has the longer arm and can be first to engage the enemy". Rommel had found the perfect weapon in the 88mm guns and their experienced crews.

As for infantry, they were needed to hold ground and block enemy advances. Like the artillery, the infantry needed to have great mobility and flexibility.[76] For Rommel, the infantry and artillery were part of the same mobile army that would ensure victory. He rejected wholly the British idea of tanks as a separate entity from the rest of the army.

Rommel, although a bold commander who took risks, was no gambler with the lives of his men. Only under the most desperate of circumstances would a gamble be justified. Whatever the situation, Rommel hated compromises and fighting by committee. After all, he was the commander and he made the necessary decisions.[77]

The Commander as a driving force

What was the role of the commander in Rommel's opinion? No surprises here since Rommel believed that the role was crucial. He felt that many subordinates were apathetic and subject to inertia without an active commander at the helm. An active and energetic commander who was close to the front and to the troops would not allow subordinate officers to slacken. As an old army instructor, Rommel believed strongly in the dictum of training the troops hard and thereby keeping casualties down. The commander had to stay close to the front, not only to keep the officers and troops on their toes, but also to prevent the battle becoming an academic game of chess. It was also vital for the commander to have close contact with the troops, to build confidence and trust, but without spouting false sentiments that the troops would instinctively realize and resent.[78]

How was Rommel as a commander of his men, and how did they perceive him? One key was the endless enthusiasm, drive and boundless optimism that Rommel possessed. Any officer who did not share his enthusiasm was quickly and mercilessly shipped back to Germany. He was intolerant of failure and could be completely ruthless when he felt an officer was not trying his best or avoiding doing his duty. He drove much younger men to exhaustion through his relentless pace and stupendous drive to win. Often his driver would be too tired to drive so Rommel took over the wheel himself.

Like his British counterpart at the later battle of El Alamein, General Montgomery, Rommel was not much for rich food or drink. In fact, his staff remembered him as extremely spartan in his tastes and most frugal in his living quarters. Again, he believed in "live as you expect others to live", and therefore shared his men's rations and living quarters.[79]

He believed in the efficacy of personal inspections, which had to be frequent but entirely unexpected. These were justifiably feared, and created an atmosphere of having to do one's best. Woe betide an officer whose unit, or camp, was not up to scratch, when the "old man" was on the prowl. Rommel's driver, Schmidt, recalled one inspection tour when they approached a camp and the sentry did not salute at first. Rommel's anger at this sloppiness turned to fury when he asked for the commander and was told he was asleep. Rommel, by now in a rage, turned "sleeping beauty" out of his bed and asked him what the local situation was like. Told that there was nothing new, Rommel snapped back: "How do you know? You have been asleep!" Rommel then went through a whole list of shortcomings with the camp, demanding immediate rectification. Rommel turned to the commander and told him not to be asleep the next time he dropped by for an impromptu inspection.[80]

What have the historians made of Rommel and his command talents? Most, including this author, have nothing but praise for an exceptional leader of men, who took a small and motley army of Germans and Italians to victory under trying circumstances and against great odds. None have heaped more praise on his qualities than his former enemies, the British, as represented by Sir Basil Liddell Hart and Kenneth Mackesy. Rommel was, by the standards of any war, an exceptionally talented and inspired leader of men – and a great commander.

Below: Most would agree that Rommel, seen here in his armoured personnel carrier "Greif", was a great leader of men, sharing their conditions and placing himself equally at risk during his drive for victory.

Others have not been as impressed. Len Deighton, for example, does not see Rommel as one of the great commanders of World War II. In fact, according to Deighton, his exceptional string of victories was due more to his talented subordinates, such as Walter Nehring, Fritz Bayerlein and Ludwig Cruewell. It is argued that Rommel's one fatal error was that he ignored the problems of logistics and supplies which were, most ungenerously, blamed on the failure of the Italian Navy to protect the supply ships.[81]

The German military historian, Wolf Heckmann, goes even further by reducing Rommel's reputation to the product of Nazi propaganda. In Heckmann's view, Rommel was too close to Hitler in personality to be truly admirable. He views Rommel as being addicted to illusions, vanity and the unhappy pursuit of glory. Once the British could match his strength, Rommel's luck ran out and he was defeated at El Alamein.[82]

In this author's opinion both Deighton and Heckmann are well off the mark. It is one thing as an armchair strategist to criticize a field commander with the benefit of hindsight. It is another to face the realities of war. It was here, on the battlefields of North Africa, that Rommel was tested and tried.

Below: Like his later adversary, Montgomery, Rommel (second from left) had little time for luxuries but subjected himself to the same hardships as his subordinates and soldiers. In this way he earned their respect.

Chapter notes

1 Moorehead, p.251; D.G. Chandler, *The Fight for Gazala: Western Desert, February–June 1942*, p.932.
2 Neillands, p.102.
3 Liddell Hart, p.278.
4 Liddell Hart, p.278; Neillands, pp.102-103; RP.180, Rommel's diary.
5 RP.181, Rommel to Lucie, 22 Jan. 1942.
6 George Forty, *Tanks across the Desert*, p.70.
7 Neillands, p.103.
8 Ibid.
9 RP.181, Rommel's diary.
10 RP.181, Rommel to Lucie, 22 Jan. 1942.
11 Salmaggi, p.209.
12 Liddell Hart, p.279; RP.182, Rommel's diary.
13 RP.182, Rommel to Lucie, 25 Jan. 1942.
14 Neillands, p.103.
15 RP, Rommel to Lucie, 27 Jan. 1942.
16 Neillands, p.103; Salmaggi, p.214.
17 RP.183, Bayerlein's notes.
18 Liddell Hart, p.279.
19 Salmaggi, pp.215-216.
20 Neillands, p.103.
21 RP.183, Rommel to Lucie, 4 Feb. 1942.
22 Salmaggi.
23 RP.183, Rommel to Lucie, 7 Feb. 1942.
24 RP.183, Rommel to Lucie, 10 Feb. 1942.
25 Salmaggi, pp.217-218.
26 Ibid, pp.222-223, 225, 231.
27 RP.183, Rommel to Lucie, 31 Mar. 1942.
28 RP.183, Rommel to Lucie, 10 Apr. 1942.
29 RP.187, Rommel to Lucie, 25 Apr. 1942.
30 RP.187, Rommel to Lucie, 27 Apr. 1942.
31 Neillands, pp.106-107; Chandler, pp.934-935.
32 Chandler, p.934.
33 RP.202, Rommel's diary.
34 Chandler, pp.934, 938; Neillands, pp.107-108.
35 Chandler, p.939.
36 Forty, p.71; Neillands, p.109.
37 Neillands, p.109.
38 Chandler, p.940.
39 Ibid, p.941.
40 Ibid, pp.939, 941.
41 Ibid, p.942.
42 Chandler, pp.941-942; RP.212, Rommel's diary; RP.213, Rommel to Lucie, 1 June 1942.
43 Chandler, p.943.
44 Moorehead, p.332. All Free French troops were viewed as deserters and traitors by Pétain's collaborationist Vichy regime, and were liable to be executed if they fell into the hands of Vichy officials.
45 Forty, p.73.
46 Ibid, p.72. A far better version would be the rude "F" version of this expression.
47 Moorehead, p.333.
48 RP.218, Rommel's diary.
49 RP.213, Rommel's diary.
50 Moorehead, pp.333-334.
51 Forty, p77. Jake Wardrop, the Eighth Army veteran, gave Koenig the highest praise by calling him "a very tough gent".
52 RP.214, Rommel's diary.
53 Salmaggi, p.250.
54 Neillands, p.111.
55 Chandler, p.943; Salmaggi, p.257; RP.220, Rommel's diary. He had wanted to crown this siege by taking the French prisoner, but their escape had succeeded (to his chagrin) and soured the German victory.
56 Neillands, p.110.
57 Chandler, p.943.
British engineers were laying a minefield line from Acroma down to the coast.
58 RP.220, Rommel's diary.
59 Chandler, pp.943-944.
60 Schmidt, p.142.
61 RP, Rommel's diary.
62 Salmaggi, p.259.
63 Chandler, p.934.
64 Ibid, p.945.
65 Salmaggi, p.259.
66 RP, 229, 231.
67 Salmaggi, p.262; Chandler, p.945; RP.231, Rommel's diary.
68 RP.232, Rommel's diary.
69 Chandler, p.945.
70 RP.231, Rommel to Lucie, 21 June 1942.
71 Chandler, p.948.
72 Ibid.
73 RP.197, Rommel's diary notes.
74 RP.198, Rommel's diary notes.
75 RP.200, Rommel's diary notes.
76 Ibid.
77 RP.201, Rommel's diary notes.
78 RP.226, Rommel's diary notes.
79 Schmidt, pp.42, 70.
80 Ibid, p.75.
81 Deighton, p.301.
82 Heckmann, pp.8-10.

CHAPTER 7

Twilight

The battles of Mersa Matruh, Alam Halfa and El Alamein (*June–November 1942*)

O n 24 June 1942 Rommel was given permission by Rome and Berlin to proceed with his advance into Egypt. The ultimate goal was for him to take Cairo and the Nile Delta.[1] This decision was not without controversy: a lengthy discussion raged at the time and afterwards over whether it was the correct strategy.

Back in Rome, the Germans and Italians had, prior to the fall of Tobruk, decided that it was more important to deal with Malta than chase the British into Egypt. As long as the British held Malta, Rommel's supply situation would continue to be precarious. Kesselring and General Cavallero had worked out an invasion plan called Operation C3 (later Hercules). Malta would be invaded by paratroopers and commando units, specially trained in Livorno to scale steep cliffs. By June everything was set for Hercules to be unleashed a month later. Rommel did not see Malta as warranting such attention – he had his sights set on Egypt, Suez and, ultimately, the Persian Gulf and its oil fields.

On 22 June the British had withdrawn to Mersa Matruh, and Auchinleck flew to Ritchie's frontline HQ on a tour of inspection. The day after, the DAK reached Sollum. Hitler persuaded Mussolini that the Malta operation should be dropped and that Rommel should be permitted to invade Egypt. Mussolini put the troops earmarked for the invasion of Malta at Rommel's disposal.[2]

To Rommel, Malta didn't matter much. It wasn't in his field of responsibility, being the concern of Kesselring and the Italians. He was determined to attack the Eighth Army before it had time to recover. Rommel dismissed those critics who later criticized his renewed offensive as foolhardy. At Sollum the British would, claimed Rommel, have been in a far stronger position than at El Alamein.[3] As he set out, he was supremely confident of victory as long as he could keep the momentum of the offensive going.[4]

On 26 June, Bastico, Cavallero, Kesselring and German liaison officer General Rintelen arrived at Rommel's HQ. Rommel thought that the Italians

Left: Decorated not only by Germany, but also by the Italian high command, Rommel claimed repeatedly that he would have traded all his medals for reinforcements and supplies for his precious panzer army.

135

Above: July 1942 sees Rommel (saluting) refusing to rest and remaining alongside his dwindling troops at the heart of the desert war.

had come to put a brake on his advance since "These beggars don't change".[5] For once, his intuition about the Italians was wrong.

Rommel outlined his plan to outflank the British at Mersa Matruh: he would cut the coastal road, thus isolating the town; and then, from the southwest, storm and take it. In other words, a repetition of his successful tactic at Tobruk. To his surprise, the Italians had no objections and Bastico gave Rommel permission to advance as far as El Alamein. The following day, Mussolini, feeling most confident, expanded the scope of operations as far as Cairo and Ismailia on the Suez Canal. Rommel was delighted and supremely confident that Mersa Matruh could be taken with ease.

Following the fall of Mersa Matruh, there was no solid British defence before Rommel reached Suez. Egypt controlled the entire Middle East, and General Alan Brooke, the Chief of the Imperial General Staff (CIGS), believed that Hitler should have reinforced Rommel instead of advancing on the Baku oil fields in the Russian Caucasus. If Egypt fell to Rommel, then only the 9th Australian Division in Syria stood between him and the Gulf oil fields.

On 25 June, despite his misgivings, Auchinleck replaced Ritchie and took personal command of the Eighth Army.[6] By then, it was a mere shadow of its former self, having lost 50,000 troops (half its strength) during the battle for Gazala. Its morale was at rock bottom. The British had no confidence in the

Mersa Matruh position, fearing that they could not hold it against any advance from Rommel.

Since Wavell's time as commander-in-chief, the British had believed that the enemy had to be held west of Mersa Matruh, i.e. at the Egyptian frontier. If that position was broken, then the only option was for the British to evacuate the Delta. They now faced that unenviable choice. On 23 June, the Middle East Defence Committee gave Auchinleck permission to evacuate Mersa. It was just in the nick of time, since two days later Rommel, with 30,000 troops and 200 tanks (so British intelligence believed), was within striking distance of the town.

Ritchie had planned to hold the line from Sidi Hamza to Mersa. The Mersa box was to be held by the 10th Indian Division, the "Charing Cross" box by the 25th Infantry Brigade, and the 50th Division would be deployed southeast of Mersa. In total, X Corps would occupy and defend 160 square km (100 square miles) of territory. Gott's XIII Corps held the desert to the south while the 5th Indian Division held Sidi Hamza.[7] Rommel knew that the British had fortified Mersa, but without the skill and thoroughness applied at Tobruk. He therefore welcomed a battle to annihilate the Eighth Army.[8]

As it was, Auchinleck was far too experienced and cautious a commander to fall into the Mersa trap. He had learnt the lesson of trying to hold a continuous line of fortifications made up of brigade boxes at Gazala. Despite the tremendous efforts that went into building that seemingly formidable line of defences, it had failed to stop Rommel's advance. The Mersa–Sidi Hamza line had not been properly fortified, and it was just as bad as the Gazala line in terms of natural defences.

Rommel could outflank this line by an offensive through the desert that could trap the entire X Corps against the sea. In short, Mersa Matruh was another Tobruk, and Auchinleck could not afford a defeat such as that again. He was determined to withdraw farther east, closer to his supply base at Alexandria and to a stronger natural defence line, such as El Alamein, where Rommel could not use his outflanking trick again. This time, the British response, under his personal command, would be a strong and aggressive version of mobile defence combining artillery, infantry, tanks and close aerial

Below: The British forces had poor radio discipline. Rommel's radio interceptors, shown here, could often overhear key orders and commands that helped him maintain his tactical advantage on the battlefield.

Bottom: Rommel's Afrika Korps remained at the heart of the panzer army during the desert war in 1942, but it was constantly under-supplied. These are German officers near Mersa Matruh.

support. In other words, to use Rommel's tactics against himself. On 25 June, Auchinleck consulted his chief of staff, General Dorman-Smith, and pointed out that the Eighth Army was too weak and dispersed at Mersa Matruh to withstand a full attack by Rommel. Dorman-Smith agreed.[9]

Two days later, Rommel was preparing for what he hoped would be a knock-out blow to the British at Mersa. The moment of truth had arrived. "It takes a lot out of one, of course, but it's the chance of a lifetime," Rommel wrote. "The enemy is fighting back desperately with his air force."[10] Rommel had very slender frontline forces available, comprising 6500 troops and 94 tanks. He made good headway as he threatened the coastal road and thereby the garrison of Mersa Matruh's escape route eastwards.

Orders were given for the Allied army to retire to the Fuka line. General Freyberg, the commander of the New Zealand Division, had insisted on this as he had no wish to share Klopper's dismal fate at Tobruk. Unfortunately, Freyberg was wounded and replaced by General Inglis, who seemed jittery to Auchinleck. Worse was the decision by Gott to withdraw XII Corps without first notifying headquarters. Since this retreat now threatened X Corps' position, Auchinleck gave permission, at noon on 28 June, for both corps to retire.

The illusion of victory

Rommel swept onwards and believed he had trapped the bulk of the Eighth Army. This was not the case. Instead he captured Mersa without much of a fight and took only 7000 prisoners,[11] but a huge booty of supplies. He was now close to his first objective, Alexandria. This could no doubt be reached with ease since the Eighth Army seemed to be demoralized, and Rommel could now utilize the excellent road and railway system of western Egypt.

He was sure that the worst ordeals for his army were over,[12] but the battle for Mersa Matruh was a huge disappointment to Rommel since his encirclement had not trapped the British. It would have been most gratifying to have captured the élite New Zealanders and their tough commander Freyberg. As it was, the British were able to fall back and prepare a much stronger defence line farther east.[13] But Rommel was now only 201km (125 miles) from Alexandria.[14]

On 29 June, the 90th Light Division reached Sidi Abd al-Rahman, only 32km (20 miles) west of El Alamein. It seemed only a question of time before the whole of Egypt was in Rommel's grasp.

Below: A unit of Rommel's 90th Light Division, always a key element of the Fox's high-speed offensives, seeks shelter from the desert sun.

Later that day, Mussolini, in anticipation of the greatest Axis victory in North Africa, arrived in Cyrenaica to await the expected fall of Cairo.

The British, by now demoralized and seemingly utterly defeated, earmarked X Corps for the defence of the Nile Delta and renamed it Delta Force. It seemed that the British had no confidence in their own troops and in the plan to hold Rommel's victorious army west of Alexandria.[15] There was, seemingly, only one man who had the competence, confidence and stubbornness to believe in a last stand before Alexandria. That was Auchinleck himself. He was determined that Rommel would be stopped decisively at El Alamein.

Auchinleck had ordered that the outer defence works of Alexandria were to be erected between Mena and Wadi Natrun. He deployed the 1st South African Division inside the El Alamein box, while the El Alamein line was manned by the 1st Armoured Division and two infantry divisions. The box was far from complete, and the line was more of a crayon mark on the staff map than a physical reality. Auchinleck did not seem to be too perturbed by all this since he had lost faith in fixed defences and now trusted his forces to use the tactics of a mobile defence in depth to stop Rommel's advance and defeat his forces.

The problem was that his army was torn to shreds, morale was at rock bottom and few of his officers had any confidence that Auchinleck would be able to stop Rommel's seemingly inexorable advance. Auchinleck's subordinate commanders lacked the experience, skills and self-confidence to carry out their commander's orders. The infantry was deficient in training, command and equipment to defeat Rommel's veteran panzer units.

As for the British armour, the same was true to an even greater degree. British armour was trained and deployed to fight a tank battle and had, during previous encounters with Rommel, shown no skill in fighting as part of a combined-arms force. Great Britain had no close air support and dive-bombers.

Below: An 88mm gun on the move. It is being towed by an SdKfz halftrack. Note the jerry cans in the rear of the vehicle.

Far right: Crusader III tanks of
the British Eighth Army head
into battle at El Alamein. Later
in the campaign, half of the
Allied tank force would comprise
US-designed Shermans
and Grants.

The coordination between air and ground forces was poor. Furthermore, the command structure was not sound. The commanders weren't as skilled or experienced as their German counterparts. Only the field artillery was good but, deployed in an anti-tank role, it did not have the appropriate training.[16] No one believed that Auchinleck's battle plan would work. In Egypt the jittery British residents, surrounded by either indifferent or hostile Egyptians, chose to flee the country. Their favourite places of exile were Palestine or Syria.

Wednesday 1 July became known as "Ash Wednesday"[17] because of all the papers, documents and files that were burnt at the British Embassy and the British HQ in Cairo. These confidential documents could not be allowed to fall into enemy hands when Rommel's tanks rolled into the Egyptian capital. Meanwhile, the most crucial battle of the Desert War was beginning to unfold.

The Italian XIX and XXI Corps were stationed between Daaba and Mersa Matruh, XX Corps was farther west, while Rommel's DAK had reached El Quseir. But the 1st Armoured Division straddled the lines between the Germans and the Italians southwest of Daaba. The 7th British Motor Brigade attacked and held the entire XX Corps, and Rommel berated the Italians for being humiliated by "so contemptible an enemy".

Only a sandstorm interrupted a British armoured attack against the 21st Panzer Division and the *Littorio* Division. This attack was most unexpected since it came from the direction of the "friendly" west. The 4th and 22nd Armoured Brigades came to rest around El Alamein, and Auchinleck's Order of the Day stated: "The enemy is stretched to his limit and thinks we are a broken army. He hopes to take Egypt by bluff. Show him where he gets off."

Below: British troops during the
First Battle of El Alamein in 1942.
Here, infantry seek what little
cover the desert provides as they
approach enemy positions.

The troops may have been impressed with this stirring stuff, but their commanders were not. General Corbett sent a note to Gott saying that they had to evacuate Egypt since the South Africans were demoralized. As if to confirm this unfounded slur, their commander, General Peinaar, with the support of Free French General de Larminat, criticized Auchinleck's decision to make a stand west of the Nile.

These defeatists were wrong, and Auchinleck closer to the mark. Rommel had only 55 tanks and was desperately short of troops as well. The condition of the Italians was, if anything, worse than the Germans since the combined strength of their three corps was a miserable 5500 infantry, 30 tanks and 200 guns.

Despite his weakness, Rommel was confident that he could brush aside the British XXX Corps at El Alamein. He chose to repeat his plan from Mersa Matruh, by sending the 90th Light Division south of El Alamein to cut the coast road. The Italian XXI Corps would attack El Alamein from the west while X Corps would resume its attack on the "box" itself, and the 20th Italian MIC would provide flank protection.

There was no British armour present. Nevertheless, Rommel's plan had two major flaws. First, it assumed the enemy's morale was broken. Second, he

Above: The Panzer III remained Rommel's most numerous tank model during the battles of El Alamein, in spite of more advanced machines being introduced by the Allies.

underestimated the enemy's strength and positions through poor reconnaissance. The 90th Light Division attacked at dawn on 1 July. For once, Rommel's panzers didn't perform well. The DAK panzers attacked at 06:45 hours, about four hours late because of the need to refuel. This delay was fatal to Rommel's plan. By noon, the 90th Light broke off its offensive and tried an outflanking move. This was halted by heavy British fire. Ominously, the German infantry showed signs of exhaustion and panic.[18]

If Rommel had every reason to feel uncertain about the future, Auchinleck had far more reason to be pleased since the course of the battle had developed as he had predicted. But the 1st Armoured Division had not reached its proper place on the battlefield, and the 4th Armoured Brigade, showing characteristic weaknesses of orientation and inexperience with the desert, floundered inside the sandtrap of Alam el Onsol and was only extracted by late afternoon.

Rommel's attack falters

An elated and over-optimistic Rommel now gave orders for the panzers to pursue the enemy during the early part of the afternoon, while the Italian XX Corps and 90th Light Division combined were supposed to clean out the entire El Alamein area. By 18:00 hours, the DAK had broken British defences at Deir el Shein but had lost 18 of its 55 panzers. An hour earlier, the 22nd Armoured Brigade, on Ruweisat Ridge, attacked the 15th Panzer Division driving west.

Rommel, after a day's intensive fighting, with relatively heavy and irreplaceable losses of tanks, had made only small gains. Auchinleck had fought him to a standstill through a combination of massed armour, heavy artillery fire and defensive infantry tactics. In fact, Auchinleck had defeated Rommel's desert Blitzkrieg tactics. Auchinleck phoned Gott (XIII Corps) with a plan to attack the southern flank of the DAK with all available British armour.

The following day, 2 July, Rommel changed his plans and ordered the DAK panzers to attack towards the coast instead of the 90th Light. Because the troops were exhausted and morale was probably in decline, the attack was not begun until the afternoon. The 15th Panzers made no progress at all against Ruweisat, which was held by the 1st South African Division and New Zealand artillery in deadly combination.

Pienaar was anxious about his position and wanted to pull his 1st Infantry Brigade back to Alam el Onsol. He called Auchinleck for permission to do so. Auchinleck, while friendly, told Pienaar that his division would have to hold the ridge at all costs and was not permitted under any circumstances to pull back. By evening, it was obvious that Rommel had shot his bolt and it was time for the 1st Armoured Division and the rest of XIII Corps to take the offensive.

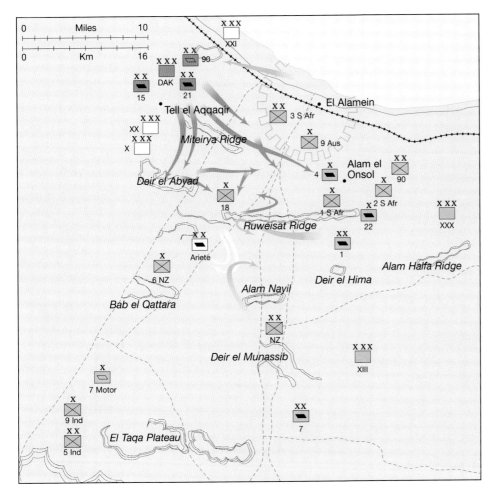

Left: Despite being understrength, Rommel believed his Afrika Korps was strong enough to punch through the British lines at El Alamein. The British fought well, however, and inflicted serious losses on the Germans, and they were forced to withdraw. Auchinleck missed an opportunity to hit back at Rommel, and Churchill lost patience, replacing him with Alexander as C-in-C Near East, and Montgomery as commander of the Eighth Army.

Rommel was so impressed with Auchinleck's command and the new fighting spirit of the British that he cancelled plans for a general offensive on 3 July. Instead, the DAK panzers and the 90th Light Division were to attack towards the coast, while the Italian *Ariete* and *Trieste* Divisions were to hold XIII Corps. But the 1st Armoured Division halted the DAK while the New Zealanders attacked the *Ariete*, leaving it with only five tanks and two guns. Rommel was shocked since he viewed the *Ariete* as his only reliable Italian formation.[19]

Rommel made the DAK stage one final effort which, during the afternoon, brought it to within 14.5km (9 miles) of Deir el Shein, which left Rommel's army in a long exposed arch without solid defences and several large holes. At this point, it might have been wiser for the Italian high command to call a halt to the proceedings. But Axis prestige was at stake since Mussolini was still in Cyrenaica, awaiting the triumphant entry of Rommel's army into Cairo.

This was the right time to launch the invasion of Malta, but Mussolini had staked everything on Rommel who was now faltering despite his confident talk.[20] Rommel admitted that this was a tough struggle, and he blamed much

Above: July 1942, and a Rhodesian anti-tank battery, equipped with the six-pounder gun, takes on Rommel's Panzer IV tanks.

of his trouble on the RAF pinning down the DAK. British air activity had reduced him personally to living in a hole in the ground for much of the day, like the rest of his troops.[21] Auchinleck, in the ascendancy, was not impressed by Rommel's latest move and was determined to counterattack with the whole of the Eighth Army. But he was handicapped by a sluggish and defeatist command and by the intelligence service, both of which overestimated Rommel's strength.

Rommel, aware of his own limitations, ordered his forces back on 4 July. The 21st Division retreated from Ruweisat to El Mreir with the 90th Light filling the gap. Suspecting a general withdrawal on the part of the enemy, Auchinleck ordered the 1st Armoured Division to attack the 15th Panzer Division, which was reduced to 15 tanks and 200 men. The division was almost overrun, and saved only by their skilled use of the 88s.

Had the British armour been commanded with greater skill and aggression, Rommel would have been in deep trouble. As it was, his Italian formations were threatened on a wide front. What saved the Germans from disaster was the fact that their army was by now so small that Rommel could command all units in person. Auchinleck couldn't transmit his fighting spirit to the troops on the ground thanks to a cumbersome command structure.[22] Rommel admitted, in private, that the enemy's resistance was too great and that his own exhaustion was matched only by that of his men. The battle was not going well.[23] The question was, nevertheless, whether the British lines, only 97km (60 miles) from Alexandria, would actually hold.[24] Rommel had little fuel and none en route. His troops were exhausted, and there was little hope of reinforcements.

Auchinleck, while both the Eighth Army and the DAK rested, laid plans for a counterattack. While XIII Corps (Gott) kept Rommel occupied, XXX Corps was to attack the enemy's weakly held rear areas. To make this possible, Auchinleck removed Norrie from command and replaced him with Ramsden, which unfortunately paralyzed the entire corps during 6–7 July.

On 7 July, the counterattack was under way, as the New Zealanders took Munga Wahla, and the 7th Armoured Division took Fuka. Meanwhile, Rommel had planned to attack XIII Corps with the DAK, which would open the road to Cairo and leave XXX Corps stranded at El Alamein. This suited Auchinleck's purposes since he wanted to lure Rommel into a trap by leaving the Italians exposed to an attack in the north. On 9 July, Rommel attacked the empty Bab al Qattara box. Instead of viewing XIII Corps as a possible trap, Rommel believed his plan was working. He was disastrously wrong.

During the evening of 9 July, Rommel laid plans for an offensive to overrun and outflank the El Alamein position. Auchinleck now had Rommel where he wanted him – stretched out from the Qattara Depression all the way to the coast. With the bulk of his army in the north, Auchinleck was ready to strike – and strike he did. On 10 July, at 03:00 hours, XXX Corps attacked. A distant rumble of artillery alerted Rommel to the unpleasant fact that the enemy had seized the initiative.

Seven hours later, the 9th Australian Division, supported by tanks, had captured the entire eastern section of the Tell el Eisa, while the 1st South African Division had taken Tell el Makh Khad. It was a glum and grim Rommel who received reports that the Italian *Sabatha* Division had broken and that the troops had fled in wild panic without any thought of defending themselves. The HQ of the DAK lay only 5km (3 miles) from Tell el Eisa, and was threatened directly by the British advance.

Main picture: German artillery in action at El Alamein. German field artillery was trained to cooperate fully with panzers and mechanized infantry.

Colonel von Mellenthin rallied the HQ staff and, with the support of the forward elements of the 164th Division (flown in from Crete), they managed just barely to put a stop to the British advance.[25] Rommel admitted privately that the British had him cornered. Here, in a confined space of desert between the Depression and the sea, the British were in their element. They had specialized in combined infantry and artillery operations, with localized attacks being their favourite tactic. Rommel had tried to escape this by attempting a breakthrough towards Cairo where the DAK could conduct operations in the open desert. But the British had struck first, since Auchinleck had realized the state of exhaustion and demoralization among Rommel's Italian troops. They were the weak link in Rommel's lines.[26]

What Rommel feared more than anything was the possibility that the British would exploit his other Achilles heel, his extended and dangerously exposed supply lines, by capturing Sidi Abd al Rahman. Cancelling any further advances to the east, Rommel sped north and launched a successful local attack that destroyed the British artillery there. But this German success was short-lived.

Early on 11 July, the Australians occupied the area west of Tell el Eisa and moved towards Deir el Abyad where they attacked and mauled the *Trieste* and *Sabatha* Divisions. The Italians broke yet again. Rommel had to rush German troops to plug this dangerous gap.[27] That day, Rommel was reduced to a mere 30 panzers while the Eighth Army had 400 tanks.

Rommel uses the right tactics

By sheer numerical preponderance the British should have been able to crush the DAK. But they were committing the same old mistake of spreading their forces too thin to cover an immense area of desert. Rommel, on the other hand, concentrated his diminutive panzer force in exactly the right spot. This knack of being in the right place at the right time had saved Rommel's neck in the past and would continue to do so.[28] At least Rommel managed during 12–14 July to stop the Australian advance on Deir al Abyad.[29] But the 21st Panzer Division, his élite unit, did not perform well since its second offensive against the Australians failed completely due to the devastating effect of British artillery fire and infantry attacks. Rommel was in a perfectly foul mood since this had been a chance to inflict a serious defeat on the enemy.[30]

The British had been entirely successful, therefore, in neutralizing the vaunted 21st Panzer Division, and had virtually destroyed two Italian divisions. It was the weakened Italian X Corps that now held the centre of Rommel's front, and it was crucial that Point 63 – where the DAK's precious supplies of oil, ammunition and reserve artillery were located – be held at all costs.

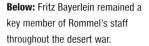

Below: Fritz Bayerlein remained a key member of Rommel's staff throughout the desert war.

Auchinleck had other plans. At one hour before midnight on 14 July, XIII Corps attacked along the Ruweisat; and by daylight the following day, the New Zealanders had taken the ridge. Even more humiliating was the capture of 1000 Axis prisoners by the 5th Indian Division, while the New Zealanders, who lost 1500 men, also captured 1600 prisoners. It showed clearly that both the Germans and Italians had begun to crack. They preferred to give themselves up rather than fight to the death. The slim consolation for Rommel was that the British armour performed badly, leading to poor relations with the New Zealand infantry who complained that the tanks left them in the lurch.

Bayerlein accepted that the failure to recapture Ruweisat, including Point 64 and Tell el Eisa, meant the battle was lost. Rommel admitted that "on that day every last German reserve had to be thrown in". "Our forces were so small in comparison with the steadily growing strength of the British that we were going to count ourselves lucky if we managed to go on holding our line at all. As a result of the immense casualties which the Italians had suffered our line was very thinly manned. We had virtually no reserves."[31] On 17 July, Rommel agreed that the situation was bad since the British had greater reserves of infantry and could pick off the Italian formations one by one.

Rommel had so few German troops left that they could not make a stand on their own. "It's enough to make one weep."[32] If the fighting – the worst Rommel had ever been through – continued, then the whole front would crack.[33]

The battle that had been fought between 1 and 17 July with such marked success by Auchinleck had not been won

Main picture: Time and again during the battles at El Alamein, German artillery broke up British tank offensives.

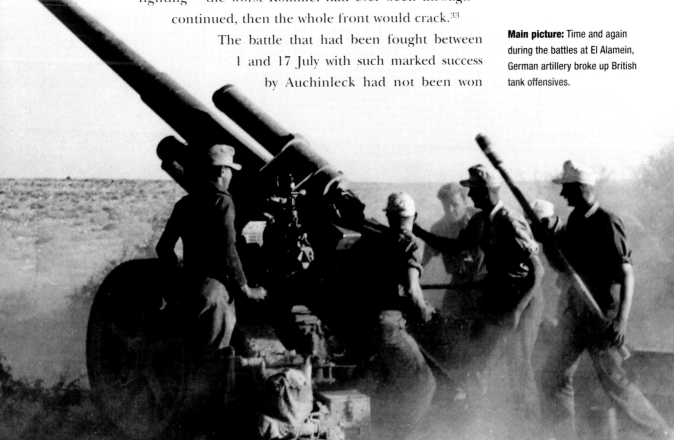

Above: Never far from the frontline, Rommel's health began to suffer under the pressure of maintaining the desert offensive with limited supplies and a lack of reinforcements.

Below: A German 88mm anti-tank gun captured at El Alamein. Note the "kill" rings around the barrel.

because of defensive fortifications such as Gazala. Neither was it, as Rommel claimed, a static battle of attrition. It was a fluid battle, but one where Rommel was unable to get to grips with the British and command events.

Rommel chose to tell Rome and his superiors his version of the unvarnished truth. The Italians could not be relied on to stand unless their formations were stiffened with German troops, and these were now reduced to 60 percent below strength. Rommel requested that the 164th Division be transferred to North Africa immediately along with any panzers that could be spared. Meanwhile, Rommel would endeavour to re-equip and rest what remained of his panzers.

Italy's CS responded quickly, on 17 July, with an order that the Ramcke and Folgore Parachute Brigades, which had been earmarked for Hercules, would be transferred to Rommel's frontline forces. The problem with this seemingly generous gesture was that it came too late, and while these troops were undoubtedly élite soldiers they were not trained for, or suited to, fighting a desert battle.

Kesselring was nearer the truth since he believed that he, and Rome, should have ignored Rommel's ideas and insisted on taking Malta to improve the DAK's appalling supply situation. Now it was too late, and the only way to save the situation was, according to Kesselring, to reinforce the DAK and for Rommel to press on with the offensive. Only by capturing Alexandria could the supply situation be remedied.[34] This opinion carried extra weight as it was expressed by one who had never been an unquestioning admirer of Rommel.

Auchinleck's success unravelled the whole Axis strategy; and Mussolini, humiliated and in a foul mood, returned to Rome without a triumphal Roman-style entry into Cairo. He was back on 20 July, and rumours immediately spread that he was near death. "Perhaps he is dying," said one of his disrespectful ministers, "but not from dysentery. It's a less commonplace disease. It's called humiliation."[35]

Auchinleck counterattacks

Meanwhile, events on other fronts had begun to shape the situation in North Africa. A month earlier, Hitler had unleashed his offensive against the Volga and the Caucasus oil field. On 9 July, the Imperial General Staff in London decided to give priority to the defence of Egypt over that of Persia (threatened from the north by the advancing Germans). This decision by the British would ensure their eventual victory in the desert war. But it came at a heavy price to Auchinleck, who in return for more troops and tanks, was forced to undertake a premature offensive.

Until Rommel was properly defeated in Egypt, the planned Allied invasion of French North Africa could not be launched. Auchinleck was under intense pressure from Churchill to smash Rommel. The most sensible plan would have been to let Rommel, equally under pressure, bleed his weak forces to death by launching his own attacks. Once these had been blunted, Auchinleck could have made local and limited counterattacks while he and the Eighth Army gained experience in beating Rommel at his own game. But there was no time for this in Churchill's plans.

Auchinleck wanted Gott (XIII Corps) to attack the enemy's centre between Deir el Shein and El Mreir. Gott had five infantry brigades, 274 tanks and the lavish support of 300 field guns when, on 21 July, he launched his offensive. The main attack was unleashed against the centre while the New Zealanders advanced north of El Mreir. This attack had not progressed beyond the minefields because they hadn't been cleared for the tanks. Gott assumed the corps had reached its

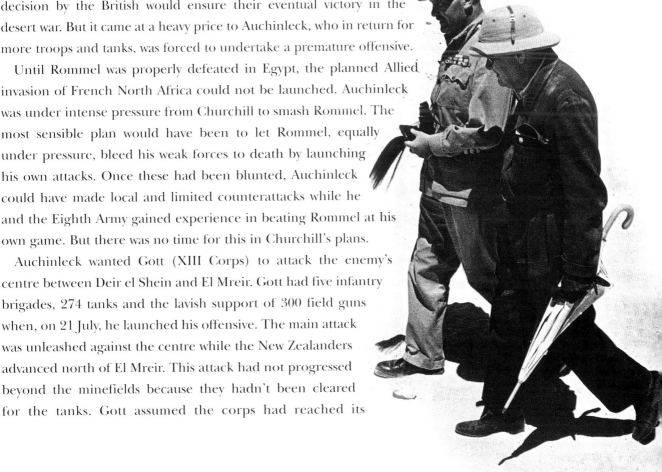

Below: Seen here with Lieutenant-General Sir Bernard Freyberg, Churchill (right) became so concerned about the fate of Egypt that he visited the Western Desert in August 1942.

secondary objectives by 08:00 hours, and when the intercepted radio messages showed the DAK was in some distress Gott ordered the offensive to continue.

Rommel's men were neither confused nor in distress. They put mines and the 88s to great effect against the British armour, which was mauled badly by the defenders. By midday, when Gott was left with 11 out of 104 tanks, it was obvious the attack had been a failure and Gott called it off. The Germans were elated at their success against a poorly coordinated and badly managed attack[36] – none more so than Rommel, who praised his men for their efforts.[37]

If Rommel was let down by his Italian ally, Auchinleck was hampered by his subordinate commanders and by Great Britain's often truculent allies. General Morshead, of Tobruk fame, refused to allow his Australian troops to join the next offensive because they doubted the resolve of the British armour to support them. Auchinleck, dismayed, invited Morshead to tea to discuss the matter. This caused a vital delay to the next offensive which, if launched during 24–25 July, might have succeeded when the DAK was off-balance. This unnecessary delay allowed Rommel to gain vital time for reinforcements to arrive, and on 25 July the Folgore Division occupied the Taqa plateau.

Having finally restored order in his ranks, Auchinleck was ready to attack. It came early on the morning of 26 July. The infantry attacked vigorously but were thrown back by the Germans, while the armour put on a poor show. Two armoured brigades were halted by the Germans, who also repelled the Australians. By 10:00 hours, the offensive was called off. Yet another British attack had failed. By 27 July, the DAK was down to its last rounds of ammunition, and if Auchinleck had attacked he might have been able to drive Rommel back into Libya. Instead, he was forced to go on to the defensive. Auchinleck would hold El Alamein even if Rommel bypassed this position, since his rear area and lines of communications would be threatened. All the ridges around El Alamein (Ruweisat and Alam Halfa) were fortified.[38]

Above: The dashing Lieutenant-General Brian Horrocks took over XIII Corps as part of Montgomery's reshuffle.

First El Alamein – an assessment

The first battle of El Alamein had been a British success. Rommel's advance had been stopped dead in its tracks, and the British had taken the initiative during much of the fighting. Rommel had suffered 13,000 casualties, and the British had taken some 6000 Italian and 1000 German prisoners.

These were losses that Rommel could not afford, given the depleted state of his stocks of troops, ammunition, tanks and supplies. He needed to avoid a battle of attrition at all costs by regaining the initiative and breaking through the British lines. But he had to admit that Auchinleck was a most skilled opponent who had succeeded in his aim of putting a halt to Rommel's advance.

What saved Rommel was that Auchinleck's subordinates were nowhere as skilled, determined or cool-headed as their commander, and Rommel pointed out that Auchinleck's excellent strategic plans failed because of third-rate execution in the field. Rommel also noted poor coordination between arms and the different contingents.[39] Auchinleck fortified the whole southern area of the Alam Halfa Ridge and planned an offensive for September. Should Rommel attack earlier than this (he had 10 August set aside for such an offensive), then he would be squared off and defeated in a triangular area contained by the Great Depression, El Hamma and El Alamein.

Above: General von Bismarck, standing in vehicle, the veteran panzer commander who had been with Rommel since France, was killed during the fighting in North Africa.

The problem was that Churchill had no time for this. The Allies had dropped the idea of a landing in northern France (Operation Sledgehammer) in favour of a landing and occupation of French North Africa called "Torch". But before Torch could proceed Rommel had to be defeated, since this would weaken Vichy French resistance considerably and remove the threat of a German occupation of Tunisia and Algeria before the Allies had a chance to take them.

General Alan Brooke argued for the dismissal of Auchinleck, who would be replaced as Commander-in-Chief Middle East by General Harold Alexander and as commander of the Eighth Army by General Bernard Law Montgomery. Churchill flew to North Africa himself on 1 August; and on 5 August he visited the frontline HQ of the Eighth Army, accompanied by Brooke.

Churchill presented his demand for an early offensive which Auchinleck and his staff, aware of the real situation, rejected as

Below: It was vital for Rommel and his staff to remain mobile and close to the action so that the commander could review tactics on the move.

completely unrealistic. Churchill was soured by what he perceived as defeatism and weakness on the part of the staff. After a conversation with Gott, Brooke came to the conclusion that he was tired and therefore not suited to replace Auchinleck should Montgomery not be available. Churchill told Brooke in private, at the breakfast table on 6 August, that he had lost all confidence in Auchinleck despite crediting him with the victories of Sid Rezegh and El Alamein. The Auch was finished. Gott was not to replace him, but Montgomery and Alexander did on 15 August. Auchinleck was demoted, in apparent disgrace, to commander of the British Army of occupation in Iraq.[40]

Rommel reckoned he had until September to launch a new offensive. After that the British would have replaced all their losses in material and men after Tobruk. He was worried that, as the Eastern Front was swallowing all the available air crews and aircraft, Kesselring would not be able to give him the vital air support he needed when the RAF was growing stronger by the day.

The supply situation

By early August, the supplies the DAK had received barely covered the daily needs of the troops and tanks. Only a fifth of the army's normal needs for petrol – 5900 tonnes (6000 tons) per day – was reaching the DAK as three-quarters of the supply ships plying the Mediterranean were being sunk by the Allies. While the British supply lines were short – only 346km (215 miles) from Suez to El Alamein, or a mere 89km (55 miles) from Alexandria to El Alamein – those of the DAK were enormous at 595km (370 miles) from Tobruk, 1060km (660 miles) from Benghazi and a staggering 2011km (1250 miles) from Tripoli.

Much of the precious fuel that Rommel so desperately needed was being consumed by the very lorries that carried it to the front. Of these trucks, most were captured British and Allied makes for which the Germans had no spare parts. Under these circumstances, a build-up of stocks was out of the question.

In Italy, huge supplies and 120 tanks were waiting for an ever-dwindling stock of heavy shipping to become available and take them to North Africa. Rommel's four German divisions were short of 17,000 men (dead and wounded) while another 17,000 veterans had to be returned to Germany for convalescence.[41] On a practical level, Rommel complained on 2 August about the failure to get the railway from Mersa Matruh to El Alamein working. He also argued that, while Kesselring was trying his best, General Ringtelen (the German officer in charge of supplies in Rome) was doing nothing to get the Italians to improve their inadequate system and supplies for the DAK.[42]

Rommel and his men were by this time suffering from fatigue and several ailments associated with a long and gruelling residence in the desert,

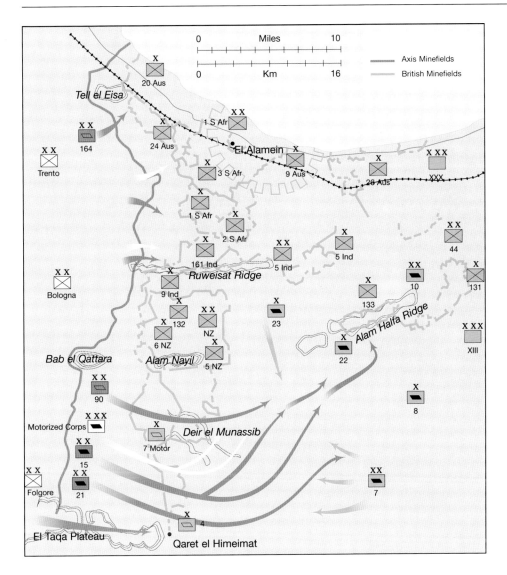

Left: Having only been in theatre for 17 days, Montgomery had to face Rommel's last attempt to break through the El Alamein position. Montgomery's men defended from the Alam Halfa Ridge, using the 7th Armoured Division as a guard against German southern offensives. Despite trying the tactics that had served him so well in the past, Rommel was unable to break the British line. Rommel retreated, then dug in and prepared to defend.

combined with continuous fighting for almost two years. Rommel's health had been poor since the Battle of Gazala, and it had not improved during the last gruelling weeks – he was suffering from high blood pressure and needed to rest. "At the rate we've been using up generals in Africa, 5 per division in 18 months, it's no wonder that I also need an overhaul some time or other." With no successor able to take command and the unsettled situation, Rommel could not relinquish command. His sense of duty prevailed, and he remained.[43]

His ADC, Lieutenant Berndt, complained that Rommel, who had been in the desert without a break for 19 months and showed remarkable physical stamina, did not take kindly to being told to take better care of himself.[44] Eventually, Rommel realized that he had reached the end of his tether, and asked the high command to replace him with Panzer General Guderian. They simply replied, "Guderian unacceptable". Rommel again remained in command.[45]

Rommel, who thought only in terms of practical military matters, had chosen Guderian as the only panzer commander who could match him in terms of determination, experience and command abilities. After all, Guderian had been instrumental in the victories in France and Russia during the previous two years, and would have been a suitable replacement. But Hitler, who had sacked Guderian for disobeying his orders during the offensive against Moscow back in December 1941, had no wish to return this military maverick and personal critic to command, even if Rommel wanted him. Rommel was stuck with his increasingly thankless task of fighting an enemy who grew ever stronger, giving him an ever-diminishing chance of winning. He had no faith in Kesselring's ability to overcome the Italians back in Rome.[16]

At least he had had some much-needed rest during the latter days of August when there was a lull in the fighting while the British changed commanders at the top. By 29 August, he felt better and his mood had improved. He had General Westphal at his side. In addition, General Vaerst, the dashing commander from the January offensives, had returned to North Africa. General Gause, however, could not stay the course because of his health.[17]

A lesser man and a far less capable commander than Rommel would have stayed on the defensive. However, Rommel realized that his slender forces could not survive another battle of attrition against the British. His army would be crushed by sheer weight of numbers unless he took the offensive and managed to break the stalemate. He greeted the dawn of 30 August with calm determination – even Hitler sent his personal best wishes for the offensive.

Below: With an ever-shrinking tank force and no supplies, Rommel found maintaining his offensive an uphill struggle.

Rommel was sure that the conditions were ideal for an offensive. "If our blow succeeds, it might go some way towards deciding the whole course of the war. If it fails, at least I hope to give the enemy a pretty thorough beating."[18] When he left his sleeping quarters the following morning, his face was troubled. A doctor (Professor Horster) had been sent from Germany to check his health. Rommel told him that "the decision to attack today is the hardest I have ever taken. Either the army in Russia succeeds in getting through to Grozny and we in Africa reach the Suez Canal, or..." He made a gesture of defeat.[19]

Above: British tanks patrol the desert during the Battle of Alam Halfa.

Alam Halfa: Rommel's last offensive

Rommel's attack at Alam Halfa was his last attempt to break through the British lines and make for Egypt, all the way to the Suez Canal. The battlefield comprised a large chunk of desert, rock, sand and desolation, between the heights of Tell el Eisa to the 200m- (656ft-) high Qaret el Himeimat, right on the edge of the Qattara Depression. It was along the Depression that Rommel, whose army was short of tanks and ammunition, attacked at night on 31 August. There was the customary diversionary attack in the north, a secondary attack at the British centre and then the main thrust in the south which aimed to outflank the British and then swing down to the coast.

Just before Rommel struck, Montgomery had moved two divisions to the Alam Halfa Ridge and ordered his tanks to dig in so that they would not be rushed into making costly attacks against Rommel's heavy artillery. He had arrived at the front to put an end to what he termed his troops' and officers' bellyaching by telling them that there would be no more retreats and that from now on every inch of territory would be fought over. Not one step back was the new general's motto.[50]

Montgomery changed the corps commanders. Lieutenant-General Oliver Leese took over XXX Corps, and the dashing Lieutenant-General Brian Horrocks took over XIII Corps. Montgomery was in a very strong position since he had 700 tanks and four infantry divisions holding a very strong fortified frontline. In spite of this material advantage, Montgomery, like Auchinleck before him, wasn't going to be bullied into a premature offensive by Churchill. He felt that Rommel could destroy himself through his constant need to attack.

The urge to mount a new offensive was strong in Rommel since he now had 200 German and 240 Italian tanks with which to attack. As the northern and central sectors were heavily fortified, the only stretch of the enemy front he could assault was in the south between Alam Nayil Ridge (held by New Zealand troops) and the Qattara Depression. Rommel wanted to launch a night attack to clear a path through the enemy minefield and then pour in his panzers.[51]

During the night, the RAF bombed the DAK's positions. The element of surprise was lost, and Rommel wanted, at first, to break off the offensive. Bayerlein, however, supported a continued advance whatever the cost. Progress was quite slow because the minefields were found to be much deeper than expected. By dawn, the DAK's objectives had still not been reached, and it was only 8 miles (12.8km) beyond the minefields. Montgomery's response was to place his brigades far apart, knowing as he did that each of his armoured

Below: Daring commando raids caused Rommel little trouble. Only Colonel Popski's raid on Barce succeeded. Seen here, originals of Popski's "private army". Popski has an eye patch.

brigades outnumbered Rommel's panzer divisions in terms of numbers of tanks.[52]

During some intensive fighting that day, Rommel suffered two major setbacks. His veteran panzer commander General von Bismarck, who been with Rommel since France, was killed. As if that were not bad enough, Nehring was wounded. The DAK's flanks were threatened by the 7th and 10th Armoured Divisions, and this forced Rommel to move his army northwards far earlier than planned.

The panzers' objective was Hill 132, and that of the Italian XX Corps was Alam Halfa itself. The actual Alam Halfa Ridge was held by the British 44th Division which had recently arrived from

Great Britain. A devastating fight ensued between this division and the attacking Axis forces which forced the DAK to ask Kesselring's Luftwaffe to lend its support. The new attack was delayed until about 13:00 hours because the DAK needed to replenish its stocks of ammunition and fuel.

Above: Britain's Special Air Service, seen here, and Long Range Desert Group conducted numerous operations, often behind enemy lines, in the Western Desert during 1942 and 1943.

The offensive, covered by a sandstorm, went well to begin with, but the Italians (*Trieste* and *Ariete* Divisions) were delayed by the British minefields. They did not begin their attack until 15:00 hours. Then the panzers ran out of petrol, and the planned attack on Hill 132 was called off at 16:00 hours. Only

Above: Supplies for the Eighth Army on their way to Alexandria.

the 90th Light Division had reached its objectives by late afternoon.

Rommel's supply lines, through the minefield, were threatened directly by the 7th Armoured Brigade. The following morning, having cancelled an all-out attack because of the worsening fuel shortage, he ordered a halt to the main offensive. Instead, local attacks were permitted, and the 15th Panzer Division, destroying the defending British armour, reached the area south of Hill 132. But it had run out of petrol.

On 2 September, some 2560 tonnes (2600 tons) of the promised 4920 tonnes (5000 tons) of petrol had been lost at sea on its way to Tripoli, and the rest was still in Italy. Without fuel, being pounded from the air by the RAF, and with only small tank forces available, Rommel called off the offensive.[53]

Montgomery's response was for his forces to stay put since he didn't believe his armoured brigades had the experience or stamina to conduct an open, mobile tank battle with Rommel's panzers. He wanted, at all costs, to avoid heavy losses until he was well prepared.

It was the combination of the RAF and the field artillery's pounding of his panzers that forced Rommel to call off the offensive on 3 September. That day, a retreat was started, continuing during the two following days. The Axis forces were almost 10km (6 miles) east of their original frontline, but they had gained only a small sliver of territory. This in no way compensated for the losses the DAK had suffered.

Below: The Allies were provided with plenty of reinforcements. Here, US-designed Shermans roll ashore to reinforce the Eighth Army.

During the night of 3–4 September the New Zealanders moved forward, encountering fierce German resistance. On 4 September, the Germans counterattacked in order to avoid being cut off. Fierce fighting continued

during 5–6 September between the minefields.[54] Rommel admitted to having lost 3000 troops, 50 tanks, 15 field guns, 35 anti-tank guns and 400 lorries. He claimed that he had inflicted heavy casualties on the British, including some 150 tanks. The real British losses were 68 tanks.[55]

The battle had been lost because of the stronger-than-expected minefields, the incessant activity of the RAF, and Rommel having lost the initiative in the early stages of the battle.[56] At least he had learnt one very important lesson from Alam Halfa, that airpower was the absolute key to modern warfare and that the DAK could not conduct mobile operations with the RAF in command of the skies.[57] That was an important admission for Rommel to make.

Alam Halfa – turning point of the desert war

One thing was clear. With the British and Allied ascendancy in the air, German-style Blitzkrieg tactics had come to an end and, with them, Rommel's golden age of mobile warfare. Alam Halfa was a splendid British defensive victory that proved decisive since Rommel now had no hope of renewing his offensives. That made this battle a major turning point in the desert war.

Monty, as he was known to the troops, chose to be cautious and postponed any idea of an offensive for seven crucial weeks. This grated on Churchill's already taut nerves, and the prime minister continued to nag Alexander for an early attack because of the needs of the Allied landings in North Africa. Had Montgomery been more adventurous, he might have had a golden opportunity to strike against a weakened and exhausted enemy. It might also have been an opportunity to trap and destroy Rommel and the DAK once and for all.[58]

The DAK's supply situation did not improve during the course of September and October. On the contrary, the RAF, in combination with the Royal Navy, wreaked havoc on Rommel's supply lines both at sea and on land. By this time the Germans could muster only 350 aircraft against 1200 enemy aircraft. The British knew exactly where to apply this aerial advantage. During September, Rommel was deprived of a third of all his supplies due to shipping losses. The following month saw only half of the army's supplies arrive safely.

All the tankers that month were lost, leaving Rommel's fuel supply strangled and his depots completely dry. Food and water, too, were now in short supply, jeopardizing the troops' health. The Italians, in their weakened state, were particularly badly affected. Dysentery, jaundice and other

Below: Shermans were fast, well-armed and had thick, sloping armour that proved resistant to the shells of most German anti-tank guns. These models are newly arrived in North Africa in September 1942.

ailments plagued the men, including Rommel, who finally felt justified in taking leave when the front had quietened down and Montgomery seemed uninterested in taking the initiative.[59]

Rommel's health had actually improved by early September, but he was in need of a rest like Gause, Westphal and Mellenthin – all of whom were out for the count. Rommel was convinced that he had about six weeks until the British attacked again, and this gave him the opportunity to take some leave. Only a victory in the Caucasus could now save Rommel's position in North Africa.[60] After all, if the Germans broke through in the Caucasus, this would not only threaten the Persian oil fields (which supplied the British with their abundance of petrol) but also the all-important lines of communication with India.[61]

Rommel was worried about the situation on the Eastern Front, where the protracted Battle for Stalingrad was taking resources and troops that he could have used.[62] As yet, there seemed little to do other than bide one's time and await events elsewhere. But in September came a spectacular reminder that the British were not remaining entirely inactive in the desert. The same commandos who had failed to kill Rommel a year earlier were back in action.

The raid on Benghazi and Tobruk
During the entire desert campaign, a secret version of the war in the Sahara was being conducted by the Long Range Desert Group (LRDG) and the Special Air Service (SAS), the latter under the command of the legendary Colonel Stirling. While these operations no doubt raised the morale of the British with their daring and panache, they were only a minor annoyance to Rommel. In September came one raid that, if successful, could have proved to be a bit more than a nuisance to Rommel and his precarious position in North Africa.

Tobruk remained Rommel's Achilles heel since it was his most important and nearest point of entry for supplies. The British, realizing this, were determined to interrupt these supply lines if possible, and at the end of August 1942 a convoy of trucks set out from the Nile for Kufra via the Dahkla Oasis. Kufra, held by the Sudan Defence Force (SDF), was the forward base of the LRDG.

The plan was for a combined LRDG/SAS attack on Benghazi and Tobruk where the commandos, supported by the Royal Navy, would land. The SDF took Jalo Oasis as a forward base for the raids. Stirling's attack on Benghazi proved a failure, and his men had to flee back to Jalo, still held by the SDF. The other raid on Tobruk also failed because of faulty intelligence and poor security.

Axis agents in Cairo had picked up rumours, and these were then pieced together by Rommel's intelligence department. Most of the raiders, including Colonel Haselden, were killed in action. The Germans congratulated the

British, especially the commandos on the shore, for a daring attack and good fight. Only Colonel Popski's raid on Barce succeeded because the local commander ignored the intelligence warning.

Rommel, while treating this as a defensive victory, was quite shaken since Tobruk was vulnerable and he was afraid that the British might have launched this as a prelude to a major offensive against his frontline. However, no major raid followed, and Rommel, directing the Italian and German naval commanders in North Africa to improve defences, breathed a sigh of relief.[63]

Götterdämerung: a battle without hope – the Second Battle of El Alamein

Rommel's replacement during his leave was General Georg Stumme, a large, good-humoured panzer commander who seemed to relish a combat command in the desert. He arrived on 16 September to be briefed by Rommel, who had taken a shine to him. Rommel did a thorough job and told Stumme that he was convinced that Montgomery would launch a night attack on the German lines, but would wait until the end of October when he would have the benefit of a full moon.

Rommel also left Stumme in charge of a formidable line of defences stretching along the El Alamein Front. This defensive line was laid in great depth in order to minimize the damage to the troops and defences alike from British aerial and artillery bombardment. Farthest out in the line lay guarded battle outposts manned by a single company from each infantry battalion. Behind these lay the main defences of the line, a series of unoccupied boxes containing thousands of mines. Behind the boxes, some 3220m (6000ft) away, were the 88mm guns and other anti-tank artillery. Yet farther back were the mobile reserves of tanks and the mechanized formations.

The DAK had laid 250,000 anti-tank mines powerful enough to cut the tracks of the enemy's vehicles, as well as 14,500 anti-personnel mines. These,

Below left: The Allied mainstay before the US tanks arrived was the Crusader II (centre).

Below right: Playing an important role by the time of Second El Alamein was the highly successful Sherman tank.

Above: One way of dealing with German minefields was by fitting flails to tanks. This is a British Great Scorpion. The fitting of flails enabled them to carve a path through enemy minefields.

if trodden on, sprang up like a deadly jack in the box, bursting and then spreading a shower of steel pellets in all directions. These giant minefields were dubbed devil's gardens and represented a formidable defence against a British offensive. Rommel had prepared an unpleasant welcome for his assailants.

His tactical plan, which Rommel wanted Stumme to follow at all costs, was to see to it that the British were bogged down in the minefields and then trapped with simultaneous counterattacks from the north and south of the line. Before departing, Rommel told Stumme that he would return the instant that Montgomery attacked.[64] This news displeased Stumme, as it seemed the master would not trust his apprentice to take on the serious tasks and inferred that only Rommel could make the right decisions.[65] Nevertheless, despite his misgivings about his task as stop-gap commander-in-chief, Stumme took formal command of Panzerarmee Afrika on 22 September.[66]

The news that Rommel had left Africa was welcome to the Allies, and President Roosevelt thought that he must have taken quite a knock. He also believed that once the intelligence leak in Cairo had been stopped there would be an end to Rommel's run of victories.[67] This was an inaccurate view of Rommel's talents, although the panzer leader had indeed taken quite a knock.

Rommel back in Germany

Once he arrived in Berlin Rommel saw the Goebbels family, whom he fascinated with tales of the desert war. Goebbels supported Hitler's intention of making Rommel commander-in-chief of the post-war German Army. On 30 September, Rommel was presented with his field marshal's baton by Hitler in person, and at 18:00 hours the "Hero of the Desert" was given a rapturous welcome from party, army and state personnel at the Berlin Sportspalats. It was the height of his career and probably his proudest moment as a soldier.

Hitler was beaming with satisfaction since he viewed Rommel as "his" soldier, and the ovations for Rommel reflected on the Führer himself. In return, Hitler promised Rommel that his army would be furnished with everything his favourite soldier wished for, including the new heavy tanks, heavy artillery and mortars, more fuel, supplies and troops. Rommel was pleased but probably sceptical since he had heard it all before. As for supplies, in the hands of the Italians these would probably not improve.

Privately, Rommel told his friend Kurt Hesse that, while he had nothing but praise for the troops, the Italian officers were worthless, their government worse and their high command was riddled with incompetents and traitors. "Give me three shiploads of gasoline for my tanks and I'll be in Cairo 48 hours later." On the morning of 3 October, Rommel held a conference for the international press in Berlin, telling them that his army was on the doorstep of Egypt and would march on Cairo as soon as possible on his return to Africa.[68]

Meanwhile, Churchill had to accept that Montgomery would not launch an offensive in September and settled for one a month later. Montgomery had been thorough, even pedantic, in his preparations. He realized that Rommel would be ready for the attack, so he opted to use Rommel's own tricks of concealment and deception. In an effort to convince his enemy that the offensive would come in the south, Montgomery built supply dumps and a dummy water pipeline into the southern sector of the front. This elaborate deception was also designed to fool German intelligence into believing that the offensive (planned for 23 October) would in fact occur two weeks later.

Montgomery reined in his more aggressive subordinates, such as General Lumsden, commander of the élite X Corps, who wanted to stage a mobile tank-dominated battle. Lumsden was put in his place by the irate and domineering Montgomery who would have no truck, unlike his predecessors, with insubordination and the questioning of his orders. At least this time there was only one man deciding strategy on the British side.

The final plan was presented on 6 October. The main attack, Operation Lightfoot, would be launched by XXX Corps (four divisions) in the north with the objective of Oxalic behind the German defence line. Two corridors would be cut through the German minefields, through which X Corps would follow XXX Corps' advance. Its task was to destroy the panzers and prevent the DAK from interfering with the advance of XXX Corps.

To mislead Rommel, a diversionary attack by XIII Corps would be launched in the south against Jebel Kalakh, Qaret el Himeimat and El Taqa. The artillery had an important role to play in laying down a smoke screen, giving covering and support fire and saturating the enemy's forward positions with shells. The RAF, led by the inspired and daring leadership of Air Marshal Cunningham, would add

Below: Augmenting the supplies of established British tanks were the Grants, derived from the US-built M3 Lee medium tank.

to enemy troubles by bombing the defence line and conducting low-level attacks. Cunningham had 200 bombers and 500 fighters for his massive aerial bombardment of Rommel's lines.

Once the plan had been laid, Montgomery, like Rommel, was a consummate military showman and extremely conscious of public relations. On 19–20 October, all the senior commanders were invited to his mobile HQ for a personal briefing. On 21–22 October, all the other officers and the troops were briefed. Montgomery had a flair for giving lectures on the objectives of the Eighth Army and how they were to achieve them. On 22 October, Montgomery held an extraordinary press conference where he exuded bombastic self-confidence and bravado. The cynical pressmen were not convinced, since they had heard talk of the last push and final victory from his predecessors. They had all failed. Why should Montgomery be any different? Perhaps he had a direct line to God Almighty![69]

If God wasn't on Monty's side then at least the big battalions were. In the air, the RAF, with 1200 planes, had a crushing superiority over Kesselring's dwindling aerial flotilla in North Africa, which was short of machines, spares, pilots, fuel and hope. Monty was equally superior on the ground. In total, the Eighth Army had 230,000 troops and some 1229 tanks available in Egypt. Of these, 195,000 troops and 1029 tanks were stationed in the battle zone ready for the offensive. They were supported by a stream of supplies and reinforcements pouring in from Great Britain, and by 2311 artillery pieces.[70]

On paper, Rommel's Panzer Army could match these formations since both sides had four tank divisions and eight infantry ones. But all of the Axis

Below: A rare opportunity for a panzer crew to rest near the battlefields of El Alamein.

formations were far below full strength. The 15th Panzer Division, which should have had a normal complement of 9180, was left with a third of that – 3300 men. The panzer army had a total of 104,000 troops, made up of 50,000 Germans and 54,000 Italians. Of the Germans, only 29,000 were actually fit for service. Rommel's once proud DAK had been reduced to a mere 489 tanks. Of these, 278 were Italian-made and almost worthless in a modern tank battle. Of the 211 German machines, only 30 were Panzer IVs with 75mm high-velocity guns. Just a few months earlier, the Panzer IV had outclassed anything the British could field. But now the Americans supplied Great Britain with a far superior machine that gave Monty more than a mere numerical advantage over Rommel.

The Sherman, which the Germans had not yet encountered, was superior in armaments, speed, engine strength and armour to the Panzer IV. Most German anti-tank guns could not knock out this behemoth – only the omnipotent 88s could penetrate the tank's thick, sloped armour. Unfortunately, the Shermans, with the Grants, amounted to only half of the British armoured strength when the battle began.[71]

Above: An officer of the 21st Panzer Division, part of the fighting heart of Rommel's army.

Decision in the desert

Both sides, whatever their strengths and weaknesses, realized what was at stake. Montgomery and his superior, Alexander, knew that the impatient Churchill would not tolerate another defeat or even half-victory that left Rommel's army intact. Rommel, too, realized that if he lost this battle of El Alamein the whole panzer army would be crushed in a battle of attrition or cut to pieces during a retreat. Neither side could afford mistakes. Now the battle that would decide the final outcome of the desert war could begin.

At 21:30 hours on 23 October, more than 1000 British artillery pieces opened up a barrage that unleashed the fires of hell on the Germans. The roar could have woken the dead. In the dark the British could see how the red glow of fires on the other side indicated destroyed German guns or ammunition sites. The air filled with whizzing projectiles and Bofors tracer bullets to guide the infantry, which 30 minutes later advanced against the German lines.[72] During the following night both corps attacked, supported by X Corps, in the north and south. The four divisions of XXX Corps attacked a narrow 10km (6-mile) front between Tell el Eisa and Miteirya Ridge, managing in the process to punch two holes in the German minefields.

The coastal road, a vital and vulnerable sector of the German front, was protected in a deep echelon by Italian units, the 90th Light Division and 164th Infantry Division. The DAK was held in reserve with the tanks, as Rommel had planned. While the 1st Australian Brigade made a feint along the coastal sector to keep the Germans on their toes, the 4th Indian Division launched a heavy raid along the Ruweisat Ridge. Where the British had managed to open a corridor, the Axis forces poured machine-gun, mortar and artillery fire into them while the 15th Panzer Division counterattacked.

Things were not going that well for the British in the south, either, and the situation had soon become critical. Free French infantry successfully assaulted and held the high ground around Himeimat, but the soft sands leading to the heights prevented the necessary support weapons from reaching the French positions. The 1st Armoured Division managed to get some tanks through the minefields but the whole of X Corps had ground to a halt.[73] It seemed as though Montgomery's simple but blunt plan for a frontal assault, reliant on brute force in a battle of attrition, was not working. Instead, as Liddell Hart pointed out, a bolder strategy should have been adopted to avoid high casualties and waste of effort. Montgomery's tactics were still more surprising given the British preponderance in numbers and quality of equipment.[74]

Rommel resumes command

Meanwhile, Rommel was convalescing in the Austrian Alps with his wife, and was completely unaware of events in North Africa. It was not until 15:00 hours on 24 October that Rommel's ADC, Berndt, managed to get through on the phone to the new field marshal. "Montgomery's offensive has begun, last night! And General Stumme has vanished without a trace!" Rommel immediately drove to the airfield at Weiner Neustadt where he phoned Hitler to tell him the bad news.

Hitler, wanting to save Rommel for possible duty on the Eastern Front, and concerned about his protégé's health, did not immediately order Rommel to return. In Stumme's absence or demise, temporary command of the army had been handed over to General Wilhelm von Thoma. Rommel hadn't met him and knew very little about him. Hitler therefore couldn't keep Rommel away.

He flew to Rome where he confronted Rintelen, the German liaison officer, about the shortage of fuel for the panzer army. The shocking news was that the fuel situation was far worse than he had expected. His army was reduced to a mere three days of supplies. It was finally at 23:25 hours on 25 October that Rommel arrived at his battle HQ and was able to signal back to Hitler and Rome, "I have taken command of the army again".[75]

Several interesting developments had obviously taken place in Rommel's absence. Stumme, although a brave soldier and a competent field commander, had committed three errors of judgement. First, he ordered the artillery to slow down or cease their counter-bombardment in order to conserve the army's depleted stocks of ammunition. In reality, those stocks were better than Krause had led Stumme to believe and his order had the unfortunate consequence of demoralizing his own troops and allowing the British an easy time picking off the forward positions of the defence line.

Second, Stumme committed his panzers in a piecemeal fashion (copying the very worst British habit), which allowed the British to destroy them in batches or tank by tank. The 15th Panzer Division was reduced, in this fashion, to a third of its original strength by the time Rommel returned. Stumme committed one final, fatal error. Despite only the most basic experience of desert conditions and topography, he set out on a tour of inspection. He got lost, was fired on by artillery and the shock gave him a fatal heart attack. He died, like many of his troops, on 24 October. His command had been short and sharp.[76]

That day XXX Corps reached the Oxalic line but X Corps failed to reach its objective, Pierson, by the end of the day.[77] By 02:00 hours on 25 October, the situation was critical in the south as the armour

Above: Dug in and waiting for the next move, 1942 found Rommel's troops all too often in a defensive, rather than offensive, role.

struggled to get through the narrow corridors in the German minefields. The tough General Freyberg took personal charge of the armour, and commanded them from his own tank. At 03:30 hours, Montgomery's chief of staff, General Francis de Guingand, called the corps commanders to a conference to discuss the precarious situation. He woke Montgomery at the same time, and his superior agreed with him and the corps commanders that the offensive should be continued at all costs despite the casualties and tank losses that would ensue. Their persistence seemed to have worked. By 08:00 hours, the corps commanders could report that the 10th Armoured Division – like the 8th Armoured Brigade and the New Zealand Division – had broken through the enemy's minefields. Only the 1st Armoured Division did not make any progress until 25–26 October.[78]

Rommel, back at his desert HQ, met General von Thoma for the first time. Thoma was an aristocratic military officer of the old school. He was gaunt, ascetic, pedantic and thoroughly unpleasant. Rommel took an instant dislike to this antithesis of himself, which didn't help cooperation between them.

Rommel wasn't pleased that Thoma and Westphal had followed Stumme's order not to fire back at the British. He pointed out that this allowed them, with little loss, to undermine the defence line by taking the outposts and minefields. Thoma argued that, as it was the German artillery that had prevented the British from advancing boldly, he believed the main attack would come in the north. Rommel agreed on that point and on the enemy's tactics.

The British, with a large troop contingent, would use their numerous infantry to create lanes, covered by smoke screens and supported by lavish artillery fire, through the minefields. Once these corridors had been created, the British would pour their mass of tanks through the lanes. Should the British armour break through his static defence line, Rommel realized it could turn into a disaster since the armour, if handled properly, could outflank and cut to pieces any Axis retreat. Given the lack of mobility of his infantry, especially the moribund Italians, Rommel's army would be destroyed by such a breakthrough so a British attack had to be deflected, and even destroyed, at all costs.

A battle of attrition

During the night, the British used Hill 28, a small elevation in the frontline, as an observation post for their artillery which allowed them to pound the Germans mercilessly. Rommel noted in the morning how this crescendo had given him only five hours' sleep. Increasing lack of sleep due to the British bombardment was not only undermining Rommel's health but also that of his troops. During the next few days Rommel observed the fierce fighting around Hill 28, which he noted sourly was hardly worth the rivers of blood expended on it by both sides.

Rommel shared Thoma's conviction that Montgomery would launch his decisive attack in the north, and he therefore moved what remained of his panzers (including the depleted 21st Panzer Division) north. The DAK's fuel reserves were now so low that this was a dangerous gamble. Should Rommel's otherwise impeccable intuition be wrong, these units could not be moved back. Luckily for the Germans his intuition was right, and during 27 October Rommel parried and blocked every British advance. Montgomery's offensive had been fought to a standstill.

There were also German reverses. A failed attack against Hill 28 left the assault troops exposed to British artillery and aerial bombardment in open terrain where there was no cover at all.[79] Rommel was now caught in a trap since his success had been built on mobility and the inspired use of tanks. His exposed position beyond the edge of the civilized world had eventually caught up with him. In terms of Rommel's neglected supply and transport problems, the chickens had come home to roost.

Without fuel, Rommel's army was forced to fight a static battle of attrition where it would simply bleed to death. The lack of fuel, exacerbated by the sinking of another two tankers, prevented him from pulling the panzer army out of British artillery range where he could have laid a trap for the British armour in a pitched panzer battle he was sure to win.[80]

Under circumstances dictated by the enemy, Rommel was sure that he faced eventual defeat. His own resources were not being replenished while the British ones, already greater than his own, were being increased continuously. If his army, which had done everything to win, was defeated the consequences would be dire. But at least the Eighth Army wasn't strong enough to take the whole of North Africa without serious resistance from his forces.[81]

Rommel was growing defeatist even though he was determined to give his old "stubborn friends" one hell of a

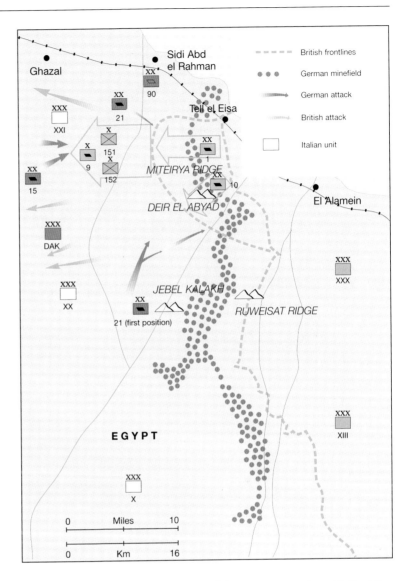

fight before he rolled over dead. On 28 October, his Order of the Day to his troops and commanders was that this was a battle of life and death that required everyone, including Rommel himself, to fight to the bitter end. Rommel's conviction that Montgomery's offensive was coming in the north was confirmed by captured enemy documents. They showed that Montgomery would attack in this sector and, once his armour had broken through, he would wheel north towards the coast at El Daba. By the afternoon, Rommel could observe how Montgomery was massing his troops for an assault in the wedge they had created in the German lines.

At 21:00 hours came the customary massive British artillery barrage that drove some troops mad with the noise. An hour later, following the established British formula, came the attack – this time spearheaded by Morshead and his veteran 9th Australian Division. All night a deadly battle raged between the

Above: The Second Battle of El Alamein was one of the turning points in the desert war. Realizing that he could not hold his position, Rommel ordered his panzers west, conducting a strategic withdrawal despite Hitler's absurd orders to stand and fight to the last man.

Above: November 1942, and a British Priest self-propelled gun edges its way past a burning enemy tank.

Aussies, respected by Rommel and all German troops as the very élite of Allied fighters, and the 2nd Battalion of the 125th Panzergrenadier Regiment. The 125th Panzergrenadiers, an élite formation itself, put up a Herculean defence that left both sides utterly exhausted. By dawn the following day, 29 October, it was obvious that the Australian attack had been blocked.

After five bloody days of fighting, the British had very little to show other than 10,000 British, Commonwealth and Allied casualties – and small dents in the German lines. In London the mood was gloomy, nowhere more so than at the British Military GHQ and in the government corridors of Whitehall.

Churchill, who had fought in the World War I, was determined that those sacrifices would not be repeated again. Now Montgomery and Alexander seemed to be repeating the same old mistakes. After a huge artillery barrage and infantry assault against an entrenched enemy, the assault had failed. This could not be allowed to go on. Churchill turned, with anger and disappointment, on General Brooke. "Why did Montgomery tell us he would break through in seven days, if all he intended to do was fight a half-hearted battle? Have we not got one single general who can win one single battle!"

Although Churchill's exasperation is understandable, no one could accuse Montgomery or the Eighth Army of fighting a half-hearted battle. He was

simply uninspired in his choice of frontal assaults and in relying on sheer mass of violent force. In his defence is the fact that there was little else he could do.

Churchill, determined to have a swift and overwhelming victory at any cost, appeared to have lost confidence in Montgomery. A meeting of the Chiefs of Staff was called at noon. Brooke, knowing Montgomery's head was on the block, chose to lie. Montgomery, or so Brooke claimed, was preparing a much larger and more impressive offensive that would at last break Rommel's defence line.

No doubt Rommel, had he known of the sombre mood among the British, would have enjoyed Montgomery's and Churchill's discomfort, caused by his army's brilliant resistance. However, he was having as bad, if not worse, a time himself.[82] Rommel was even more depressed than Churchill, and he wrote to his beloved wife that same day, "I haven't much hope left. At night I lie with my eyes open, unable to sleep, for the load that is on my shoulders. In the day I'm dead tired. What will happen if things go wrong here? That is the thought that torments me day and night. I can see no way out if that happens."[83] Insomnia drove him to take a stroll with one of Westphal's officers at 03:30 hours, and he launched into a long monologue about what he should do. Rommel said he realized that the army would be destroyed by the superior Eighth Army if it remained much longer at El Alamein. Should the British break through the defence line then the lack of fuel would doom his panzers and make mincemeat of his slow-moving Italian infantry. Despite having four days' respite, Rommel had more or less given up this "battle without hope" as lost.[84]

Below: Great Britain's Commonwealth allies were in the thick of the action during El Alamein. Here, South African troops use the cover of smoke to advance on enemy positions.

At 07:00 hours on 30 October, Rommel told Bayerlein that the battle was lost. The last straw was news that yet another tanker, whose fuel was so desperately needed, had been sunk outside Tobruk. Rommel drew a red line on the map, at Fuka, which was his army's fall-back position. He had been planning a retreat for some time, but he kept this eventuality concealed from the Italian and German high commands. In the afternoon, Rommel discussed an eventual retreat to Fuka. After the war, Westphal defended Rommel's actions vehemently against any accusation that he was behaving treasonably.

Rommel's spirits revived with the arrival of an Italian tanker with 590 tonnes (600 tons) of fuel – one day's supply for the army.[85] Rommel should have acted on his first instinct and retreated since, according to Liddell Hart, this would have caught Montgomery off-guard. But the field marshal, who had a strong paternalistic streak and was a humane commander, would not abandon the infantry to their fate. Instead, he simply hoped that Montgomery would cancel any planned offensives. Monty obliged Rommel, and the feared British attack failed to materialize. Rommel's relief was matched by Montgomery's private anxiety that he would be sacked like his predecessor for postponing an offensive.

Churchill, deeply depressed by the news from North Africa, vented his anger and frustration on the hapless General Brooke.[86] That day, Kesselring arrived at Rommel's HQ to promise him full Luftwaffe transport support to alleviate the fuel shortage. The Junkers 88 aircraft would be transferred from the equally hard-pressed air force units on the Eastern Front. Rommel wrote to Lucie that: "It's a tragedy that this sort of support only starts when things are virtually hopeless."[87]

Rommel's criticism of his superiors' lethargy and indifference to his army's needs was amply justified. Had he been given the resources, supplies and reinforcements he had asked for earlier then

Below: German artillery tries to stem the tide of the Allied assault at Second El Alamein.

he would by this time have been master of Alexandria, the Nile Delta, Cairo and even the Suez Canal. But he had not, and now Hitler and Mussolini's belated support came too late to change the outcome of the battle.

Later that day, some 30 British tanks and Australian infantry advanced to the coast – it seemed that Montgomery had finally achieved his all-important breakthrough. It was a false alarm since Rommel's panzers attacked and destroyed the tanks and captured 200 Australians. Cavellero, on Mussolini's behalf, radioed Rommel to congratulate him on a splendid local victory and to pass on Il Duce's confident predictions of a battlefield victory for Rommel.

The end at El Alamein

But the commander himself had lost all belief in such a victory, and had made a fatal backward glance in the mirror. Now the important matter was to retreat to Fuka without losing too many men and supplies. Krause had inspected the Fuka line and found it to be excellent since it was anchored on the Depression and could not be outflanked. The army had enough fuel for two days of operations and plenty of ammunition (Kesselring noted that the DAK always complained about an ammunition shortage, but when Rommel retreated he destroyed thousands of tonnes so it wouldn't fall into enemy hands[88]).

Alexander telegraphed Churchill that: "Enemy is fighting desperately, but we are hitting him hard and continuously, and boring into him without mercy. Have high hopes he will crack soon."[89] Rommel had equally high hopes that he wouldn't crack as long as he and his troops could take the strain of battle.[90]

The British, having abandoned their piecemeal approach, were ready once again to launch a massive attack. At 22:00 hours on 1 November, a mighty barrage was unleashed by 200 guns against a narrow section of the front, while other areas were pounded from the air by waves of British bombers. During that long, cold night, Rommel observed the British attack as parachute flares hung over the battlefield. British bombs and artillery shells smashed into the DAK headquarters where Thoma was wounded, the radio jammed and the telephone wires cut.[91]

Main picture: German panzers rumble into action during the Second Battle of El Alamein.

Above: General Ritter von Thoma (right), commander of the Afrika Korps, salutes General Montgomery, commander of the British Eighth Army (left). Having experienced the "insanity" of Hitler's order to stand fast, von Thoma headed to the battlefield and was captured by British troops.

A short time later, at 01:00 hours, the firestorm of artillery and bombs died down and XXX Corps launched Operation Supercharge, spearheaded by the 2nd New Zealand Division.[92] A mass of British tanks attacked on a 914m- (3000ft-) front at Hill 28 in a furious attempt to break through the German lines. The German and Italian infantry put up fierce resistance, and in the semi-darkness of the early morning a desperate battle was fought out. Soon the whole battlefield was littered with the burning hulks of British tanks. The problem for Rommel was that there were as many tanks waiting to advance against his tired troops as there were burning. Worse, several British armoured cars had broken through and were roaming around the Axis rear wreaking havoc on Rommel's soft-skinned vehicles and supply dumps.[93]

British tank losses were severe. The 9th Armoured Brigade had lost three-quarters of its tanks during this offensive.[94] The decisive day had arrived, the day that would either make or break Rommel's army. At 11:00 hours on 2 November, artillery observers phoned Rommel with the unwelcome news that a large number of British tanks had broken through southwest of Hill 28 and were advancing westwards. They estimated their number at 400, and reported a further 500 awaiting the signal to advance beyond mine boxes J and K.

Rommel faced his last large-scale panzer battle in the desert; and Lieutenant Armbruster, who saw Rommel leave his HQ, wrote down his impressions. "Today will probably decide the outcome. Poor Rommel, he has to shoulder too much responsibility and there's little he can do. Accursed gang in Rome! Pray God we pull it off."[95] Rommel, having lost three-quarters of his panzers by this time, was facing impossible odds. The British had 600 frontline tanks to his 30. It was amazing that the DAK had held out for so long.[96]

Until now the Sherman hadn't been seen in the desert war, and the tank proved almost impervious to the 88s' shells. Rommel's army had to contend not only with superior Allied tanks but also with superior airpower. In an hour of fighting Rommel noted seven consecutive bomber attacks on Hill 28.

At 13:30 hours, the radio interceptors snapped up messages from the British that made it clear Monty had ordered his tanks to turn in a northeasterly direction towards the coast at Ghazal, halfway to El Daba. Rommel moved all his available forces, the artillery and the *Ariete* Division, northwards to

Tell el Aqqaqir – Monty's intermediate objective. All afternoon the battle raged, and by 15:30 hours Rommel had seen enough to convince him that only a withdrawal would save his army from destruction. An hour later he gave his staff orders for a retreat to the combat line along the Rahman Track, as the first step towards the inevitable withdrawal to the Fuka line. That evening Thoma phoned Rommel to tell him that the DAK, once the pride of his army, was reduced to 35 tanks. That clinched it for Rommel. The retreat to Fuka was now a matter of when, not if.[97]

Rommel gave orders for Thoma and the DAK to cover the rest of the army's retreat to Fuka by holding the line until the morning of 4 November, which would give the infantry time to escape. Rommel made it quite clear to Thoma that his panzers had to conduct a fighting retreat. By 21:00 hours the whole army had orders to retreat, a withdrawal that Rommel had concealed from both Mussolini and Hitler alike.

Cavallero was informed of Rommel's orders for a retreat by the Italian liaison officer, Colonel Mancinelli, at Rommel's HQ. Cavallero radioed to Rommel Mussolini's wish for the defence line to be held at all costs. He told him that fuel would be rushed to assist Rommel's army in holding fast. The Italian general seemed to think that Rommel had 250 tanks and plentiful supplies of ammunition. Rommel's reports to the German high command spelt out the army's dire situation but did not mention the possibility of a retreat.[98] Hitler was assured that the reports he received were the same as those sent to Rome, and since they did not mention the hated word retreat Hitler had gone to bed satisfied that all was still well on the El Alamein Front.

Below: Another victim for the Allies: a German Panzer III tank sits in ruins near Tell el Eisa.

At 08:30 hours on 3 November, Hitler was woken by field marshal Keitel, his high command flunkey, with the news that Rommel's midnight report mentioned him giving permission for the infantry units to retreat. Hitler flew into a rage that he had not been woken, and vented his spleen on Jodl's deputy, General Walter Warlimont, who was responsible for informing him of developments.[99] Hitler was therefore in a fine fury when he pencilled a new set of orders for Rommel. He ordered the field marshal to stand fast and hold the El Alamein line at all costs, to the last man and the last bullet. His infamous "Death or Glory" order was sent to Rome at 11:30 hours, and shortly afterwards, thanks to the Bletchley deciphering service of Enigma, Churchill had a copy of the order on his desk.

Since 18:30 hours the previous evening, the British had dropped 1000 bombs per square mile of front on the panzer army. Rommel hadn't slept all night. By evening most of his army was in full flight to Fuka, including the *Littorio* Division which lacked officers to lead it. Rommel only had enough fuel for an orderly retreat. Leaving Westphal at his HQ, Rommel drove along the coast road. Even two hours later, the British were unaware that their enemy was pulling out of El Alamein.[100] British artillery pounded the abandoned Himeimat position. It was not until 11:30 hours that British aircraft on patrol spotted the coastal road jammed with vehicles, and Monty had the news he had wanted to hear for weeks. Rommel was retreating.

Below: While a British Honey tank passes this knocked-out Panzer III, an artillery listening post operates in its shadow.

Bayerlein reported to a depressed Rommel that the DAK (with only 32 panzers) held a semi-circular position along the Rahman Track. The good news from Thoma was that the DAK, in spite of its diminutive size, had managed to destroy 100 British tanks including many Shermans. It was while he was having lunch with Westphal that Rommel received Hitler's stand-fast order. Rommel's response was one of rage and panic. If he continued the retreat then Hitler might have him cashiered for insubordination, but to obey such an order was to condemn his army to destruction.

Rommel changes his mind

He penned several replies that were not sent, and at 14:28 hours on 3 November Rommel phoned Thoma. The DAK commander reported his formations as follows: 21st Panzer Division (12 tanks), 15th Panzer Division (10 tanks) and the Italian *Littorio* Division (17 tanks). That was all. Rommel's reply was to quote Hitler's order, to which Thoma agreed in principle but would amend in order to make minor, local withdrawals.[101]

Rommel agreed, for reasons known only to himself, to carry out Hitler's stand-fast order. The main reason was probably that he feared being replaced by another general. By obeying, he might still save his precious army from destruction. He reversed his previous order to retreat and ordered an intermediate defence along a line that wits in his army dubbed the "Telegraph-Post Runway". It lacked all natural defences, and would leave the retreating forces open to a British attack.[102]

Bayerlein, Rommel's chief of staff, was appalled that his superior chose to obey Hitler's insane order instead of disregarding it as completely inappropriate. More precious time was lost for Rommel (time that should have been spent reaching Fuka) as he radioed one desperate message after another asking permission to retreat. He pointed out that the Italian *Littorio* and *Ariete* Divisions had perished during a most courageous last stand. The DAK was reduced to 24 tanks, while the infantry units were half their normal strength and the artillery had lost almost two-thirds of its capability. If the battle continued there would soon be no army for Rommel to retreat with.

He decided to send his ADC, Berndt, to Rastenburg, Hitler's East Prussian headquarters, in order to spell out, in person, his reasons for retreating. But it would take Berndt at least a day to get to East Prussia. Rommel therefore reluctantly issued new stand-fast orders at 18:40 hours,[103] but believed that his army was doomed. "I can no longer, or scarcely any longer, believe in its [the battle] successful outcome", Rommel wrote to Lucie on 3 November. "What will become of us is in God's hands."[104]

Luckily Rommel began to come to his senses. If he disobeyed his orders there was still time to save the panzer army. He chose to mutiny, and gave orders for the army to resume its retreat. Rommel's belief in Hitler had taken a serious and ultimately fatal knock, as had Hitler's faith in his protégé. Putting the safety of his men before any oath of loyalty to his Führer, he issued the necessary orders. It was now public knowledge that Rommel denounced Hitler as mad.[105]

Had he disobeyed earlier, then his army would by now have been ensconced safely in the Fuka line. It was almost too late. Kesselring, on his way to El Alamein, was determined to carry out Hitler's orders for Rommel to stand fast. He arrived at Rommel's HQ only to be told that the panzer army was reduced to just 24 tanks. He revised his assessment since he believed that Hitler's ideas, conditioned by his experiences on the Eastern Front, were not applicable to the desert war. Rommel asked Kesselring what he should do. "Use your own judgement", was the simple answer. He could not believe Hitler intended to destroy the whole panzer army and DAK.

The Italians, who had reached Fuka by 4 November, were in full retreat, and it was now too late to slow the momentum.[106] Not all Italian troops were fleeing, though. During 3 November, the élite paratroopers of the Folgore Division fought magnificently to buy time for an infantry retreat. The next day, Rommel, standing at an observation post at Tell el Mamfsra, saw a gigantic dustbowl to the southeast. It was the *Ariete* Division making one last stand. These brave crews manned their tinpot tanks one last time. They were slaughtered with their machines. Rommel was seeing the last death throes of his once mighty army. It was supremely ironic that the much-abused Italians were making the last stand.

Around this time, von Thoma had told Bayerlein that Hitler's order to stand fast was complete madness. He walked out and sought honourable death on the battlefield. Instead, he was captured by the gleeful British, who were delighted to have ensnared the commander of the once-vaunted DAK – second prize only to Rommel himself.[107]

Rommel gave the order to retreat, and the following day came Hitler's grudging approval. It was on this sad note that the Second Battle of El Alamein ended. For Rommel it had always been a battle without hope, in which he lost almost all his tank force and the British captured 20,000 Italian and 10,000 German prisoners.[108]

Below: A poignant scene – two graves and a Sherman of the Eighth Army. Thousands of men perished to halt Rommel's drive through Egypt.

Chapter notes

1 Purnell's, Vol. 9,
E. Dorman O'Gowan, *Battle of Mersa Matruh*, p.950.
2 Salmaggi, pp.262, 266.
3 RP.233-234, Rommel's diary notes.
4 RP.235, Rommel to Lucie, 23 June 1942.
5 RP.237, Rommel to Lucie, 26 June 1942.
6 Dorman O'Gowan, p.950.
7 Ibid, pp.951-952.
8 RP.237, Rommel's diary.
9 Dorman O'Gowan, p.952.
10 RP.238, Rommel to Lucie, 27 June 1942.
11 Dorman O'Gowan, p.952.
12 RP.239, Rommel to Lucie, 29 June 1942.
13 RP.240, Rommel's diary.
14 RP.239, Rommel to Lucie, 29 June 1942.
15 Salmaggi, pp.268-269.
16 Dorman O'Gowan, pp.984-985.
17 Liddell Hart, p.295.
18 Dorman O'Gowan, p.986.
19 Dorman O'Gowan, p.987; Liddell Hart, p.295.
20 Dorman O'Gowan, p.989.
21 RP.249, Rommel to Lucie, 3 Jul. 1942.
22 Dorman O'Gowan, p.989; Liddell Hart, pp.295-296.
23 RP.250, Rommel to Lucie, 4 Jul. 1942.
24 RP.250, Rommel to Lucie, 5 Jul. 1942.
25 RP.252, Rommel's diary; Dorman O'Gowan, p.989.
26 RP.254, Rommel's diary.
27 Dorman O'Gowan, p.990.
28 Liddell Hart, p.299.
29 RP.255, Rommel to Lucie, 12, 13 Jul. 1942.
30 RP.255, Rommel's diary.
31 Dorman O'Gowan, p.990.
32 RP.257, Rommel to Lucie, 17 Jul. 1942.
33 RP.257, Rommel to Lucie, 18 Jul. 1942.

34 Dorman O'Gowan, p.991.
35 Ibid.
36 Dorman O'Gowan, pp.992-993; Liddell Hart, p.299.
37 RP.259, Rommel's diary.
38 Dorman O'Gowan, p.995; Liddell Hart, p.300; RP.275-276, Rommel to Lucie, 21, 22, 26 Jul. 1942.
39 Liddell Hart, p.301.
40 Dorman O'Gowan, pp.996-997; Salmaggi, pp.279-280; Liddell Hart, p.302.
41 RP.264-266, Rommel's diary; Purnell's, Vol.10, Bayerlein, *The Battle of Alam Halfa (Aug–Sept.1942)*, p.1065.
42 RP.263, Rommel to Lucie, 2, 5, 10 Aug. 1942.
43 RP.270, Rommel to Lucie, 24 Aug. 1942.
44 RP.270-271, Lt. Alfred I. Berndt to Frau Rommel, 26 Aug. 1942.
45 RP.271, Footnote 1.
46 RP.272, Rommel to Lucie, 27 Aug. 1942.
47 RP.272, Rommel to Lucie, 29 Aug. 1942.
48 RP.275, Rommel to Lucie, 30 Aug. 1942.
49 RP.275, footnote 1, Rommel's notes.
50 Purnell's, Vol.10, Bayerlein, *The Battle of Alam Halfa (Aug–Sept.1942)*, p.1065.
51 Liddell Hart, pp.303-304.
52 Ibid, pp.305-306.
53 Bayerlein, *Rommel's own story*, pp.1066-1067.
54 Purnell's, Vol.10, Brigadier G. Roberts (22nd Armoured Brigade), *Alam Halfa battle*, p.1068; RP.280, Rommel's diary.
55 Purnell's, Vol.10, *Rommel's own story*, p.1068.
56 RP.277, 279, Rommel's diary.

57 Purnell's, Vol.10, *Rommel's own story*, p.1068.
58 Liddell Hart, pp.308-309. Liddell Hart is quite critical of Montgomery's cautious style as a commander which contrasted with Rommel's boldness.
59 Liddell Hart, pp.311-312.
60 RP.290, Rommel to Lucie, 9 Sept. 1942.
61 RP.291, Rommel to Lucie, 11 Sept. 1942.
62 RP.291, Rommel to Lucie, 16 Sept. 1942.
63 Purnell's, Vol. 10, Major P. Livingstone, *The Great Desert Raids (September 1942)*, pp.1069-1073; RP.291, Rommel's notes; Salmaggi, p.294.
64 Irving, p.195.
65 Purnell's, Vol.10, Major-General Sir Francis de Guingand, *Alamein: The Tide Turns (October–November 1942)*, p.1074.
66 RP.292, Rommel's diary.
67 The recall of the American military attaché from Cairo had removed a vital source of intercepted messages for Rommel's intelligence service and radio surveillance unit.
68 Irving, pp.196-198.
69 Guingand, pp.1076-1077.
70 Ibid, p.1078.
71 Guingand, p.1078; Liddell Hart, pp.310-311; Irving, p.201.
72 Guingand, p.1078; Irving, p.202.
73 Guingand, p.1079.
74 Liddell Hart, p.314.
75 Irving, pp.199-200.
76 Liddell Hart, p.314.
77 Salmaggi, p.303.
78 Guingand, pp.1079-1080.
79 Irving, p.203.
80 Ibid, p.204.
81 RP.310, Rommel to Lucie, 28 Oct. 1942.

82 Irving, p.205.
83 RP.312, Rommel to Lucie, 29 Oct. 1942 (quoted by Liddell Hart), p.316.
84 Irving, p.205.
85 Ibid, p.206.
86 Liddell Hart, p.316.
87 Irving, p.206.
88 Ibid, p.207.
89 Salmaggi, p.310.
90 RP.316, Rommel to Lucie, 1 Nov. 1942.
91 Irving, p.207.
92 Salmaggi, p.311.
93 Irving, p.207.
94 Salmaggi, p.311.
95 Irving, p.208.
96 Liddell Hart, p.317.
97 Irving, p.208; RP.317, Rommel to Lucie, 2 Nov. 1942.
98 Irving, p.209.
99 Ibid, p.210.
100 Ibid, p.211.
101 Ibid, p.212.
102 Purnell's, Vol.11, Freiherr von der Heydte, *Afrika Korps Escapes, North Africa, October–November 1942*, pp.1146-1147. Von der Heydte was in command of the Panzer Army's rearguard during the entire retreat from Egypt to Tunisia.
103 Irving, p.213.
104 RP.322, Rommel to Lucie, 3 Nov. 1942.
105 Irving, p.213.
106 Ibid, p.214.
107 Ibid, p.215. Irving claims that von Thoma had in fact intended to desert to the British. Rommel seemed to have believed the rumour since he told his staff to shut up about it for fear of reprisals against von Thoma's innocent family should the rumours of treason reach Hitler's ear.
108 Salmaggi, p.312.

CHAPTER 8

Decline And Fall

The great retreat after El Alamein, Tunisia and the invasion of France
(November 1942–October 1944)

Rommel had shot his bolt, and he had no alternative other than to escape the trap that Montgomery wanted to spring on him. The "Desert Fox", cunning to the end, saved himself and his army to fight on. But Rommel was a realist and a practically minded professional soldier. He could read the writing on the wall, and knew that Germany had lost the war. It was only a question of when. Rommel chose to fight on in the spirit of the loyal soldier he was, despite the lessons of El Alamein. It took further setbacks and Hitler's increasingly paranoid intransigence to make Rommel become defeatist and more openly defiant of his former idol. In the end, Rommel chose to serve his country's interests, rather than those of his former Führer. For this, he paid with his life. From the latter part of 1942, time was running out not only for the Fox but for Germany as a whole.

The Desert Fox escapes, part I: the great retreat from Egypt to Agheila

Rommel had set up a temporary "stop line" at Fuka, and Montgomery gave orders for his armour to begin the pursuit of the enemy. As usual, the British advance was both slow and hesitant. Montgomery lost a golden opportunity to trap and capture what remained of Rommel's defeated army.[1] The Fox had justified his retreat by the enemy's weight of numbers, and he had lost much sleep wondering how he was to save his precious army.[2] He had, of course, been in tight spots before. A year earlier, he had managed to get the DAK out of Cyrenaica without much trouble. The difference this time was that Rommel had lost hope.

During the night of 3–4 November the British armour halted and wasted its chance to capture Rommel's army. A similar chance was lost on 5 November. The British reached Fuka by dawn, when it was already too late.[3] Nevertheless, the British captured 20,000 Italian and 10,000 German prisoners.[4] In general,

Left: While Rommel will be remembered for his remarkable exploits during the desert war, he had another major challenge facing him as Germany readied its defences against the inevitable Allied invasion of France. Once again, lack of support and respect from his superiors and peers meant frustration for the Fox.

the British advance was clumsy and overly cautious. The armour's advance was slowed by a general fuel shortage, and it seemed that God was on Rommel's side. During the afternoon of 6 November, the desert experienced an unusual phenomenon, a massive downpour that created mudslides and transformed the dirt "roads" into mud-filled ditches. Rommel could escape. During the night of 7 November, the Axis troops left Mersa Matruh for Sidi Barrani without making more than a token stand. The RAF's deadly Desert Air Force, meanwhile, bombed Sollum and the Halfaya Pass.[5]

Torch: the Allied invasion of French North Africa

Meanwhile, the strategic situation for Rommel deteriorated further when the Allies sprang a nasty surprise on him by invading French North Africa. The USA had joined the Allied cause after Japan's surprise attack on Pearl Harbor in December 1941. It was in North Africa that the Germans were first to feel the presence of this new and dangerous foe. Since entering the war on the side of Great Britain and Russia, the Americans had poured an ever-increasing stream of supplies and arms into assisting her allies. Now, for the first time, American troops and arms would face the Germans in a head-on confrontation.

The Americans had wanted to launch an invasion of mainland Europe (Operation Sledgehammer), which had been discussed during Churchill's August 1941 meeting with Roosevelt in Newfoundland. Churchill believed Sledgehammer was premature and bound to fail. On 17 June 1942, Churchill's view prevailed and the Allies decided to invade French North Africa instead.[6]

Below: German soldiers, taken prisoner by Great Britain's Black Watch regiment, wait in the desert for their ride to captivity.

The European war hadn't seen the like. Some 500 warships and 350 transports had been collected to land the Anglo-American invasion army on the shores of Morocco and Algeria. Officially, the Vichy French leader, Marshal Pétain, had assured the Germans that his forces in North Africa, led by Admiral Jean Darlan, would resist the Allied landing. The Germans were sceptical and quite right to be suspicious, since Pétain had given orders for Darlan not to resist "too much".[7]

Above: Fighting on for a lost cause, MG34 machine gunners of Rommel's 21st Panzer Division.

On 8 November, General George Patton's Western Task Force (sailing direct from the USA) landed at Safi, Fedala and Mehdia. General Fredendall (Centre Task Force) landed at Oran, while the Eastern Task Force (General Ryder) landed at Algiers.[8] It was lucky for the Allied forces that it wasn't Rommel's veterans that were waiting for them at the beaches. Instead, the Allies faced poorly equipped and demoralized Vichy French troops. Patton, never a man to mince his words, was outraged at the bungling of his inexperienced troops and officers. He reserved his worst tongue-lashing for the US Navy's poor handling of the landings and fire support for his troops.

The Americans, who had expected a warm welcome as liberators by the French, were shocked to find themselves pinned down by fierce local French resistance at Oran and Mehdia.[9] But the show of Allied might, albeit rather

Below: Even the remainder of Rommel's troops, experienced in desert warfare, couldn't overcome the overwhelming number of Allied soldiers, tanks and aircraft once the US had joined the war. This is an observation post in Tunisia.

Above: German Junkers
Ju 52 military transport
aircraft cross the Mediterranean
with much-needed supplies
and reinforcements.

Below: Rommel's rival and joint
commander of Axis forces in
Tunisia, General von Armin (left).
The two men had a difficult
relationship that set back the Axis
defence of French North Africa.

feeble, impressed the French. On 9 November, Darlan ordered his forces to lay down their arms. The German response was predictably swift and ruthless. They began to occupy Tunisia and marched into the Vichy zone of metropolitan France on 11 November.[10]

Tunisia: bridgehead or deathtrap?

The Allied invasion had come as an unpleasant surprise to Hitler and the German high command. The Allies already controlled Morocco and Algeria, but Hitler was determined to hold Tunisia at all costs. Much was at stake. The fall of Vichy France and its colonies in North Africa heralded the inevitable collapse of Italy. If Tunisia fell to the Allies without a fight, not only would Rommel's army be trapped and forced to surrender, but the Allies would then invade Sicily. This would signal the fall of Mussolini, Italy's desertion from the war and the unravelling of the entire southern sector of Hitler's empire.[11]

On 25 November, General Nehring (who had served under Rommel) arrived in Tunisia to organize the tactical HQ of the newly established XC Army Corps. At the same time, black-painted Junker Ju 52s, flying in shuttle traffic between Sicily and the African shore, brought 1000 Axis troops a day into Tunisia. Hitler was truly determined to hold Tunisia. He was equally keen to avoid further disappointments such as Rommel, and decided to appoint two conventional German generals to command his new army.

For the Fifth Panzer Army, Lieutenant-General Heinz Ziegler would nominally serve under Colonel-General Jürgen von Arnim. He had served as commander of the XXXIXth Panzer Corps on the Eastern Front with an obstinate and unrelenting energy that must have endeared him to Hitler. Arnim, unlike Rommel, was a conservative, diehard Prussian Junker officer of the old school, who was to clash with the Desert Fox as soon as they clapped eyes on each other.[12]

When Ziegler and Arnim arrived by plane at Hitler's

Rastenburg HQ in East Prussia, Keitel told them that they would be lavishly provided with troops and tanks comprising three panzer divisions and three motorized divisions (including the élite *Hermann Göring* Division). Arnim, while sceptical about his precarious supply lines, believed that Tunisia was a viable bridgehead if he was given the supplies he needed. Ever the false optimist, Hitler assured Arnim he had nothing to worry about and that his supplies would be forthcoming.[13]

Nothing could have been further from the truth, as Hitler's decision was to be a military disaster possibly even greater than the setback at Stalingrad. Rommel wondered why this mass of material and troops had not been forthcoming at an earlier stage of the campaign, when it might have secured a German victory. Now, when it was too late, precious resources were poured into a lost front, simply to stave off the fall of Italy and a possible Allied presence on the mainland of Europe.

Countless troops were eventually sacrificed to hold the bridgehead. For Army Group Afrika, the writing was on the wall.[14] In fact, the outcome had become

Above: US troops landing in North Africa were well-equipped but extremely inexperienced, particularly in desert warfare.

Below: Rommel played a vital role in the defence of Tunisia, but was handicapped by lack of supplies and reinforcements.

inevitable right after El Alamein, and Rommel was quite right to try to save his army from complete annihilation.

The news, on 8 November, that the Allies had landed in North Africa made Rommel cancel plans for a stand at Halfaya Pass. He would instead make a stand at El Agheila, which was more defensible and allowed him to shorten his supply lines. The day after, Rommel abandoned Sidi Barrani, evacuated Halfaya on 11 November, and British advance forces entered Tobruk two days later. It was obvious by now that the British had failed to trap the DAK.[15] In fact, the German dash made the British even more cautious. Would not the Desert Fox, in his usual manner, spring a trap on them as they followed him westwards?

Montgomery set up a Special Pursuit Force, made up of the 7th Armoured Division and the New Zealand divisions. By this time, Rommel was reduced to some 5000 German and 2500 effective Italian combat troops in his rearguard.[16] He hoped that he could hold the advancing British at El Agheila, where the Wadi Faregh protected the flank; Italian-built field works dominated the hills; and the salt lakes made an approach difficult from Mersa Brega. Rommel ordered his troops to lay deep minefields between the stop lines to slow the British advance. The German sappers, short of mines, used tins and surplus helmets as decoys. These looked like mines when dug into the sand.

Below: February 1943, and soldiers of the 8th Field Squadron, Royal Engineers, probe the heavily mined Thala to Kasserine road.

Above: January 1943, and tanks of the Eighth Army roll through the tree-lined streets of Tripoli.

The British marched into Benghazi on 20 November, and Montgomery ordered the Eighth Army to halt in order to bring up supplies and reorganize his forces for the ultimate advance on Tripoli. Not for Montgomery a mad dash across the desert without a care for his supplies. Had Rommel been leading the Eighth Army things would have been different. As it was, Rommel and his tired troops were given a valuable respite of three weeks. It was not until 12 December that the British attacked again, and by dawn the Germans had abandoned Mersa Brega.

Two days later, the two New Zealand divisions made a sudden and most unexpected flanking attack at El Agheila, which caught Rommel off-guard. To prevent his forward echelons being encircled, Rommel ordered them to abandon what he had hoped would have been his holding position. It was a stunning and sudden reverse. To gain time, Rommel mustered his remaining panzers and launched a sudden counterattack against the 7th Armoured Division that was advancing along the coastal road. Although valuable time was gained, Rommel lost a fifth of his small and dwindling tank force.

During the following days (15–16 December), the British advance guard and the German rearguard clashed continuously along the coastal road, with the most important skirmish taking place at Merduma. By 17 December, the main part of Rommel's army had escaped, but fighting continued between the New

Zealanders and the Germans at Mersa Brega until 18 December. Thus, the battle for El Agheila had ended. Rommel had made a stand there only at the insistence of Hitler, who wanted his troops at all times to stand, fight and perish, rather than yield any territory.[17] Rommel noted, in private, that there was little hope of success as the DAK was short of everything and Bastico was deeply depressed about the overall situation.[18]

After the fall of El Agheila, Rommel's main task was to defend Tripoli. But Rommel and Hitler had very different ideas about how this was to be achieved. Hitler, to save his ally from embarrassment, and for reasons of political prestige, wanted to save as much Italian territory in Libya as possible. He therefore ordered Rommel to stand at Bouerat. This was a weak defence line without natural cover and could be outflanked from the south.

Rommel had found a better line between Homs and Tarhuna, which ran along the low-lying hills of Jebel Nafusa south of Tripoli. Here Rommel, courtesy of Montgomery's slow advance, could prepare fortified positions. Against his better judgement, Rommel again allowed himself to be persuaded by Hitler into making a futile stand – this time at Bouerat. It was the "stand fast" order of El Alamein all over again, and it could only have the same consequences for the DAK.

The fall of Tripoli

The British reached Sirte only on 21 December, and after heavy fighting took the town four days later.[19] Rommel and his fellow officers tried to hide any sign of depression, so that troop morale remained high. Nevertheless, the situation was hopeless and the high command's promises of support worthless. "They can't be kept because the enemy puts his pencil through all our supply calculations."[20] Rommel was far more worried about the situation at Stalingrad (which showed the way the fighting was heading on this important front),[21] and shared other Germans' fears about the direction the war was taking.

Again there was a lull in the fighting. At dawn on 15 January, the 7th Armoured Division broke through the German lines at Sirte and made a wide outflanking advance south towards Tarhuna. Fifteen hours later, the 51st Division attacked the German lines as a diversion. Rommel ordered his troops to fall back but, this time, Montgomery wasn't going to let the Fox escape so easily. He was determined, for once, not to let up and that the advance would continue both day and night. This would prevent Rommel from gaining time to prepare the defences of the Homs–Tarhuna line. The latter place fell to the 51st on 19 January. The road to Tripoli was now wide open, and despite Hitler's orders to hold the Libyan capital Rommel ordered the retreat to continue.

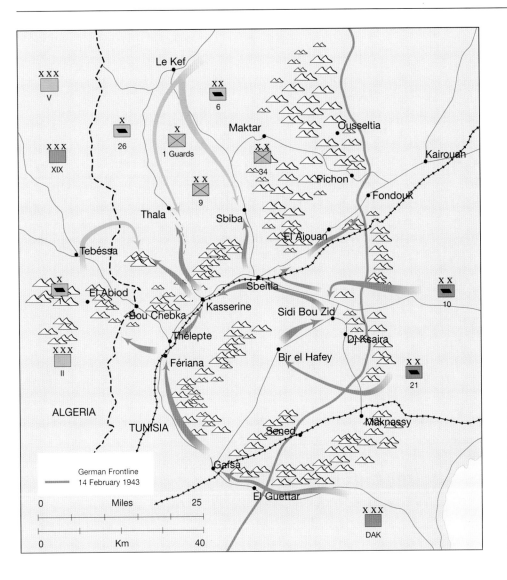

Le Kef

XXX V

XX 6

X 26

Maktar

Ousseltia

X 1 Guards

XXX XIX

Kairouan

X.X 34

Pichon

Fondouk

XX 9

Thala

Sbiba

El Aiouan

Tebéssa

Sbeitla

X El Abiod

Bou Chebka

Kasserine

Sidi Bou Zid

XX 10

Dj Ksaira

Thélepte

Bir el Hafey

XX 21

Fériana

XXX II

ALGERIA

Maknassy

TUNISIA

Sened

Gafsa

El Guettar

XXX DAK

German Frontline
14 February 1943

0   Miles   25

0   Km   40

Left: With the Eighth Army stretched out, Rommel decided that a concerted attack should be launched to relieve the Allied pressure on Tunisia. On 14 February 1943, Rommel launched two thrusts at the British and US lines. He achieved initial success at Kasserine, but was forced back by dogged resistance from the defenders.

Two years after O'Connor had hoped to reach it, the British finally marched into Tripoli on 23 January 1943, with bagpipes blaring, drums rolling and boots thumping. They had reached their final objective after a long and hard-fought campaign against their most determined foe. But they did not reach the Tunisian border until February because of fierce rearguard action by the DAK.[22]

Rommel fell back on Tunisia in the hope that his army could recover, recoup its losses and possibly call a halt to the Allied advance. In December 1942, the Allies had failed to take Tunis and dropped the ambitious plan to trap Rommel's army between General Anderson's First Army and Monty's Eighth Army. In fact, as Arnim's Fifth Panzer Army and Rommel's DAK came ever closer, the German position improved. First, the frontline the Germans needed to defend shrank. Second, they could coordinate their defences and counterattacks against an enemy whose supply lines were over-extended.

Rommel, an avid admirer of Napoleon, recognized that this position was ideal in order to strike and defeat his enemies, one by one. General Eisenhower, the Allied supreme commander, had very different ideas and wanted to launch Operation Satin, with his raw US troops, in order to capture Sfax and thus threaten Rommel's rear area.[23]

The Mareth Line

The Mareth Line in Tunisia, while nowhere near as famous or well fortified as the Maginot Line in France, had a certain allure to the Germans. Having retreated for months and across desert, the Axis troops would be glad to have a safe haven for a while and enjoy the luxury of prepared positions from which to fight. But this renowned "Maginot of the Desert" was a bluff. It had been built by the French (1934–39) to keep the Italians out of Tunisia, and extended from Jebel Dahar on the coast to Mareth. It consisted of a single row of concrete pillboxes and some barbed wire. That was all.[24]

Rommel wasn't impressed with the Mareth Line (he never had any confidence in concrete pillboxes and fixed defences) since it could be outflanked from the south should Montgomery be bold enough to try. Rommel wanted instead to fall back on Wadi Akarit, which was a natural, deep obstacle to any tank offensive and (unlike the Mareth) could not be outflanked since it was anchored deep in the desert at the massive salt marsh of Chott el Jerid.

Neither Mussolini nor Hitler liked the idea. As usual, the dictators wanted to fight for every yard of ground, and this time it was Mussolini who was most insistent. He was still smarting from the humiliation of seeing Tripoli fall, and he had fired Bastico and Cavallero to vent his spleen. Bastico was replaced by General Ambrosio.[25]

Having not been fired, unlike his hapless Italian colleagues, Rommel hoped to hold the Tunisian bridgehead indefinitely with 30,000 German and 48,000

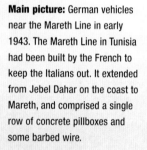

Main picture: German vehicles near the Mareth Line in early 1943. The Mareth Line in Tunisia had been built by the French to keep the Italians out. It extended from Jebel Dahar on the coast to Mareth, and comprised a single row of concrete pillboxes and some barbed wire.

Italian troops. He believed that Montgomery would advance only slowly and not until he had made his painstaking preparations. He was also sure that the Mareth Line would be enough to hold Montgomery while he dealt with the advancing Anglo-American army from Algeria. Thus, he would strike against the First Army before turning against the Eighth Army. Unfortunately, Rommel had only Colonel von Lieberstein's division to do the job, while the 21st Panzer Division had been transferred to Arnim's command.

By the beginning of February, there were 100,000 German and 26,000 Italian soldiers in Tunisia. But only three-quarters of these were combat troops, and the Axis forces had only 280 tanks. By contrast, the US 1st Armoured Division alone had 300 tanks, and the flow of supplies to both Allied armies was escalating.[26] As usual, it was Rommel's precarious and unsatisfactory supply situation that worried him the most, as well as the deplorable situation on the Eastern Front. On 20 January 1943 Rommel wrote to Lucie: "Paulus is perhaps even worse off than I am. He has a more inhuman enemy. We can only hope that God does not desert us altogether."[27]

The initiative was in the hands of Arnim, who made a series of attacks and probes against the Allied frontline during the latter part of January. On 31 January, the 21st Panzer Division (Colonel Hans Hildebrandt) had managed to capture Faid Pass as a springboard for an all-out onslaught on the First Army. By 1 February, Arnim held two key passes into Algeria, and it seemed that the combined Axis armies could defeat the Allies. But there was one fatal flaw in the command structure since Arnim was not subordinate to Rommel, and neither had any sympathy for the other.

Above: Rommel, centre, with Kesselring on the right. The two men held each other in great respect during the North African campaign.

Arnim, the quintessential Prussian officer, saw Rommel as a figure of Nazi propaganda and one of Hitler's stooges. Rommel saw Arnim as a conservative Prussian plodder of the worst sort, stodgy, slow and without imagination. Arnim refused to subordinate himself to Rommel and vice versa. To add to the confusion, the Italian First Army was under the independent command of General Giovanni Messe. Worst of all, Rommel was ill. He was suffering from insomnia and circulation problems. He hadn't, however, lost his sense of timing and judgement.

Rommel believed Arnim should strike from the Faid Pass, through Gafsa, against the Eastern Dorsale and towards Tebessa. In Rome, Rommel's offensive ideas were liked, and a reluctant Arnim – who refused to hand over his panzer divisions to Rommel – was prevailed upon to attack the US forces holding Tebessa and Gafsa.[28]

Rommel distrusted the Italians. In his opinion, they had no fight left in them and seemed quite defeatist. They would, he was sure, desert Germany at the last moment since, in his opinion, "people and nations don't change".[29] He couldn't pull the 15th Panzer Division from the Mareth if the DAK was to hold the line against Montgomery.

On 9 February, Kesselring flew to Tunisia to mediate between the squabbling generals. He made them agree that they would take the offensive with what they had against the Allied First Army's positions at Gafsa and Sidbour Zid.[30] But nothing had been resolved, since Rommel and Arnim's dislike of each other and refusal to cooperate continued. This on-going conflict was to have a devastating effect on the outcome of the German counteroffensive, and be one of the main reasons for its ultimate failure.

Conditions on the Allied side were far worse than the Axis could have imagined, preoccupied as they were with their own problems. The American forces, while well-equipped and lavishly supplied, were deficient in combat experience and were therefore completely unprepared to face Rommel's tough desert veterans. The British were in no better shape, but they played a subordinate role in what was a mainly American-run operation. The French forces were poorly equipped and led by an officer corps tainted with Vichy service and devoid of expertise in modern warfare. Pure French and native North African courage was no compensation for inexperience and obsolete equipment. What made matters worse was the choice of commanders.

To head the incongruous First Army Eisenhower had picked (probably to soothe Churchill) a dour and uninspiring Scotsman, General Kenneth Anderson, who did not have much sympathy for his allies. The French weren't pleased, to put it mildly, at being under British command. French feelings were still brittle from what they saw as British betrayals at Dunkirk, Dakar and Oran. The commander of the US II Corps, Major-General Lloyd R. Fredendall, had nothing but contempt for his French counterparts, but nevertheless shared their dislike for the British commander.[31] Even if Rommel and his veterans hadn't been exceptionally good, it seemed the Allies would be easy meat.

The Battle of Kasserine Pass: Rommel's lesson learnt

On 12 February 1943, Stukas bombed the village of Sidi bou Zid while Battle Group (Kampfgruppe) Gebhardt swept aside all opposition. The Arab and French civilian population fled towards the Algerian border. Rommel had a bold plan. If Arnim struck hard and fast through the lines, then he could converge with Rommel's forces from the south. Together they would advance behind the Allied lines and capture all of eastern Algeria, including the strategic port of Constantine. As in France in 1940, and in the desert a year later, once the Allies were on the run they could be kept off-balance until they were completely defeated. This might turn the tide in Germany's favour yet again.

Arnim refused to transfer the 21st Panzer Division to support Rommel's attack against Tebessa. This was most unfortunate since its crews were experienced veterans and had been equipped with the new and formidable heavy Tiger tanks.[32] Rome, liking Rommel's bold strategy, backed him against

Below: German paratroopers march through Tunis during their futile quest to keep the Allies out of French North Africa.

Arnim and transferred the panzers and Messe's army to Rommel's command on 19 February. Despite direct orders to effect the transfer, Arnim claimed the Tigers were being repaired – and they remained outside Rommel's command.[33]

That day, Rommel received Rome's orders to attack. Rommel ordered the 21st Panzer Division against Sbiba and Ksour, supported by the DAK Assault Group, while the 10th Panzer Division would attack Sbeitla. The French commander, General Welvert, organized a defence line with French and US troops. Rommel noted that while the Americans were clumsy and inexperienced they also had an alarming ability to learn fast and hit back hard. It was like Tobruk again since Hildebrandt (21st Panzers) failed to break through Welvert's defence line of artillery and minefields. Further attacks were called off, and preparations were made overnight for a new assault the next morning. Rommel also switched his attention to the Kasserine Pass.[34]

Kasserine – last victory in Africa

Kasserine is a typical small Arab village nestling in the foothills of the Atlas Mountains some 32km (20 miles) southwest of Sbeitla on a flat, arid and rock-strewn plain covered with cacti. Flowing through the middle of the plain is the River Hatab. The pass itself is narrow and squeezed between two mountains. There had been no time for the Allies to lay mines so these were simply lying on the surface. The pass was held by 4000 American and French troops supported by howitzers and 75mm guns.

On 18 February, Rommel had sent forward reconnaissance patrols into the pass – some of the jittery and green US troops fled at the mere sight of the Germans. During the morning, Colonel Alexander N. Stark ("Old Stark") arrived at the pass to keep the troops in line and provide much-needed leadership. Heavy rain turned the ground into a quagmire, and the mist obscured vision. Despite this, the 8th Panzer Regiment drove the French troops from the mountains. The DAK Assault Group, led by Colonel Karl Bülowis, made an unsuccessful attack in the afternoon. He was driven back by heavy US artillery fire. By dusk the pass was still in Allied hands.

The Americans had overcome their initial nervousness and were now fighting back. But German troops were infiltrating the American positions, and this sowed seeds of confusion among the Allied units. While the engineers (19th Engineering Regiment) held fast, the artillery wasn't particularly good. In contrast, the French artillery kept up remorseless fire against the advancing Germans. Nevertheless, Allied defences along the Thala road collapsed.

Rommel was now awaiting only the arrival of the 10th Panzer Division (General Freiherr Fritz von Broich), which would attack towards Thala while

Bülowis moved against Tebessa. Only the advance guard of the 10th Panzer had arrived, and Rommel was now aware that Montgomery's forces were advancing to attack the Mareth. Furthermore, Arnim still hadn't transferred his 24 Tiger tanks, while the Allies made the defences of the pass ever stronger. Rommel ordered the only Italian troops he trusted, the Bersaglieri, to attack.[35]

The 20th of February was not a good day for Rommel. The Bersaglieri, even with the support of the DAK Assault Group, were stopped on the Thala road by Gore Force, and the Axis commanders were sharply reprimanded by Rommel for the slowness of the advance. Meanwhile, Bülowis had made substantial headway on the Tebessa road, while the 10th Panzer Division captured Kasserine village. Rommel arrived at Sbiba, where he found Hildebrandt's troops pinned down by heavy enemy artillery fire. Rommel returned to Kasserine Pass, where he received the ominous news that Montgomery had finally reached the Mareth.

For three days the Allied troops had held out despite mounting German artillery and tank fire. Finally, Gore Force broke when its commander was killed, and on Saturday 21 February the whole of Kasserine Pass was in German hands. That morning, Rommel ordered Broich to attack Thala and Bülowis to deal with the Allies at Jebel Hamra. Rommel counted on the two commanders being able to support each other. But the peevish Arnim had, despite Kesselring's constant badgering, still not handed over his tank forces to Rommel, and this prevented Rommel from making a double-pronged attack following the fall of the pass. Instead, he decided to concentrate his forces against Thala and aim for Le Kef.

It was late afternoon when Hildebrandt, reinforced by the 10th Panzers, attacked Jebel Hamra. The 10th Panzers took 571 prisoners, 28 guns and destroyed 38 tanks. The Allies had been defeated in less than a week. Rommel's reputation, tarnished by El Alamein, soared. Kesselring, in Rome, recommended that the Desert Fox be given full command of the African theatre.[36]

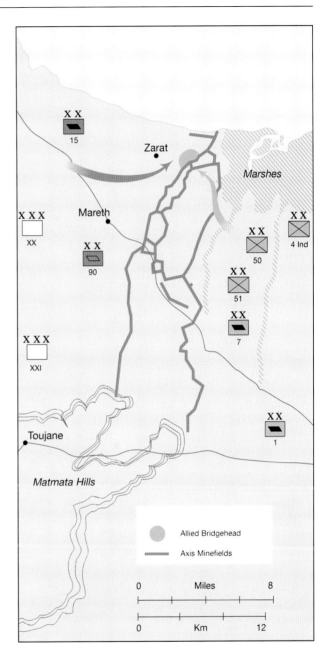

Above: The breaking of the Mareth Line in March 1943 was Rommel's last battle in North Africa. He was recalled to Europe days after his forces has been driven back by Montgomery's advances, though the Axis units were able to disengage without suffering a massive defeat.

Rommel had no illusions about the final outcome of this uneven battle, as the Allies would soon gain enough in experience to counterattack. With their growing material superiority, they could then crush the Axis armies in Tunisia. The massive Allied use of artillery and their growing strength convinced Rommel that they were preparing a counterattack at the earliest opportunity.

Bülowis, bogged down by heavy rain, missed Jebel Hamra, and the Allies began to recover from their earlier disarray. The battle tipped in their favour and Rommel, already impressed with US equipment, was astonished at how quickly the Americans could reinforce and re-supply their frontline units.

On 22 February, the weather cleared. Despite the Allies having only one minor airfield (Youks les Bains) near the frontline, they launched a series of savage air strikes against the Axis lines. The Allied forces going on the offensive had even taken a few Italian and German prisoners by that evening. Rommel was convinced more than ever that the Axis forces would be defeated by the Allied superiority in troop numbers and material. He also believed that the over-extended frontline was an open invitation to the Allies to attack.

Rommel, physically in poor shape and also deeply depressed, gave permission for Broich to break off his attack, and reported his misgivings to Kesselring. On 23 February, Rommel handed back command of the Axis armies to Arnim and Messe. The following day, the Germans pulled out of Kasserine Pass – that same evening, the pass was back in Allied hands.

By that time, Rommel had returned to the threatened Axis position along the Mareth.[37] Thus, the last German throw of the dice in Africa had landed and they had lost. The campaign might have succeeded had Rommel been sole commander on the spot and had his plan of attack been adhered to. Then the US airfields and supply dumps would have been captured.[38] The Americans, like the British in

Below: Rommel's most effective tank during the bulk of the desert war was the Panzer IV with the long-barrelled 75mm main gun.

1941–42, would have been severely mauled by the Fox's offensives.

It was just as well that Rommel returned to command what was left of his forces along the Mareth. He had weak Italian divisions holding the line itself; and behind them some 10,000 German infantry, 200 guns and 160 tanks, being the combined strength of three panzer divisions (10th, 15th and 21st).[39] This shows how his forces had shrunk, but it was nothing short of a miracle that he had even these available. Montgomery had only one division at Medenine and, fearing that Rommel was preparing some trick, rushed reinforcements

there – the 2nd New Zealand Division, the 201st Guards Brigade and the 8th Armoured Brigade.

By 3 March, Montgomery had completed his defences at Medenine. Rommel was quite ill and depressed by now. His preparations for the attack on Medenine were not up to his usual meticulous standards, and failure resulted. His exhortations to his troops carried little conviction. Neither he, nor his staff, had much confidence in the plan drawn up, and he was forced to attack along a broad front from three separate directions.

Above: Infantry from the British Eighth Army move through a wired section of the Mareth Line during March 1943.

Below: The Kasserine Pass in Tunisia, 14 February 1943. Rommel initially had great success here, but was eventually overwhelmed by the Allies.

Above: Some of the Axis soldiers taken prisoner during the fighting on the Mareth line in April 1943.

Main picture: The arrival of the Americans in the North African theatre of war made a huge difference. Here, US tanks support British infantry.

On the early morning of 6 March, a combined assault by Stukas and Nebelwerfer rocket launchers hit the British lines. At 09:00 hours, the German tanks attacked in massed formation and managed to reach the British lines unmolested until the British artillery opened devastating point-blank fire against the advancing Germans. The infantry fell back, leaving the tanks at the mercy of the British anti-tank guns. The British had copied and perfected Rommel's own tactics to deadly effect. Three hours later, the offensive was winding down; and Rommel, having failed to command and direct his panzer commanders up close, was forced to call a halt to proceedings.

At 15:30 hours, a new attack was launched with the infantry in the lead, supported by artillery and Stukas, while the panzers moved discretely behind the troops. This attack was stopped in its tracks by intensive British artillery fire. By the evening, the German force was in full and disorganized retreat. Had Montgomery shown greater aggression, Rommel's forces would have been pulverized. But Monty chose not to pursue his defeated enemy, and continued his methodical advance on the Mareth Line.[10]

For Rommel the battle for Africa was now at an end. His last offensive had failed, and he had lost 52 out of 150 precious panzers. The question now was when, and under what circumstances, the Axis troops would be forced to capitulate. Rommel was saved this ultimate humiliation and disaster. He was too precious a symbol of former victories, and his reputation had to be saved.

On 9 March, Rommel handed over all his command responsibilities to Arnim, and took well-earned sick leave in the Fatherland. On his way back home, he stopped off in Rome to persuade Il Duce that Tunisia was lost and that the Axis armies should be pulled out.[11]

The battle for Tunisia continued for another two hard-fought and desperate months. On 12 May 1943, Arnim capitulated to General Alexander. The following day, Messe – promoted to field marshal by Mussolini – followed suit. Some quarter of a million Axis troops now became prisoners to no purpose, when Hitler and Mussolini might have saved them to fight another day.[12] In terms of troops and equipment lost, it was another Stalingrad.

An inglorious interlude: Rommel deals with Italy (May–November 1943)

It took Rommel until May 1943 to recover. His poor state of health and depression no doubt reflected a far greater ill, namely the state of Germany and her armed forces in early 1943. Her manpower resources had peaked, and even then the country kept some 900,000 troops (a third of the total number on the Eastern Front) in Germany to man 20,000 anti-aircraft guns against Allied bombing raids.

On 9 May, Hitler met Rommel at his HQ. They discussed Africa, and Hitler, for once candid and honest, admitted that he should have listened to Rommel all along. He also admitted that Rommel was right about the Italians, whose army was no good. While he trusted Mussolini's loyalty, that did not extend to any other figures in his Fascist regime. Constantin von Neurath, Hitler's advisor on foreign affairs, was aware of the intrigues in Rome but his statements about the realities of Mussolini's ramshackle regime did not suit an angry Foreign Minister Ribbentrop. Neurath told Rommel that Ribbentrop was without doubt the greatest idiot in the entire Reich when it came to foreign affairs – notwithstanding that Ribbentrop was Hitler's foreign minister. No doubt Rommel agreed.

Above: Even Germany's most powerful tank, the Tiger, had an unhappy time in Tunisia.

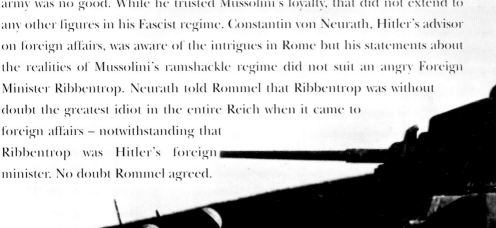

During the next two months, Rommel stayed at Hitler's side in the hope of being given a new command. Rommel, who had stated openly to his staff after El Alamein that only the removal of Hitler would save Germany from disaster, was yet again under his Führer's spell.[13] In July 1943, Rommel chanced on Manstein, and told him with no small amount of sarcasm that, "I am here for a sunray cure. I am soaking up sun and faith."[14] But Rommel had not lost his wits or his honest bluntness, even with Hitler. He was convinced that Germany had lost the war, and Hitler appeared to listen to his favourite commander's views. He even told Rommel that nobody would make peace with him even if he had wanted to negotiate. Rommel, a practical and realistic man of action, was shocked by Hitler's lack of realism and his suicidal fatalism. He told Lucie in strictest confidence that Hitler, in his opinion, was no longer quite "normal".[15]

Rommel, who hated to be inactive, was given command of the German forces stationed in Austria with the task of infiltrating troops into northern Italy. Luckily, Rommel had trusted old DAK veterans such as Gause and von Bonin serving under him. Rommel was also charged with the disarmament of the Italian armed forces (Operation Alaric) should Mussolini be toppled.

In Sicily, XIV Panzer Corps (some 70,000 troops) under General Hube conducted a well-fought defensive campaign against the invading Allied armies. But with Italy wobbling badly, as Mussolini lost control over the domestic

Below: German Tiger I tanks in Italy during the Nazi takeover of the country in September 1943.

situation, XIV Corps was in a very precarious and exposed position. On 15 July, Rommel was appointed to command Army Group B, and he flew to Saloniki in northern Greece.

On 25 July, at a meeting in Rome, the fate of Mussolini was decided. A vote of no confidence in Il Duce was passed. By some 18 votes out of 28, including that of his son-in-law, Count Ciano, Mussolini's 20-year dictatorship was at an end. Marshal Badoglio took over. No German, especially Hitler and Rommel, believed for one moment in Badoglio's goodwill and honesty. German intelligence knew that the Italians had treacherous contacts with Eisenhower, and that it was only a question of time until Italy laid down her arms.

On 30 July, German troops, under orders from Rommel to enter Italy in the spirit of a good "ally", began to occupy all strategic points and passes into the northern part of the country – economically, the most important part of Italy. Rommel suggested that the southern part of the country should not be defended but a series of defensive lines be constructed across central Italy – at Salerno, Cassino and the Appenines. On 15 August, Rommel, accompanied by Hitler's military henchman, General Alfred Jodl, flew to Bologna, where they had a mutually hostile and suspicious meeting with the Italian high command represented by General Roatta. Despite his reputation as an Italian hater, and in the face of ineffective Italian protests, Rommel set up his HQ at Lake Garda.

Below: September 1943, and *Ariete* troops at Bracciano, near Rome, applaud Badoglio's radio broadcast of an armistice.

The Allies began landing in Calabria on 3 September, and five days later – to the rapturous applause and support of the Italian populace – Radio Rome announced in its morning broadcast that Italy had signed an armistice with the Allies. At 10:00 hours, orders were radioed from Hitler's HQ to begin Operation Achse, the occupation of Italy. Rommel had eight divisions and began immediately to disarm the Italians. The following morning, 9 September, the Allies landed at Salerno. Ten days later, Rommel could report that he had bagged 82 Italian generals, 13,000 officers and 430,000 troops.

By now the Tenth Army (six divisions) was holding the line south of Rome and at Salerno; and on 23 September Rommel dropped the pretence of friendship by ordering his troops to treat the Italians as enemies.[16]

Rommel was not cut out to be a harsh occupation commandant: he stopped suspected saboteurs being shot, and punished those troops that mistreated Italians and Jews, while showing his dislike of the Fascists. In October, Rommel had a final meeting with Mussolini at Garda. It was with few regrets that Rommel departed the country on 21 November. He thus left the entire Mediterranean Front, which had been his military home for more than two years. He was never to see its blue waters again.[17]

Yet again, a well-timed departure had saved his personal honour and military standing for posterity. Rommel had performed an essentially non-military task to perfection, which no doubt saved the Germans from a potentially great disaster. But he was fortunate that his old sparring partner, Kesselring, took over the command of the Italian Front. Defensive and positional warfare was to be Kesselring's masterpiece, and this was not a task at which Rommel, the panzer general, excelled.

Preparations for the last stand: Rommel in France (1944)

Hitler could not afford to keep a commander of Rommel's experience and brilliance unemployed for too long. Sooner or later, as 1943 drew to a close, the Allies would cross the English Channel and invade France. Here was a task that suited Rommel down to the ground: to prepare defences, make plans for a counterattack and defeat the Allied invasion. In November 1943, Rommel was appointed Inspector General of Atlantic Coast Defences from Holland in the north to the Spanish frontier in the south.[18]

Rommel was under the nominal leadership of his former campaign commander Field Marshal Gerd von Rundstedt who, as a stalwart Prussian officer, shared many of the prejudices about Rommel. To Rundstedt's utter relief, he found that all his ideas regarding the Fox's Nazi sympathies and ardent Hitler worship were wrong.

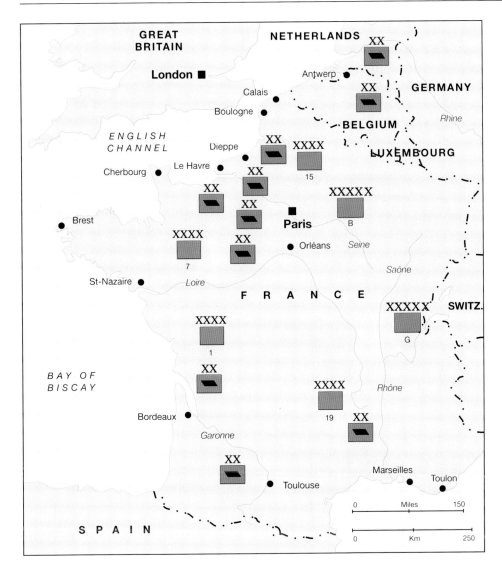

Left: The disposition of German armies and panzer divisions on the eve of the Allied invasion of Normandy. Rommel tried his best to prepare the defences for imminent attack, but had too little time to finish the task. His proposed plans were sound, but due to Hitler's interference and lack of time they were never carried out as Rommel would have wished.

In fact, Rundstedt found Rommel to be exceptionally courageous, loyal, honest and honourable. In short, a man who could be trusted. Furthermore, his direct access to Hitler would come in handy should problems arise. Rundstedt, in contrast to Rommel, had never been more than a token supporter of the Nazis and had the deepest contempt for Hitler, whom he dismissed as "that Bohemian Corporal".[19]

Having had a year in which to recover his health, Rommel was delighted to be given a new command and a job that he felt was important. He focused completely on the task at hand. He was back to his former glory days as he returned to the routines of that campaign. He ate simple meals from the canteen, did not waste his time with bureaucracy and did more work in weeks than his colleagues had done in years. On 15 January 1944, Rommel was appointed commander of Army Group B. His first Order of the Day was for the erection of shore defences. This work had been on the cards for years under the unenthusiastic control of High Command West. Now it was to be given the highest priority and the work begun as quickly as possible.

After giving the orders for construction to begin, Rommel set out on an extensive tour of inspection that stretched from Holland in the north to the Somme River in the south. He admonished his commanders for the poor coordination between the different arms, and was shocked at the poor state of the coastal artillery. Outside the main ports there were hardly any fortifications at all.[50] The fortification of the coast was now urgent as, on 8 January, German intelligence in Ankara had picked up information about an Allied operation called Overlock to invade western Europe during the spring of 1944. A month later, the Germans knew that the operation was called Overlord and that there were only two possible areas where the Allies could land, Normandy or the Pas de Calais. They also knew that the Allies would land between May and August 1944.[51]

The Germans were divided about which area would be invaded and what would be the best response to an invasion. Rommel, like Hitler, did not believe that the Allies would choose the obvious route across the Pas de Calais but would land in the more distant region of Normandy. Rommel wanted to concentrate all his panzer units as close to the coast as possible. He believed, correctly, that once the battle started the tanks would be unable to move during daytime due to the overwhelming airpower of the Allies.

Rundstedt disagreed completely with Rommel's analysis. He believed the Allies would land along the Pas de Calais, and that the panzers should be concentrated far inland to deliver a massive counterstroke that would throw the Allies back into the Channel. Rundstedt's view was shared by none other than Guderian, the tank genius of the 1940–41 campaigns.

Below: Rommel on an inspection tour of the Atlantic Wall defences in early 1944.

Guderian was shocked by Rommel's ideas, and on his return from an inspection of the "Atlantic Wall" defences he protested to Hitler about them. Hitler asked Guderian to return to Rommel's HQ at La Roche Gayon[52] and discuss the matter. He did so, but Rommel would not budge. He told Guderian that the Allied landing would come in Normandy, and that it had to be destroyed on the beaches before the Allies had a chance to consolidate a bridgehead since their airpower

made it impossible for the Germans to conduct a battle of mobility.[53]

Only time could vindicate Rommel's views. The problem was that he did not possess enough aircraft to send on spying missions above England to find out where the Allies were amassing the invasion army. Neither had German intelligence been able to penetrate Great Britain and find out whether Patton's Army Group, supposedly stationed in East Anglia for an attack against the Pas de Calais, was a bluff or not. In effect, the Germans were blind.[54]

There were a mere five divisions holding 400km (250 miles) of coastline.[55] There was some consolation for Rommel as these troops were hardened Eastern Front veterans who would fight back with all the ferocity they had learnt in Russia. It was also fortunate that General Dollmann (Seventh Army) and General Marcks (commanding the troops in Normandy) shared Rommel's ideas

Top: A string of reinforced bunkers was built to provide shelter for machine gunners and to keep the Allies off the French beaches.

Above: Rommel struggled to find labour for the construction of trenches and fortifications.

about how to tackle an invasion. This didn't apply to the commander in Holland who, as late as March 1944, reported that nothing had yet been done about coastal defences. He was reprimanded, and so were the troops that had been put to work on the fortifications but showed no sense of urgency.

As in the desert, Rommel was travelling all the time, inspecting, inspiring, cajoling and reprimanding his subordinates. He gave any commander whose quota of mines had not been fulfilled a tongue-lashing that they would never forget.[56]

Meanwhile, the arguments continued to rumble on between Rommel and his opponents in high command and at the frontline. Hitler was convinced that the Allies would invade Normandy, since they had concentrated their troops in southwest England. But he had a nagging fear that they might stage a second, and even more powerful, invasion against the Pas de Calais. Unfortunately for Rommel, the commander of Panzer Group West, General Geyr von Schweppenburg, shared Rundstedt's and Guderian's view and managed to convince Hitler to keep the five panzer divisions in northern France[57] close to Paris. This was entirely against Rommel's recommendation, and would prove, when the invasion came, to be one of the main reasons why the Germans failed to crush the Allied landing in Normandy.

Below: Rommel with SS-General Sepp Dietrich, commander of the 1st SS-Panzer Division.

Neither the naval forces (60 vessels) nor Luftflotte III (400 aircraft) were strong enough to repel or inflict serious damage on the Allied invasion army. Rommel persisted in his views, and while Hitler shared many of them he chose disastrously to compromise and thus ensured that the German forces were spread too thinly trying to defend too many points on the coast.[58]

Forbidden to fly by Hitler, because of the risk of being shot down, Rommel was forced to take the train to Berchtesgaden and here, on 19–20 March, he had an important conference with Hitler. Rommel wanted to get command over the panzers so that he could move the 21st Panzer Division closer to Normandy and the 10th SS Panzer Division north of the Seine to support the Pas de Calais area. Hitler, in his usual fashion, dithered and would not hand over control to the one man who knew how to command massed tank formations.[59]

Rommel continued with his own plans, and drove his men to exhaustion by building obstacles, bunkers, firing points, artillery positions and trenches wherever the terrain was suitable. Many of the underwater obstacles that were constructed and erected on the beaches were Rommel's own ideas, and built according to his wishes. He planned to sow some 50 million mines on the beaches: in fact, only six million were ever laid.

He cancelled Rundstedt's plans for a second line of defences, and concentrated everything on the beaches. Rommel believed that the battle for western Europe would be won or lost during the first day of the landings right there on the beaches of Normandy. It was not only sabotage by the resistance movements, Allied bombings and an acute shortage of labour that wrecked Rommel's plans, but also Göring's refusal to cooperate. Göring had 300,000 useless ground troops and 50,000 communication soldiers that Rommel wanted to employ in building coastal fortifications. For reasons of prestige and pride, Göring refused to allow his men to be used in such menial tasks and he also refused to give Rommel command over his artillery forces in France.[60]

The German command in the west would be divided and confused when the Allies struck. In addition, Rommel was hampered by the lack of support from his subordinate commanders. He also had no control over much of the coastal artillery or the air support (due to Göring's sabotage). Worst of all, the tanks

Above: The commander of Panzer Group West, General Geyr von Schweppenburg, disagreed with Rommel's view about the landing site for the Allied invasion.

Above: German dead and their equipment litter a courtyard in the bitterly defended Fort du Roule after Cherbourg had fallen to US forces in late June 1944.

remained outside his immediate control due to Schweppenburg's opposition. Nevertheless, during the six to eight months he had been given, Rommel had improved considerably the defences in the West.

He had command over 43 of the 60 divisions in the West, and he had placed six divisions in Normandy. Of these, the 352nd, 709th and 716th Infantry Divisions were right on the invasion beaches. Crucially, Rommel had managed to move the 21st Panzer Division to Caen, and three of Schweppenburg's panzer divisions closer to Normandy.[61] It was now just a matter of watching and waiting until the Allies struck.

Rommel's military logic convinced him that the Allies would strike at dawn, when weather and the tide were favourable. Judging a landing to be, for the moment, out of the question, Rommel travelled back to his villa in Herrlingen to celebrate Lucie's 50th birthday. He was sure that the Allies would not strike in such foul weather conditions. He was wrong.

Invasion: D-Day (6 June 1944)

The 6th of June was Lucie's birthday, and Rommel had set this day aside for rest, relaxation and spending time with his neglected family. How different it turned out to be. At around 07:30 hours the telephone rang. It was

Below: A US infantryman heading for Cherbourg stays low to avoid sniper bullets and splinters from shellfire.

Left: Summer 1944, and German Tiger I tanks are on the move to take on the Allies.

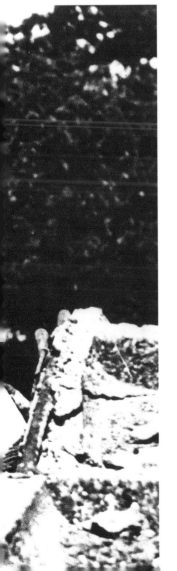

General Speidel, his chief of staff, who reported that Allied paratroopers had landed in Normandy. When he called back an hour later, a serious Speidel confirmed Rommel's worst fears. This was the invasion. Wave after wave of Allied troops waded ashore in Normandy while the paratroopers, flown in during the night and early morning, had created pockets deep behind the Allied beachhead. As at El Alamein, Rommel was absent from the front when the enemy struck. By the time he reached the frontline, 100,000 Allied troops were ashore on the continent of Europe.[62] Germany had a second front, and defeat was staring the Reich in the face.

Rommel's absence was an unmitigated disaster for the Germans. Had he been at his HQ, he could have cut through the Gordian knots of the German military bureaucracy. Had he led, in person, the available panzer divisions in a concentrated counterattack, then the Allies might have been defeated, crushed and thrown back into the Channel during the first 48 hours of the invasion. As it was, there was no one to lead the panzers or the infantry on the beaches, and no one to prevent the Allies establishing a bridgehead in Normandy.

An example of this confusion and lack of leadership was the failure to send the 21st Panzer Division from Caen to the beaches during the first half of D-Day. It would have taken only hours to move the tanks against the British. When Rommel heard of this, he exploded and ordered Speidel, on the phone, to "get the division moving into the attack right now! Don't await further reinforcements; attack at once!"

Only the courageous General Marcks, directing the tanks from his BMW, led in person an attack from Caen against the Allies. But Feuchtinger (commander of the 21st) failed to provide leadership and cancelled the attack. When Colonel Bodo Zimmerman, of Rundstedt's staff, was asked what had been done, he said, "So far, a load of shit. Feuchtinger took to his heels".[63]

Driving at breakneck speed across Germany and France, Rommel was back at his HQ at La Roche Gayon by 10:00 hours on 6 June. He looked grim but determined. Since the landings, his troops had inflicted 10,000 casualties on the enemy. However, the Allied forces had managed, disastrously, to establish a 130-square-kilometre (80-square-mile) bridgehead with 155,000 troops. The invasion would clearly succeed unless Rommel could activate the panzers and strike back as quickly as possible.

Rommel wanted the 21st Panzer Division and 12th SS Panzer Division, under SS-General Sepp Dietrich, to combine and attack the vulnerable Allied frontline during the morning of 7 June. But Dietrich got cold feet and postponed the offensive. This reflected a strange German complacency, both among the civilian population back home and among the military, that the Allies had stuck their heads in a noose.

Rommel did not share this view. He reprimanded Dietrich for his lacklustre leadership, but it was obvious that Allied airpower was overwhelming. Panzer Lehr (one of Rommel's more powerful tank divisions) lost through aerial attacks alone some five tanks, 85 armoured vehicles and 123 trucks. The 21st

Below: Fighting was particularly fierce in the Saint Lô sector, which Rommel visited on 13 July, reporting that the situation was desperate.

Panzer Division was reduced to a mere 55 tanks.[64] Rommel's fears about Allied airpower had been vindicated, as had his concern that the battle would be lost or won on the beaches. Since the Allies had been able to establish a beachhead, the battle was already lost.

Battle for the beachhead (8–24 June)

By 8 June, the British and American beachhead had been joined and the Americans were aiming to take Cherbourg and the entire Contentin Peninsula on which this strategic port stands. Unfortunately, Rommel, given faulty intelligence, believed there would be a second landing at the Pas de Calais by

Above: An American task force, complete with Sherman tank, advances warily through the main street of Saint Lô. The town fell in July after an eight-day siege.

Patton's First US Army Group supposedly stationed in East Anglia. As a result, no troops were moved from the Fifteenth Army area to Normandy where they were needed if Rommel was to succeed in throwing the Allies back into the sea.

The Germans had battle-hardened infantry (mostly in their thirties) while the tank crews were teenage boys and young men in their twenties. The latter were quite skilled, fearless and had superb machines in the mammoth Tigers and Panthers. The tank battles, such as those around the village of Lingèries on 9 June, were short, sharp affairs, with the tanks firing at each other at short range.

Rommel spent that day at the Le Mans HQ of the Seventh Army. Unfortunately, Hitler believed a rumour that the Pas de Calais was about to be attacked. He therefore withdrew Rommel's most powerful panzer division, the 1st SS Panzer with 21,000 troops, to Belgium to counter this "threat". The Americans broke out from Sainte-Mére-Eglise and began their offensive against Cherbourg.

By 10 June, Rommel, despite having a four-to-one superiority in tanks, had still not launched his counterattack. The following day, Schweppenburg, who believed that his tank forces could be concentrated for a big strike, had a deadly demonstration of Allied airpower. US bombers attacked his HQ, killing his entire staff. By some miracle, the general escaped unscathed. In speaking with his naval commander, Admiral Ruge, Rommel believed it was time to reach a compromise peace with the Allies before it was too late. There were further setbacks that day. Carentan was abandoned, and General Marcks, Rommel's most competent and courageous commander, was killed by an Allied fighter.[65]

Rommel wanted to concentrate all available forces for a major drive against the Americans on the southern tip of the Contentin Peninsula before they reached Cherbourg. Hitler wanted Rommel to strike against the British instead,

Above: A German Tiger I tank that fought to the bitter end amidst the devastation.

on 12 June. Rommel grew more pessimistic and still believed that the Pas de Calais might be attacked. Hitler feared his favourite general was showing signs of defeatism, and invited him to his Soissons HQ on 17 June. Rommel briefed Hitler on the situation, and praised his young troops for fighting "like tigers". He warned that courage was no compensation for reinforcements and supplies.

Rommel wanted to save his troops in the peninsula, and he got Rundstedt's support for pulling them out. Hitler agreed to a withdrawal in return for Cherbourg being held until the middle of July. While Rommel and Hitler were taking shelter during an air-raid warning, they talked further. Rommel asked that Hitler use diplomacy and find a political solution to a military situation that was getting out of hand. Hitler was taken aback and snapped at Rommel: "That is a matter which is no concern of yours. You must leave that to me."[66] This was the beginning of the end of the remarkable relationship between Hitler and his foremost commander. Rommel grew ever more disillusioned with the Führer who, for his part, began to distrust Rommel.

On 18 June, the German troops on the Contentin Peninsula were cut off from the rest of Rommel's armies. At least Rommel managed to save the 77th Infantry Division. Four days later the situation at Cherbourg, which was held by three shattered and weak divisions, was desperate. On 24 June, Panzer Lehr lost 2600 troops in a battle that seemed ever more hopeless in the face of Allied numerical superiority. Rommel and Ruge spoke again about the need to remove Hitler from power before it was too late to seek a political solution to Germany's problems. Cherbourg fell the following day, and Rommel was deeply depressed by the news. Dollmann, the commander of the Seventh Army, committed suicide. Rommel ordered that his death be ascribed to battle wounds, and that he receive a state funeral in Paris. Little did he know that he was to suffer the same fate a few months later, with a covered-up suicide and a state funeral.[67]

The battle of Normandy (25 June–17 July): a last victory and near death

The end of June and beginning of July was an eventful period in Rommel's career. On 28 June, he attended a conference with Hitler at Berchtesgaden. When he tried to look at the overall strategic situation, a furious Hitler cut him short and ordered him to return to a strictly military report on the situation in Normandy. Rommel complied but returned, yet again, to the strategic-political state of Germany. This time, Hitler was so infuriated that he asked Rommel to leave the conference room. He was not asked back, and left the day after without having been reconciled with Hitler.

That day, Montgomery's tank forces mauled Dietrich's SS panzers around Caen. Rommel, back in Normandy, received another "stand or die" order from Hitler to hold Caen at all costs. Schweppenburg was now replaced by General Heinrich Eberbach as commander of Panzer Group West. But an even greater shock was the news, on 2 July, that Rundstedt had been fired and replaced, not by Rommel but by Field Marshal Günther Hans von Kluge, as General Commander-in-Chief West. "Clever Hans", as he was known to his troops and admirers, arrived at Rommel's HQ on 3 July. Kluge was a thoroughbred Prussian Junker of the most arrogant kind. He was harsh, unyielding, uncompromising, yet resourceful and courageous.

Kluge had been a successful commander on the Eastern Front. Rommel hated him on sight, and the feeling was mutual. Kluge had the nerve to tell Rommel that he had been allowed too much independence and that Kluge, unlike Rundstedt, would require Rommel to follow his orders. Kluge made it quite clear that he had arrived to put some steel and determination into Rommel's armies.

When Rommel protested at this outrageous claim, Kluge retorted: "Up to now you haven't really commanded any units bigger than a division." This was not only untrue but deeply insulting to Rommel as commander of an entire army group. He lost his temper and, if anything, Rommel's relations with Kluge were worse even than those with Hitler.[68]

Two days later, Rommel had a better meeting with far more congenial company, namely General Eberbach who arrived at Rommel's HQ to discuss the situation at the front. Eberbach was cheerful, plucky and resourceful. Better still, he was a Swabian like Rommel. The two men liked each other and could cooperate closely. Like Rommel, Eberbach was convinced that the superior German tank crews and panzers were more than a match for the Allies.

On 7 July, they were proven right when the British poured 80,000 shells into the German lines. The 16th Luftwaffe Division fled but the teenage troops of the 12th SS Panzer Division, with a handful of Tigers, destroyed 103 British tanks. This ended Monty's hopes of an early breakthrough at Caen. It was a splendid tactical German victory, and boosted German morale, albeit temporarily.

On 9 July, Rommel was visited by Caesar von Hofacker at his HQ. Hofacker had been sent by the Military Governor of France, General Stülpnagel, to get Rommel's support for the planned coup against Hitler. Rommel listened but refused to be involved. He had more pressing matters on his hands.

By 12 July, after a mere five weeks of fighting, Rommel had lost 97,000 troops, including 2400 officers and 225 tanks. He had received only 6000 troops and a paltry 17 tanks as replacements. His armies were bleeding to death, and the war appeared to be lost. In the Saint Lô sector, which Rommel visited on 13 July, the situation was desperate, and he concluded in his report to Kluge that "everywhere our troops are fighting heroically but the unequal struggle is drawing to its close. In my view the political consequences of this have just got to be

Below: At Caen the Germans had constructed a series of defensive lines featuring infantry, tanks and anti-aircraft guns. This is a four-barrelled Flak 38.

drawn. As Commander-in-Chief of the Army Group, I feel obliged to make myself quite plain."[69] For Rommel, like his armies, the day of reckoning was fast approaching. On 17 July, troops under his command fought their last battle at Caen. Here, the Germans had constructed a series of defensive lines. The first line was made up of infantry positions, the second of Tigers and 88s, and the third of fortified villages held by German infantry. Behind this lay yet one more line made up of 80 88mm guns, a dozen even heavier anti-aircraft guns, 194 field guns and 272 Nebelwerfer rocket launchers.

When the British armour attacked, they had to fight for every inch of ground with the blood of their crews and the strewn wrecks of their tanks. It was only by late afternoon that a few bold and reckless British tank crews managed finally to reach the fourth defence line. They couldn't, despite their most valiant efforts, break through. Even if they had, a final line awaited them beyond the fourth, made up of 80 SS panzers (Tigers and Panthers), manned by the youth soldiers of the *Hitlerjugend*.

By the evening, 126 British tanks (mainly Shermans) had been destroyed. The British had to admit that the attack had failed. Rommel's panzers had scored

Above: The multi-barrelled German Nebelwerfer rocket launchers were used to good effect at Caen.

Below: The fighting around Caen was part of Montgomery's plan to draw in German armour and wear it down.

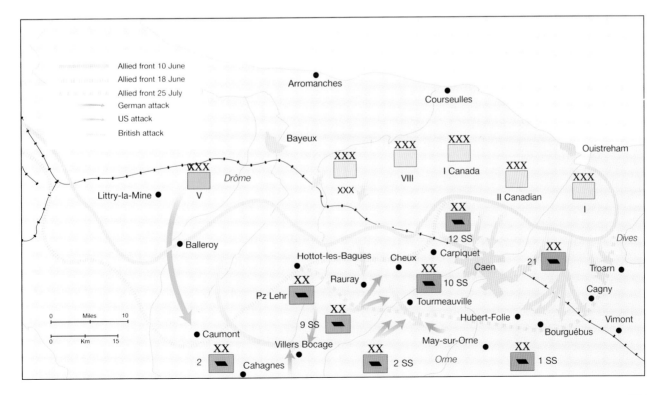

one final victory against their most determined and stubborn foe, the British tank corps. It must have warmed Rommel's heart that he had given his arch foe, Field Marshal Bernard Law Montgomery, one final bloody nose.

That morning, Rommel had a meeting with Sepp Dietrich, who was willing to talk politics. When Rommel asked him if he could rely on his obedience, Dietrich replied emphatically: "You're the boss, Herr Feldmarschall. I obey only you, whatever it is you're planning." Was Rommel planning some sort of military move against Hitler or not? We will probably never know, but Rommel told his staff that he had won over Dietrich.

As he drove back, French refugees fleeing the fighting in Normandy seemed more angered at the Allies than at the Germans for this invasion. Many of the refugees recognized Rommel, and greeted him with respect and admiration. His last driver, Corporal Daniel, took only secondary roads to head back to HQ. Rommel's luck finally ran out, and he was strafed and wounded by a passing Allied aircraft. Rommel was out of action, this time for good. Kluge grabbed his chance and made himself, with Hitler's permission, commander of Army Group B.[70]

Below: British infantry move through the rubble of Caen in July 1944.

The end: coups, conspiracies and cyanide

As Rommel, suffering from severe head injuries, was transported back to Germany for treatment and rest, the Americans took Saint Lô. By 18 July, Rommel's army group had suffered 110,000 casualties but destroyed 2117 enemy tanks.

Two days later, a routine meeting at Hitler's HQ in East Prussia was interrupted by a massive explosion that wounded several of Hitler's entourage but left the leader unscathed. The assassin was Colonel Count Claus Schenk Graf von Stauffenberg, a 37-year-old highly decorated, but crippled, war veteran. He left the Wolf's Lair immediately after the explosion and flew back to Berlin, convinced he had killed the tyrant. The army conspirators had finally acted, but they bungled the military and political takeover in Berlin.

The conspirators were apprehended and shot by a still loyal army. There followed the usual Nazi terror as thousands were arrested on the most spurious grounds for being implicated in the conspiracy to murder the "beloved" Führer. Two of them, Generals Hofacker and Speidel, implicated Rommel whose house in Herrlingen was being watched by the Gestapo day and night. Speidel's arrest disgusted Rommel, who believed that he was innocent. He wrote a letter to Hitler on 1 October praising Speidel and defending his innocence. Nothing could have been more damaging for Rommel's own survival than his defence of one of the conspirators. In Hitler's eyes, it meant that Rommel was guilty of treason.

Rommel did not help himself when, a few days later, he told a local Nazi official that Hitler was not quite right in the head. This was reported immediately to the official's superior, the sinister Martin Bormann. Unfortunately, Bormann had borne Rommel a grudge since 1939, when Rommel had snubbed him. He now saw a golden opportunity for revenge. Hitler was quickly convinced that Rommel was guilty, with his insulting remarks being the last straw.

On 10 October, Hitler invited Rommel to clear his name by coming to his HQ. Thinking that this was simply to explain his command and conduct of operations in Normandy, Rommel declined. Four days later, Generals Burgdorf and Meisel, known as Hitler's "angels of death", arrived in Heerlingen.

Rommel, who knew Burgdorf personally, invited them into his home with usual Swabian hospitality. The three men went into the parlour, where they engaged in a low-key and seemingly friendly chat. But Rommel was shocked by the generals' message, directly from Hitler. Commit suicide and spare yourself and your family the embarrassment of a public show trial, or choose the latter and your family will face a concentration camp. Rommel, who had confronted death in two wars, had an unenviable choice. He chose to die in order to spare his family. Speeding off in a Mercedes, Rommel bit into a cyanide capsule and died instantly. The Fox was finally cornered and killed, not by the enemy but by Hitler, the man who had created him.[71]

Below: Rommel's grave at Heerlingen Cemetery.

Rommel, Germany's most popular general, and a symbol of the country's once great military might, was dead. He was given a state funeral attended by Rundstedt, but not by Hitler, who was unwilling to play the hypocrite's role in a carefully orchestrated charade. When Winnrich Behr ventured to tell General Krebs that Rommel had been murdered by Hitler, Krebs told Behr to shut up. "My dear Behr, don't deceive yourself you'll get a state funeral".[72]

It was only after the war that the truth could be revealed concerning the real circumstances surrounding Rommel's death. Even today, Rommel is the only German general of World War II whom both Germans and Allies can still admire without a trace of hesitation or embarrassment. To friend and foe alike, Erwin Rommel was the quintessential soldier, gentleman and the immortal Desert Fox.

Chapter notes

1 Liddell Hart, p.317.
2 RP.320, Rommel to Lucie, 3 Nov. 1942.
3 Liddell Hart, p.318.
4 Salmaggi, p.312. Rommel had saved 70,000 out of his 90,000 troops.
5 Liddell Hart, p.319.
6 Purnell's, Vol. 11, Liddell Hart, *Operation Torch, French North Africa, July–November 1942*, p.1122.
7 Salmaggi, p.313.
8 Liddell Hart, p.1127.
9 Ibid, p.1132.
10 Ibid, p.1127.
11 Ward Rutherford, *Kasserine*, pp.10, 23.
12 Ibid, pp.23, 26.
13 Ibid, p.27.
14 Purnell's, Vol. 12, Von der Heydte, *Chase to the Mareth Line, November 1942-February 1943*, p.1245.
15 Purnell's, Vol. 11, Von der Heydte, *Afrika Korps Escapes North Africa, October–December 1942*, p.1148.
16 Liddell Hart, pp.319-320.
17 Von der Heydte, *Afrika Korps Escapes*, p.1148.
18 RP.376, Rommel to Lucie, 18 Dec. 1942.
19 Purnell's, Vol. 12, Von der Heydte, *Chase to the Mareth Line*, p.1244.
20 RP.379, Rommel to Lucie, 24 Dec. 1942.

21 RP.381, Rommel to Lucie, 31 Dec.1942
22 Von der Heydte, *Chase to the Mareth Line*, p.1244.
23 Liddell Hart, p.415.
24 Salmaggi, p.353.
25 Liddell Hart, p.419.
26 Ibid, pp.420-421.
27 RP.388, Rommel to Lucie, 20 Jan. 1942. Paulus' situation was totally different from Rommel's since he and the Sixth Army were trapped in Stalingrad – doomed to destruction at the hands of a now vengeful and victorious Red Army. Paulus' fate was a warning to Rommel, and the capitulation of Stalingrad to the Red Army despite Hitler's express orders only made the German despot even more suspicious of his generals, including Rommel.
28 Rutherford, pp.55, 61, 63, 65.
29 RP.390, Rommel to Lucie, 22 Jan. 1942.
30 Rutherford, p.66.
31 Ibid, pp.37-39.
32 The Tiger Tank was a brand-new, heavy German model that had gone into production during 1942 to match the Russian T-34.
33 Rutherford, pp.107, 109.
34 Ibid, pp.110-111.
35 Ibid, pp.113-119.

36 Ibid, pp.121-125.
37 Ibid, pp.130-132, 136, 139-141, 147.
38 Liddell Hart, p.429.
39 Liddell Hart, p.430.
40 Purnell's, Vol. 12, Kenneth Macksey, *Breaking the Mareth Line (March 1943)*, pp.1252-1253.
41 Liddell Hart, p.431.
42 Salmaggi, pp.376-377.
43 Fraser, pp.432, 436.
44 Ibid, p.433.
45 Ibid, p.435. Fraser's caustic comment is that Rommel deceived himself if he thought that Hitler had ever been normal.
46 Ibid, pp.437-446.
47 Ibid, pp.450-451.
48 Purnell's, Vol. 16, R.W. Thompson, *Fortress Europe*, p.1728.
49 Thompson, p.1729.
50 Friedrich Ruge, *Rommel in Normandy* (London, 1979), pp.31, 53.
51 Thompson, pp.1727, 1729.
52 Rommel chose this chateau because it was close to Normandy.
53 Thompson, p.1729.
54 TV documentary, "The Real Rommel", interview with Behr.
55 The 319th Division occupied the Channel Islands, and was called the

"Canada" division because of its isolated position, cut off from the mainland by Allied aerial attacks. Another of the divisions, the 243rd, was also a fortress unit with almost no mobility.
56 Ruge, pp.65-67, 71, 82, 85, 97.
57 2nd, 21st, 16th Panzer Divisions, 7th SS-Panzer Division and Panzer Lehr. The 1st SS-Panzer Division was stationed in Belgium, and the 19th Panzer Division in Holland.
58 Thompson, p.1730.
59 Ruge, pp.108-109.
60 Thompson, pp.1731, 1734.
61 Ibid, p.1734.
62 TV documentary, "The Real Rommel".
63 Irving, p.338.
64 Ibid, pp.339-341.
65 Irving, pp.340, 342-347; Ruge, p.183.
66 Irving, pp.348, 350-353, quote from p.353.
67 Ibid, pp.355-359.
68 Ibid, pp.363-367.
69 Ibid, pp.369-371, 374-375.
70 Ibid, pp.380-383.
71 Ibid, pp.387, 394-395, 397-398, 400-401, 405.
72 TV documentary, "The Real Rommel", interview with Behr.

Bibliography

Blumenson, Martin, *Rommel's Last Victory: The Battle of Kasserine Pass.* London, Allen & Unwin, 1968

Brantigan, Richard, *Rommel drives deep into Egypt.* New York, Dell, 1970

Clifford, Alexander, *Three against Rommel: The Campaigns of Wavell, Auchinleck and Alexander.* London, Harrap, 1943

Crawley, Aidan, *De Gaulle.* London, Collins, 1969

Deighton, Len, *Blitzkrieg: From the Rise of Hitler to the Fall of Dunkirk.* London, Panther Books, 1985

Deighton, Len, *Blood, Tears and Folly. An objective look at World War II.* London, Pimlico, 1995

Douglas-Home, Charles, *Rommel.* London, Weidenfeld & Nicolson, 1973

Douglas-Home, Charles, *The War Lords. Military Commanders of the Twentieth Century.* London, Weidenfeld & Nicolson, 1976

Eppler, John, *Operation Condor: Rommel's Spy.* London, Futura, 1978

Forty, George (ed.), *Tanks across the Desert. The War Diary of Jake Wardrop.* London, Kimber, 1981

Fraser, David, *Knight's Cross. A Life of Field Marshal Erwin Rommel.* London, Harper-Collins, 1994

Heckman, Wolf, *Rommel's War in Africa.* London, Grenada, 1981

Horne, Alastair, *To Lose a Battle: France 1940.* London, Penguin, 1988

Irving, David, *The Trail of the Fox: Rommel.* London, 1977

Jackson, W.G.F., *The North African Campaign 1940–43.* London, Batsford, 1975

Jentz, Thomas L., *Panzertruppen.* Atgeln, Schiffer Publishing, 1996

Koch, Lutz, *Erwin Rommel: die Wandlung eines grossen Soldaten.* Stuttgart, Bauer, 1970

Kühn, Volkmar, *Mit Rommel in der Wüste: Kampf und Untergang der deutschen Afrika-Korps 1941–1943.* Stuttgart, Motorbuch, 1975

Lewin, Ronald, *Rommel as Military Commander.* London, Batsford, 1968

Liddell Hart, Basil (ed.), *The Rommel Papers.* London, Collins, 1950

Liddell Hart, Basil, *History of the Second World War.* London, Papermac, 1997

Macksey, Kenneth, *Afrika Korps.* London, Pan Books, 1972

Macksey, Kenneth, *Rommel: Battles and Campaigns.* New York, Da Capo, 1997

Mitcham, Samuel W., *Rommel's Last Battle: the Desert Fox and the Normandy Campaign.* New York, Stein and Day, 1983

Moorehead, Alan, *African Trilogy. The North African Campaign 1940–43.* London, Hamish Hamilton, 1965

Neillands, Robert, *The Desert Rats: 7th Armoured Division 1940–1945.* London, Orion, 1997

Pitt, Barrie (ed.), *Purnell's History of the Second World War.* London, Phoebus. Volumes 2, 6–12, 16

Ruge, Friedrich, *Rommel in Normandy.* London, MacDonald & Jane, 1979

Rutherford, Ward, *Kasserine: Baptism of Fire.* London, MacDonald, 1971

Schroetter, Hellmuth, *Panzer rollen in Afrika: mit Rommel von Tripolis bis El Alamein.* Wiesbaden, Limes, 1985

Schmidt, Heinz W., *With Rommel in the Desert.* London, Harrap, 1980

Shirer, William L., *The Collapse of the Third Republic.* London, Heinemann, 1970

Sibley, Roger, and Fry, Michael, *Rommel.* London, Random House, 1974

Swinson, Arthur, *The Raiders: Desert Strike Force.* London, MacDonald, 1968

Toland, John, *Adolf Hitler.* New York, Ballantine, 1976

Williams, John, *France: Summer 1940.* London, Aldus, 1973

Windrow, Martin, *Rommel's Desert Army.* London, Osprey, 1976

Young, Desmond, *Rommel.* London, Collins, 1959